Moral Reason

What is it to have a reason to do something? is one sort of question; *what is it we have reason to do?* is another. These questions are often explored separately. But our answers to them may not be independent: what reasons *are* may have implications for what reasons *there are*. So the door is opened to a troubling tension—the account of what reasons are that is most plausible in its own right could entail a view of what we have reason to do that is independently implausible. In fact, it *looks* like this is the case.

In the first half of *Moral Reason*, Julia Markovits develops and defends a version of a desire-based, internalist, account of *what normative reasons are*. But does that account entail that there are no moral reasons that apply to all of us, regardless of what we happen to desire? It may look obvious that it does—that a bullet must be bitten somewhere. If what we have reason to do depends on what we antecedently desire, corrected only for misinformation and procedural irrationalities, and if desires differ from person to person, there seems to be no basis for assuming that everyone has reason to be moral. But the bullet may yet be avoided. In the second half of the book, Markovits shows how we may do so, building on Kant's argument for his formula of humanity to provide an internalist defense of universal moral reasons. In doing so, she provides a more satisfying answer to the age-old question: *why be moral?*

Julia Markovits is Associate Professor of Philosophy at Cornell University.

OXFORD PHILOSOPHICAL MONOGRAPHS

Moral Reason

Julia Markovits

OXFORD
UNIVERSITY PRESS

OXFORD
UNIVERSITY PRESS

Great Clarendon Street, Oxford, OX2 6DP,
United Kingdom

Oxford University Press is a department of the University of Oxford.
It furthers the University's objective of excellence in research, scholarship,
and education by publishing worldwide. Oxford is a registered trade mark of
Oxford University Press in the UK and in certain other countries

© Julia Markovits 2014

The moral rights of the author have been asserted

First published 2014
First published in paperback 2017

Published in the United States of America by Oxford University Press
198 Madison Avenue, New York, NY 10016, United States of America

British Library Cataloguing in Publication Data
Data available

Library of Congress Cataloging in Publication Data
Data available

ISBN 978-0-19-956717-1 (Hbk.)
ISBN 978-0-19-879840-8 (Pbk.)

For Inga and Dick

Acknowledgements

I would like to thank the following for permission to reproduce previously published material:

- Palgrave MacMillan for permission to reprint "Internal Reasons and the Motivating Intuition," first published in *New Waves in Metaethics* (edited by Michael Brady) in 2011, which appears here as §2.1-3.1, in slightly amended form;
- Oxford University Press for permission to reprint significant portions of "Why Be An Internalist About Reasons?," first published in *Oxford Studies in Metaethics, Vol. 6* (edited by Russ Shafer-Landau) in 2011, which appear here as §3.2-3.5 in slightly amended form.

This book has been many years in the making. It began as a masters' thesis, written during my time as a B.Phil student at Oxford, which then formed the core of my doctoral dissertation, also completed at Oxford. During that time I benefitted from the generous financial support of a number of institutions. The Philosophy Faculty and Somerville College, Oxford provided me with a graduate scholarship, which, in conjunction with grants from the Overseas Research Studentship Award Scheme and the Oxford University Clarendon Fund Bursaries, supported my first three years of study. Christ Church, Oxford, funded my last two years of research by providing me with a Senior Scholarship. I look back on my time as a graduate student at Oxford with great fondness, and I owe all of these institutions heartfelt thanks.

After completing my doctorate, I was lucky enough to receive a Junior Fellowship at the Harvard Society of Fellows. The fellowship provided me with a rare luxury for a post-doctoral philosopher: three years of uninterrupted research time. This meant I had time to begin reworking my dissertation project into a book; but also, and just as crucially, it meant I had time, for a while, to ignore it completely and think about new topics. By the time I returned to the manuscript in the second half of my fellowship, I was able to see it with the clearer sight afforded by distance. In that time and in the years since, with the benefit of the supportive philosophical community at MIT, I have rewritten much of it entirely. But the basic outlines of the project and the motivating thoughts behind it remain the same.

Two people in particular helped me to write this book. The first is my doctoral thesis advisor Derek Parfit. I would not have thought it possible for someone to be so generous in his encouragement of a project built on premises so at odds with his own philosophical convictions. The defense of a philosophical position can only benefit from repeated collisions with the most forceful and persuasive arguments for the opposite view. I hope some such benefit will be evident in this book, and that I have managed at least to address, if not allay, some of Parfit's worries about internalism. That I share many of those doubts will be readily evident to the reader. So too, I hope, will be the pervasive influence of Parfit's thought throughout the book, despite the distance between the conclusions for which I argue and his own. Our philosophical instincts are, I think, not so far apart as those conclusions make them seem.

Just as indispensable to my completion of this book has been the help I have received, in a less formal capacity, from Stephen Kearns. He has read and talked through with me every argument in it. Many of the ideas developed in the book began as conversations with him, during our time as graduate students together at Oxford. I was quite concerned, when I left Oxford, about how I would learn to do philosophy without him. I needn't have worried. Skype does wonders for expanding the reach of philosophical conversations, and Stephen's advice has been as crucial to the final formulation of the ideas in this book as it was to their origination. I consider myself extremely lucky to have him as a long-distance sounding board.

In addition to these two, a number of people gave me very generous and helpful comments, either in writing or in person, on large parts of the manuscript at various stages of development. For such help I owe thanks to Ruth Chang, Roger Crisp, Kate Manne, Rebecca Markovits, Adrian Moore, Philip Stratton-Lake, and Kurt Sylvan. I have also benefitted greatly from numerous conversations about this work, in settings both formal and informal, over the years. Unfortunately, I won't be able now to recall all the people who have helped me in this way, but the list includes at *least* Robert Adams, Brian Ball, Terence Cuneo, Stephen Darwall, Jamie Dreier, David Enoch, Caspar Hare, Niko Kolodny, Rae Langton, Ofra Magidor, Graham Oddie, Michael Smith, Daniel Star, Nicholas Sturgeon, Mark van Roojen, and R. Jay Wallace.

I've had opportunities to present some of the work represented in the book to audiences at Berkeley, Brown, Carnegie Mellon, Cornell, MIT, NYU-Abu Dhabi, Oxford, Rice, Rutgers, UC-Santa Barbara, the University of British Columbia, the University of Melbourne, the University of Nebraska-Lincoln, the University of Oslo's Center for the Study of Mind in Nature, the University of Texas-Austin, and the Wisconsin Metaethics Workshop. I know that many of the suggestions and concerns raised by audience members in those talks have made their way directly into the book. The same is true of comments made by the excellent graduate students at MIT, from whom I have been fortunate to learn. Though many of these people no doubt deserve to be acknowledged by name, my porous memory forces me to settle instead for this general thanks.

For thoughtful help in preparing the index, much better than I could have done myself, and for other sound suggestions, I thank Brendan Dill. Thanks also go to Peter Momtchiloff, my editor, and the staff at OUP, for their advice, patience, and support, as well as to an anonymous reader for OUP, whose very helpful comments on the initial draft of the book revealed an eye that is at once generous and critical—in other words, just what any author would hope to find in a referee.

And I am more grateful than I can say to Sally Haslanger, whose advice and reassurance have helped me to finish this book, and helped me in so many other ways as well.

I have said that this book has been many years in the making. In fact, the earliest seed of the project was a term paper I wrote when I was a Yale undergraduate for a class on Kant's ethics taught by Allen Wood.

He introduced me to a very likeable Immanuel Kant, in whose thinking the value of rational nature as an end in itself plays the central role.
I am grateful for the introduction.

A final word of thanks goes to my family: Rebecca, Benjamin,
Stefanie, and Daniel (and their families), and especially to my parents, Inga and Dick, and my partner, Jeff Moses: without their good
will, steadfast support, skills in crisis management, and stubborn faith
in my abilities, any undertaking would be a great deal more difficult
than it is.

Contents

1

Reasons and Moral Relativism

1.1 Two Sorts of Questions

What are reasons for action? The question is multiply ambiguous.

First, the term "reason" is itself infamously ambiguous. A reason for an action might be a fact that *explains why* an agent acted, or a fact that *motivates* the agent to act, or a fact that helps *justify* an agent's action. An example may help: the fact that I haven't gotten enough sleep lately may (partly) explain why I snap at you. But it doesn't *motivate* me to snap at you—it's not the consideration on the basis of which I choose to do so. Perhaps I choose to snap at you because your voice is rather shrill for this time of the morning, and it's getting on my nerves, and my snapping at you will get you to stop talking. These facts are what motivate me to act as I do.[1] But these facts don't *justify* what I do—after all, it's not your fault that I haven't been sleeping, and you can't (and shouldn't) change the register of your voice just to suit me. I ought not to snap at you as I do. So my motivating reasons are not, in this case, justifying reasons. Things would be different, perhaps, if you *were* to blame for my lack of sleep—if I'm sleep-deprived because you keep waking me up, at 5 a.m., by practicing arias under my bedroom window in your unsteady soprano. In that case, the early hour and the shrillness of your voice may well justify my telling you to put a lid on it.[2]

---

[1] Motivating reasons are also a species of explanatory reasons: they feature in explanations of what agents do that operate at the level of the agents' intentions.

[2] Sometimes, when I'm motivated to act by the consideration that justifies my acting, the same fact is an explanatory, motivating, and justifying reason.

My focus in this book will be on this last kind of reason—the *justifying*, or "normative," kind, though its relation to the other kinds of reasons will sometimes be of interest, too. My question is: *what are normative reasons for action?*

There is a second source of ambiguity in my question, even after we restrict our topic to normative reasons: it can be read as an *analytic* or a *substantive* inquiry, as asking *what reasons are* or *what reasons there are*.

So, for example, someone might offer as an answer to the substantive question—the question of what we have reason to do—the thesis that only facts about the (agent-neutral) value of the consequences of an action are reasons to perform it. Or that what we have reason to do depends on what others can consent to our doing. Or that only facts about how the action would satisfy the desires of the agent provide the agent with reasons to perform it.

There is in fact a lot of disagreement about how to answer the substantive question. But even if we disagree about this, we should be able to agree on an answer to the analytic question—the question about *what reasons are*. Indeed, we will have to agree about this on some level, more or less, at least implicitly, if our differing answers to the substantive question are to count as *disagreements* at all: as *rival* answers to *the same question*.

Fortunately, we do, most of us, agree on an answer of sorts to the analytic question: it's commonly accepted that a normative reason for action is *a consideration that counts in favor of the action*. Some philosophers argue that nothing else useful can be said about what a reason is. (" 'Counts in favor of how?' " Scanlon famously asked; and replied, " 'By providing a reason for it' seems to be the only answer."[3]) But other philosophers—sometimes called *reasons-internalists*—think there is more we can say. They have offered a kind of desire-based view as an account, not of *what reasons there are* but of *what reasons are*: they've suggested that what it *is* for a consideration to count in favor of an action is for it to show that performing the action stands in the right

---

[3] See Scanlon, *What We Owe to Each Other*, p. 17.

relation to the agent's desires, broadly understood: archetypically, by showing that the action will help satisfy one of those desires.

So: *What is it to have a reason to do something?* is one sort of question; *What is it we have reason to do?* is another. The two questions can be, and often are, explored separately. This seems quite natural. After all, on the face of it, it seems like quite different sorts of considerations would be relevant each of them. The first question falls into the domain of metaethics; the second, into "normative," or first-order, ethics. Arguments about the nature of normativity—about what we're talking about when we talk about normative reasons—seem to operate at a different level from arguments about whether, say, we have reason to override the will of a resistant patient to perform surgery that's necessary for her future health.

But our answers to these two different questions may turn out not to be independent. What reasons *are* may have implications for what reasons *there are*. (In fact, this wouldn't be surprising.) So the door is opened to a troubling kind of tension: it could be that the account of what reasons are that is most plausible in its own right entails a view of what we have reason to do that is independently *im*plausible. In fact, as I will argue, it *looks* very much like this is the case. That would leave us with some unpalatable choices; we'd have to bite some bullets in one theory or the other.

The first half of this book addresses the analytic question: I will be exploring and then defending a version of a (loosely-speaking) desire-based, internalist, account of *what normative reasons are*. But I'm quite unsympathetic to the (more narrowly-speaking) desire-based view about *what reasons there are*. I firmly believe we have reasons, especially moral reasons, to do many things we have no desire to do, and even when we do desire to do these things, our reason to do them isn't that doing them will satisfy our desires. There are moral reasons that apply to all of us, regardless of what we happen to desire.

Does the internalist account of what reasons are entail that there are no such reasons—and that we have no reason to do what we don't want to do? It may look obvious that it does, and that a bullet must be bitten somewhere, either in our metaethical or in our first-order moral theory. If having a reason depends on having a relevant desire, and if desires differ from person to person, there seems to be no basis for assuming that everyone has reason to be moral. But looks can be deceiving, and the bullet may yet be avoided. It may be that the independently plausible answers to the analytic and substantive questions are more compatible than they at first appear. That, in any case, is what I hope to suggest. So after defending the loosely-speaking desire-based account of what reasons are, I will argue, in the second half of this book, that it doesn't commit us to a problematically desire-based account of what reasons there are. In other words, I will try to provide an internalist defense of universal, or categorical, moral reasons.

If such a defense is available, then, I will suggest, what appeared to be a weakness of the internalist account of reasons may turn out to be its greatest strength. One of the appealing features of the internalist analysis of reasons is, as I will argue in Chapter 3, that it offers us something non-question-begging to say in defense of our reasons ascriptions—a kind of "Archimedean point" (to borrow a phrase from Bernard Williams) against which we can brace ourselves in disputes about reasons. The internalist defends her claims about what someone has reason to do by appealing to that person's own commitments.

Moral philosophers have long been concerned about how to respond to the *amoralist*—the person who recognizes what morality requires of him, but wonders *why he should do* what morality requires. The *moral ought*, this amoralist might concede, is certainly *about* him—it *refers to* him. But it doesn't follow merely from this that it has a *proper, normative hold on him* (whatever that comes to), any more than the fact that the dictates of some old-fashioned religion—a religion that in no way reflects what I care about—refer to me entails that I have any *real reason* to comply with them. Because internalist accounts of reasons ground reasons in facts about our desires, broadly understood, an internalist defense of moral reasons may allow us to provide a more satisfying answer to the amoralist. Or so I will argue.

1.2 The Analytic Question

I've been characterizing internalism about reasons as a "loosely-speaking desire-based account" of what reasons for action are, according to which our having a reason to perform some action depends on our having some desire that performing the action will help us satisfy. But I should begin to speak less loosely. The essential feature of an internalist account of reasons is that it ties the truth of a reasons claim to the presence of a suitable element in what Bernard Williams called the agent's motivational set: "the set of his desires, evaluations, attitudes, projects, and so on."[4]

The loose formulation I have been working with is too loose in at least two ways. Firstly, *not all* and *not only* our desires give us reasons. Not all of our desires give us reasons because unjustified false beliefs or bad reasoning can give us desires we have no reason to fulfill. (So, for example, my unjustified false belief in the efficacy of some quack cure may give rise to a desire to try it, but that desire would give me no reason to do so.) And not *only* our *desires* give us reasons, because we value and act for the sake of many things we can't properly be said to desire, because they aren't the kinds of ends we could achieve or come to possess; for example, we often act for the sake of other people. Our "motivational set" contains everything for the sake of which we act, everything we pursue, promote, protect, and respect.

Secondly, and relatedly, linking what we have reason to do with what satisfies our desires suggests that reason plays a purely instrumental role. I'll follow Williams, however, in allowing for the possibility that we have reason to act in ways that serve our ends non-instrumentally—perhaps the action in question is constitutive of some end or commitment, or expresses that commitment.[5]

Internalism about reasons might be generally formulated as the view that what we have reason to do depends fundamentally on what ends, understood in this broad way, we already have. It follows from the

---

[4] Williams, "Internal Reasons and the Obscurity of Blame," p. 35.
[5] Williams, "Internal and External Reasons," in *Moral Luck*, p. 104.

internalist picture that if we are rational relative to our ends (broadly understood), then we are rational, all things considered. On the *externalist* view, defended, for example, by Derek Parfit, what reasons we have need be in no way connected to the ends that we in fact hold.

It may be helpful to take a particular spelling-out of the internalist thesis as a starting point (it will not be our ending point). Williams' formulation of the view has been influential. According to Williams' version of internalism, for some agent A to have a reason to perform some action ϕ, that action must be related to A's "motivational set" in a particular way. Specifically, Williams says, it must be the case that "A could reach the conclusion that he should ϕ. . . by a sound deliberative route from the motivations that he has in his actual motivational set—that is, the set of his desires, evaluations, attitudes, projects, and so on."[6] Put in an oversimplified way, an internal interpretation of reasons is one that takes an agent A to have a reason to ϕ only if A would after procedurally rational deliberation have some end the attainment of which will be served by his ϕ-ing.[7] (Remember that Williams understands both the notion of an *end* and that of *serving an end* quite broadly.)

One element of following a "sound deliberative route" is, according to Williams, possessing the relevant information. In this way he allows that an agent who is otherwise deliberating rationally may have a reason of which she is unaware, or may think she has a reason that she in fact does not have. Williams is here describing what might be called "objective reasons." Roughly speaking, his view is that we have *objective reason* to do whatever we would be motivated to do if we were deliberating procedurally rationally and were fully informed. The

---

[6] Williams, "Internal Reasons and the Obscurity of Blame," p. 35.

[7] Williams, "Internal and External Reasons," p. 101. In "Internal and External Reasons," Williams states the internalist thesis as a biconditional: "*A* has a reason to ϕ *iff A* has some desire the satisfaction of which will be served by his ϕ–ing." (Williams later qualifies this simple statement of the thesis to allow that desires based on false beliefs or bad reasoning aren't reason-giving (pp. 102–103).) In "Internal Reasons and the Obscurity of Blame," Williams explicitly defends only the "only if" half of this biconditional—the claim that connection to the agent's motivations is a *necessary* condition for her having a reason—though he notes that he thinks the sufficiency half of the claim is also true (pp. 35–36).

reason I have to jump out the window of the building I'm in to escape a fire of which I have no evidence provides one example.

There is, however, a second class of internal reasons that we can call "subjective reasons." Consider the reason I have to jump out the window when I have a justified *false* belief that the building is on fire. Because I would not be motivated to jump out the window if I were fully informed, we need to supplement the conception of a reason just discussed with one that does not build the full information requirement into the notion of a sound deliberative route. Roughly speaking, we have *subjective reason* to do whatever we would be motivated to do if we were deliberating soundly from our current epistemic position. The two classes of reasons intersect—for example, the reason I have to escape through the window when I know or ought to know the building is on fire is both an objective and a subjective reason. But each class also contains some reasons not found in the other. Both objective and subjective reasons are, on this account, internal reasons: they link facts about what reasons we have to facts about our existing motivations.

It's plausible that we are morally obligated to do only what we have sufficient evidence to believe it would be best to do, not what it would (in fact) be best to do. For example, a doctor is morally obligated to prescribe the course of treatment her evidence tells her is most likely to cure her patient, not the treatment that (against all evidence) happens to be best; if all the evidence suggests that I need penicillin, and my doctor has no evidence that I'm allergic, she fails to fulfill her obligations if she refuses me penicillin, even if it turns out I am allergic. So the reasons grounding moral obligations are subjective reasons. (Unless I specify otherwise, I will, in what follows, use "reason" to refer to subjective reasons.)

So according to Williams' version of internalism: *a consideration can be a reason for me to φ only if it would motivate me to φ if I were deliberating in a procedurally rational way from my antecedent ends.*

I should dispatch an initial worry by making a clarification. Derek Parfit has distinguished (as I did above) between analytic and substantive versions of the internalist thesis. He finds the substantive version of the internalist thesis no more appealing than I find it. But, Parfit worries, if the internalist thesis is intended to state an *analytic* truth, then it merely stipulates a *definition* of the internalists' term "reason," and so states a "concealed tautology." In that case, he argues, internalists and externalists may simply be talking past one another when they argue about what reasons are and what reasons people have, as their use of the word "reason" may be merely homonymous. Here the real dispute, as Parfit later suggests, is about which sense of "reason" is the important one: the one that interests us, for example, when we are discussing what ought to be done (Parfit goes on to call analytic internal reason claims "true but trivial").[8]

My own view is that the internalist thesis should be read neither as stipulating a definition nor as making a substantive normative claim about what we have reason to do. Instead, it makes a claim about *what it is* for some fact to be a reason in a sense of "reason" that is shared by both internalists and externalists, according to which a reason is simply *a consideration that counts in favor of doing something.*

I don't deny that some internalists explicitly defend internalism as true in virtue of meaning. Williams sometimes seems to argue for this view in "Internal and External Reasons." Even these internalists aren't *stipulating* a definition of "reason," as Parfit suggests. Rather, they're defending a view about how a particular English word, one used synonymously by internalists and externalists, is defined.[9]

Parfit might concede this is what such internalists think of themselves as doing, but he finds the internalist account of what our shared word means deeply implausible: how could his own meaning be so hidden from him? That is why he has begun to suspect internalists and externalists of talking past each other—fooled into thinking they're discussing the same topic by a homonym. But I'm not interested in

---

[8] Parfit, *On What Matters*, Volume Two, pp. 275–277. See also Volume One, p. 72.

[9] An exception here is Kate Manne, whose "Internalism About Reasons: Sad But True" argues that there may be multiple common and useful senses of the term "reason," at least one of which is distinctively subjectivist. Manne allows that the general idea of a consideration counting in favor of an action may be broader than the distinctively subjectivist concept of a reason, but thinks that general idea elides some important distinctions.

defending internalism as a thesis about *how "reason" is defined* or *what our reasons-claims mean*. Instead, I'm interested in defending internalism as a thesis about *what reasons are*.

Understood in this way, the internalist thesis represents an analysis not in the linguistic sense that philosophers often have in mind, but rather in the sense that is more familiar from chemistry—the sense, for example, in which water has been analyzed as bonded hydrogen and oxygen. Similarly, internalism aims to provide an informative account of what property the property of being a reason—the property of being a consideration that counts in favor of something—is identical to. It need not aim to provide a rival theory of what we mean by the term "reason," any more than the theory that water is bonded hydrogen and oxygen represented an attempt to explain what we meant by the term "water." Internalism, in other words, concerns the *reference*, not the *sense*, of "reason." Parfit may be right that the *meaning* of his terms could not be so hidden from him; but history has taught us that the fundamental nature of the things our terms pick out often is hidden from us.[10]

So analyses in this sense can, like the analysis of water as H_2O, be *surprising*; and they needn't strike us as obviously true once we hear them. (This can be true even of non-empirical analyses, as the venerable philosophical debate about the correct analysis of *knowledge* brings out.) But analyses that are *too surprising* threaten to eliminate their object. Consider an "analysis" of mermaids that shows them to be

---

[10] Parfit might resist this analogy. He might reply that the pre-theoretical concept *water* had "an *explicit gap* that [was] *waiting to be filled*," and so was, in a sense, crying out for further analysis: that even our pre-theoretical concept of water was of *some substance—whatever it is*—that runs in our streams and fills our lakes and oceans and falls from the sky and is odorless, colorless, and potable, etc. *Reason*, he might say, is not "gappy" in this way. Parfit makes precisely this move in rejecting reductive naturalist utilitarian accounts of *rightness; rightness*, he says, is not gappy in the way that our pre-theoretical concept of *heat* left a gap—that property, *whatever it is*, that causes water to boil, and certain sensations in us, etc.—before scientists discovered it to be molecular kinetic energy. (*On What Matters*, Volume Two, pp. 301–302.) But I am much less confident than Parfit seems to be in our ability to recognize which of our concepts are or aren't gappy—candidates for further reduction or analysis. It's not at all clear to me, for example, that *heat* would have struck me, pre-theoretically, as gappy. (I am, however, much more sympathetic with Parfit's view that *some* proposed reductive analyses, such as naturalistic reductions of normative concepts, threaten to eliminate their objects, as I go on to discuss above.)

manatees, or an investigation of the monster under the bed that shows it to be my big brother.[11] Parfit, naturally, might worry that if the internalist analysis of reasons proves to be the right one, that'll amount to showing that reasons as he took them to be don't exist after all. Indeed, some versions of reasons-internalism strike me as eliminativist in just this way. Some *reductive naturalist* versions of internalism, for example, take normative reasons to be facts that would motivate us if we attended to them.[12] According to these theories, there are no irreducibly normative reasons: normative-reasons-ascriptions report purely psychological facts.

This view may have the virtue of side-stepping some of the metaphysical mysteriousness that seems to cling to the idea of a normative reason. But I share Parfit's suspicion that the reasons-theorist who "analyzes" normative reasons in this way has changed the subject. When I ascribe a normative reason to someone, I am not merely saying that certain considerations would *cause* her to act in some way if she were to attend to them. I am saying those considerations *count in favor of* her acting in that way. I am not merely making a prediction about how she will act, or would act under other circumstances. I am holding her to a *normative standard* she can fail to live up to. I am saying that if she is not motivated accordingly, she has *gone wrong—acted irrationally.*

But non-reductive versions of internalism, like Williams', do not seem to me to raise the same eliminativist worries that reductive versions raise. Williams' thesis does not equate reasons with merely psychological properties, and it appeals to a genuinely normative standard—the standard of procedural rationality. This normative standard and psychological facts about the agent's antecedent ends *jointly* determine her reasons.[13] On Williams' view, the person who fails to be motivated by her reasons has gone wrong: she has failed to deliberate *soundly.*

---

[11] Parfit offers the example of an analysis of *God* that determines that *God* is simply *the love some people feel for others.* (*On What Matters,* Volume Two, pp. 304–305.)

[12] W.D. Falk, for example, defends a version of this claim in "'Ought' and Motivation." See p. 116.

[13] Similarly, if I believe that at least some of my reasons for belief are jointly determined by facts about what I already believe and by the (genuinely normative) rules of inference, my account of the nature of these reasons won't reduce them to merely psychological facts.

Some externalists have found the account of reasons we're considering unsatisfactory in a different way. Although the non-reductive internalist account of reasons recognizes reasons to be irreducibly normative, and does not equate reasons with merely psychological facts, Parfit has suggested that even the non-reductive internalist concept of a reason is not *relevantly normative*. Employing that concept may, according to Parfit, allow us to make genuinely normative claims "about which ways of deliberating are procedurally rational, and in other ways ideal." But it would not allow us to make any genuinely normative claims "about reasons, or about what we should or ought to choose, or to do."[14]

And indeed, it may seem unsatisfying to suggest that someone who has failed to act as she has a *moral* reason to act is merely guilty of a *procedural* irrationality—like an error in logic, say. Someone who acts wrongly seems to be doing something more—something worse—than behaving irrationally. So even the non-reductive internalist account of reasons we're considering here might seem *too* reductive. But it seems to me that whether the internalist account of normative reasons is too reductive, or not relevantly normative, will depend very much on the details of the view, and on what failing to live up to the normative standard it establishes can look like. This worry should, therefore, be postponed until the real work of developing the internalist analysis of reasons is behind us.

1.3 The Threat of Relativism

There are, I have said, ways of *going wrong* with respect to our reasons, on the internalist view. Most obviously, if I'm deliberating soundly from my existing ends and motivations, I will take the means necessary to achieving them (or, if I'm not willing to, abandon the end in question). I'm procedurally irrational if I intend to catch the 6 o'clock train home, know that it takes me 10 minutes to reach the station, and

---

[14] Parfit, *On What Matters*, Volume Two, pp. 285–288.

still haven't left my office by 5:50. I have an (internal) reason to leave my office to which I am failing to respond. If internalism is right, we can have reason to do certain things *given* that we have certain ends, whether or not we do them.

But what if we're missing the relevant ends? Internalists have traditionally turned to Hume to underwrite their view that the scope of the normativity of practical reason does not extend to the adoption of our most fundamental ends. "Reason alone can never be a motive to any action of the will," Hume insists. He goes on to explain:

> Where...objects themselves do not affect us, their connexion [of effect to cause, which reason makes evident to us] can never give them any influence; and 'tis plain, that as reason is nothing but the discovery of this connexion, it cannot be by its means that the objects are able to affect us.[15]

Hume is talking here about the scope of the *motivating* force of reason. But his skepticism about the possibility that reason could motivate us to adopt new ends is due to his views about the limits of the scope of the *normative* force of reason.[16] Reason doesn't motivate us to adopt new ends because recommending new ends—ends that aren't derived from our old ones—is not part of its job description: Hume identified practical reason as nothing but the discovery of the connection of effect to cause, and thereby confined it to playing an instrumental role.[17] This is why he says, elsewhere, that "the ultimate ends of human actions can never, in any case, be accounted for by *reason,* but recommend themselves entirely to the sentiments and affections of mankind,"[18] and

---

[15] Hume, *A Treatise of Human Nature*, pp. 413–414 (II, 3, iii).

[16] As Christine Korsgaard has argued: she points out in "Skepticism about Practical Reason" (reprinted in *Creating the Kingdom of Ends*) that Hume's "motivational skepticism" – doubts about the scope of reason as a motive – derives from his "content skepticism" – doubts about whether principles of reason have any content that could give substantive guidance to choice and action. See especially *Creating the Kingdom of Ends*, pp. 311-314.

[17] Some scholars (notably Elijah Millgram) have argued that Hume rejected even instrumentalism about practical reason, in favor of a more thoroughgoing skepticism, but I will set this (and other) questions of textual interpretation of Hume aside. (See Millgram, "Was Hume a Humean?," especially §1.)

[18] Hume, *Enquiries Concerning Human Understanding and Concerning the Principles of Morals*, (hereafter, "*Enquiry*"), p. 293 (Second Enquiry, Appendix I), emphasis in the original.

famously concludes: "Reason is, and ought only to be, the slave of the passions, and can never pretend to any other office than to serve and obey them."[19]

The task of reason is to recognize the appropriate means to take to achieve our ends, and to transfer motivational force from our ends to those means. That is, if we are motivated to pursue the ends, we should be motivated to pursue the means. If our reasoning faculty is performing this task then we are behaving rationally. And if, furthermore, our deliberative process does not stumble over any false beliefs or informational gaps, we will not fail to act on the reasons that apply to us, regardless of the ends we start out with.

Williams more or less agrees:

> The internalist proposal sticks with its Humean origins to the extent of making correction of fact and reasoning part of the notion of 'a sound deliberative route to this act' but not, from the outside, prudential and moral considerations.[20]

So on both Williams' and Hume's accounts, the scope of the normativity of internal reasons extends to corrections of instrumental reasoning, but does not necessarily extend to prudential and moral concerns, since whether we have reason to pursue our own good or the interests of others will depend on what we care about going in. Thus Hume has infamously written of prudence,

> 'Tis [not] contrary to reason to prefer even my own acknowledg'd lesser good to my greater,[21]

and of morality,

> 'Tis not contrary to reason to prefer the destruction of the whole world to the scratching of my finger.[22]

---

[19] Hume, *A Treatise of Human Nature*, p. 415 (II, 3, iii).
[20] Williams, "Internal Reasons and the Obscurity of Blame," pp. 36–38. Williams adds, "To the extent that the agent already has prudential and moral considerations in his S, of course, they will be involved in what he has a reason to do. They will contribute to an internal reason."
[21] Hume, *A Treatise of Human Nature*, p. 415 (II, 3, iii).
[22] Hume, *A Treatise of Human Nature*, p. 415 (II, 3, iii).

Although Williams points out (as Hume certainly allowed) that the motivational sets of most agents do in fact contain prudential ends and moral commitments, and even more have ends to the achievement of which prudential and moral behavior is instrumental—he essentially agrees with Hume. He writes of the prudential case,

> If an agent really is uninterested in pursuing what he needs; and this is not the product of false belief; and he could not reach any such motive from motives he has by the kind of deliberative processes we have discussed; then I think we do have to say that in the internal sense he indeed has no reason to pursue these things.[23]

And he reaches a similar conclusion in the moral case, as his discussion of the following example brings out:

> Suppose, for instance, I think someone (I use 'ought' in an unspecific way here) ought to be nicer to his wife. I say, 'You have a reason to be nicer to her'. He says, 'What reason?' I say, 'Because she is your wife.' He says—and he is a very hard case—'I don't care. Don't you understand? I really do not care.' I try various things on him, and try to involve him in this business; and I find that he really is a hard case: there is *nothing* in his motivational set that gives him a reason to be nicer to his wife as things are.
>
> There are many things I can say about or to this man: that he is ungrateful, inconsiderate, hard, sexist, nasty, selfish, brutal, and many other disadvantageous things.... There is one specific thing the external reasons theorist wants me to say, that the man has a reason to be nicer.[24]

And this, Williams concedes, the internalist about reasons cannot claim. To put the point more finely, the internalist cannot even say of the cruel husband that he *ought* to be nicer to his wife without abandoning the plausible tie between what a person ought to do and what he has reason to do.

Williams is not the only internalist willing to bite one of these bullets. Philippa Foot's internalism led her to reject the claim that everyone need have reason to do as morality requires, and as a result, to reject

---

[23] Williams, "Internal and External Reasons," p. 105.
[24] Williams, "Internal Reasons and the Obscurity of Blame," p. 39.

the connection between what we ought to do and what we have reason to do.[25] (I'll return to that possibility in the next section.) And Gilbert Harman has famously taken the truth of internalism to imply a kind of moral relativism. In "Moral Relativism Defended," Harman argues (first) that moral ought judgments (at least judgments of the form "A ought to φ" or "It's wrong of A to f") imply the existence of moral reasons; (second) that such reasons must be rooted in the goals, desires, or intentions of the subject of such judgments, so that a rational and fully informed agent would be motivated to accept the moral principle to which the judgment appeals; and (third) that a rational agent may fail to have the relevant desires and ends underlying any particular moral principle, and so fail to have the reasons the corresponding judgment ascribes to him.[26]

Harman concludes that it would be false to say of cannibals that they ought not to eat a stranded shipwreck survivor, false to say of a contented assassin employee of Murder, Inc. that he ought not to kill his next victim, and even false to say of Hitler (assuming that his value system differed in sufficiently dramatic ways from ours) that he ought not to have ordered the extermination of the Jews. Derivatively, Harman thinks we can't say of any of these agents that *they were wrong* to act as they did.[27]

Harman's chosen bullet is moral relativism. His conclusions strike me as unacceptable. If we are to avoid them, we seem to be left facing the following dilemma: either we must, like Foot, give up on the tie

---

[25] See Foot, "Morality as a System of Hypothetical Imperatives," in *Virtues and Vices*. Foot's views on the relationship between reasons and ends changed over the course of her career.

[26] Harman, "Moral Relativism Defended," particularly pp. 3–11. Also see Harman's "What is Moral Relativism?" (especially pp. 152–159), and "Is There a Single True Morality?" Harman's version of moral relativism is actually quite complex. Because he introduces it as a kind of relativism of social agreement, it might easily be mistaken for a version of normative cultural relativism, according to which what we ought to do depends on the norms accepted by our social group. The internalist version of relativism that I describe above, by contrast, looks much more individualistic. As Harman's argument makes clear, however, he is moved to adopt relativism on internalist grounds. The element of the *group's* normative commitments is introduced, I believe, by the way Harman distinguishes *moral* reasons from *non-moral* reasons: Harman says we have *moral* reason to do something if we intend to do it on the understanding that others have the same intention. (See "Moral Relativism Defended," pp. 11–12.)

[27] Harman, "Moral Relativism Defended," pp. 5–8.

between "ought"-claims and reasons, or we must abandon internalism about reasons.

1.4 "Ought" and Reasons

In "Morality as a System of Hypothetical Imperatives,"[28] Philippa Foot distinguishes between two different "uses" of "ought" in judgments about what others ought to do: the *hypothetical* use, which presupposes that the subject of the judgment has a desire or interest, broadly understood, that would be served by his doing as we judge he ought; and the *categorical* use, which makes no such presupposition. For example, when we say someone "ought to leave now, to catch the 6 o'clock train," we presume that she wants to be on that train. If we learn she is really headed somewhere else, we withdraw the judgment. But moral judgments aren't like that: we don't, for example, withdraw our judgment that Hitler ought not to have issued his terrible orders when we learn that they fit perfectly into his plans.

Should we conclude that, since "ought" entails "has (conclusive) reason to," everyone has reason to be moral, regardless of their contingent ends and desires? Foot argues no. After all, she argues, we find the categorical use of "ought" in cases where we should clearly not conclude that categorical—universal—*reasons* follow. Her example is the "ought" of etiquette: we would not withdraw the judgment that invitations issued in the third person ought to be answered in the third person if we learn that someone has no interest in this sort of propriety. But we would never conclude, on this basis, that everyone *has reason* to be proper in this way. Despite the categorical form of the "ought" of etiquette, Foot says, someone might reasonably wonder whether he has reason to do as he *ought*$_E$, and that question, she suggests, must be answered in the usual way, by looking at the agent's ends.

---

[28]   Foot, "Morality As a System of Hypothetical Imperatives," pp. 157–173.

Foot sees no grounds for thinking the *moral* case is any different:

> The fact is that the man who rejects morality because he sees no reason to obey its rules can be convicted of villainy but not of inconsistency. Nor will his action necessarily be irrational. Irrational actions are those in which a man in some way defeats his own purposes, doing what is calculated to be disadvantageous or to frustrate his ends. Immorality does not necessarily involve any such thing. It is obvious that the normative character of moral judgment does not guarantee its reason-giving force.[29]

Could this be the solution to our dilemma? Can we avoid troubling relativist conclusions like those Harman draws by insisting that the *moral* "ought" applies to an agent independently of his reasons?

Williams, at times, seems to be suggesting something like this. In "*Ought* and moral obligation" he argues for a distinction between the moral and the "practical or deliberative" sense of *ought*: the latter, but not the former, necessarily entails that the agent has *reason*, in the internal sense, to do as we say he ought. If we discover that he does not aim to do so, and furthermore, that there is no sound deliberative route to that aim from any end he does have, we must withdraw our statement. Williams concludes that "an agent can consistently recognize that he is under a moral obligation to do a certain thing, yet conclude in his deliberation that he ought not to do that thing," where the final "ought" is the *ought* of practical reason.[30]

Williams, like Foot, thinks that not much is lost by this concession. "What weight or content is there in the thought that some [moral] obligation *applies* to [an agent who refuses to respond to it]?," he asks:

> The statement of obligation certainly *refers* to him, but that obvious truth does not capture the thought. Moreover, if he does not care about these considerations, then the commentators will feel that he ought to care about them. That distinguishes the obligations from some other *oughts*...but it does not ultimately provide any more 'hold' over the agent, since whatever question arises for the first *ought* must also arise about this second one. Beyond those facts, however, there are no

---

[29] Foot, "Morality As a System of Hypothetical Imperatives," pp. 161–162.
[30] Williams, "*Ought* and Moral Obligation," in *Moral Luck*, p. 120.

more—except the rage, frustration, sorrow, and fear of someone who sees someone else blandly doing what the first person morally thinks they ought not to be doing. In some sense, this critic deeply wants this *ought* to stick to the agent; but the only glue there is for this purpose is social and psychological.[31]

This glue, Williams suggests, is all we should be looking for. The issue is not whether our wrongdoer has normative reasons to act better, but whether we can, by any means, trigger his reformation.

The externalist, he acknowledges, wants more. She wants to express, with the judgment that an agent, regardless of his ends, morally ought to do something, the thought that there is an "external reason" for him to do so: "[t]his would seek to 'stick' the *ought* to the agent by presenting him as irrational if he ignored it, in a sense in which he is certainly concerned to be rational." But, Williams says,

> I doubt very much, in fact, whether this proposal does capture what the ordinary moral consciousness wants from the *ought* of moral obligation, as opposed to something read into it by a rationalistic theoretical construct.[32]

What's more, Williams thinks that even if we abandon this ambition, we still have plenty of arrows of moral criticism in our quiver. After imagining the cruel husband who, he has conceded, may have no reason to be nicer to his wife, Williams writes:

> There are many things I can say about or to this man: that he is ungrateful, inconsiderate, hard, sexist, nasty, selfish, brutal, and many other disadvantageous things.... There is one specific thing the external reasons theorist wants me to say, that the man has a reason to be nicer.... But if [this form of words] is thought to be appropriate, what is supposed to make it appropriate, as opposed to (or in addition to) all those other things that may be said? The question is: what is the difference supposed to be between saying that the agent has a reason to act more considerately, and saying one of the many other things we can say to people whose behaviour does not accord with what you think it should be? As, for instance, that it would be better if they acted otherwise.[33]

[31] Williams, "*Ought* and Moral Obligation," p. 122.
[32] Williams, "*Ought* and Moral Obligation," pp. 122–123.
[33] Williams, "Internal Reasons and the Obscurity of Blame," pp. 39–40.

According to Williams, the claim that the man in his example has reason to be nicer is either simply false (if we accept the internalist picture) or hopelessly obscure (if we try to adopt the externalist one). Moreover, the restriction of our responses in the case of the cruel husband to the other expressions of moral condemnation that Williams lists does not result, Williams seems to be suggesting, in an important loss of meaning. These expressions are perfectly sufficient to express the view that the man *ought morally* to be nicer to his wife.

And Harman, too, makes a very similar move, as a way of *softening* his relativist conclusions. There may be some moral-ought judgments we *can* make of Hitler and his fellow villains, he suggests, if they are moral-ought-judgments that don't entail reasons-claims. He says, for example, that perhaps we *can* say that Hitler ought not to have issued his order if we mean no more by this than that it was a terrible thing that he did so—just as we might say that cancer ought not to kill so many people, meaning it's terrible that so many people die of the disease; in making this judgment we are, of course, imputing no reasons to cancer.[34]

But we clearly mean more than this when we judge that Hitler acted wrongly. And, as Harman himself acknowledges, even this use of "ought" does not seem quite natural unless there is *someone who ought—in the reasons-implying sense*—to have done something to stop the harm in question. He approvingly cites Thomas Nagel's observation that the claim that a certain hurricane ought not to have killed so many people usually implies the absences of safety or evacuation procedures the authorities ought to have provided.[35] Ought, that is, in the reason-implying sense. (This is certainly what we meant when we made this judgment about Hurricane Katrina.) In the cancer case, the "ought"-formulation seems most natural if we think, for

---

[34] Harman, "Moral Relativism Defended," p. 6. Harman suggests that some other kinds of moral judgments might also not entail anything about an agent's reasons—he seems to allow, for example, that Hitler's actions were *evil*. (See p. 5) But it's unclear why Harman allows himself this judgment—after all, the judgment that Hitler's actions were evil surely entails that it was wrong of him to perform them, and that he (morally) ought not to have done so. I raise a related worry about Williams' similar response below.

[35] See Harman, "Moral Relativism Defended," especially note 2.

example, that our government should be putting more funding into cancer research or screening. In Hitler's case, too, our readiness to make ought-judgments reveals our recognition of the presence of reasons. But Hitler is not like cancer or a hurricane. When we say that Hitler ought not to have ordered the extermination of the Jews, we don't, of course, *just* mean that someone (else) ought to have prevented him from doing so. We would make this judgment about Hitler's actions even if no one (else) had been in a position to prevent them. The reasons we are imputing we are imputing to Hitler himself.

Nagel's observation helps bring out the extent to which our ordinary uses of "ought" (or "should")—including the moral one—are bound up with reasons-claims: reasons seem to be lurking in the background even in uses of "ought" that appear to describe non-rational subjects. And (as Foot would acknowledge) in many non-moral cases, "ought" seems to mean something very close to "has most reason to." Consider the instrumental "ought": "she ought to use a Phillips screwdriver;"[36] or the "ought" of expectation: "he ought to have arrived by now," which might be parsed as "we have sufficient reason to expect him to have arrived by now." Why think the moral "ought" behaves differently?[37]

We should, I think, be very reluctant to cut the tie between moral-ought claims or other forms of moral assessment and reasons-ascriptions. It is worth remembering that the sense of "reason" at issue here is not some narrow, technical one, but rather the perfectly ordinary sense that, I've said, internalists and externalists share, according to which a reason is simply a consideration that counts in favor of an action. It's actually less easy than Foot's discussion suggests to hear even the "ought" of etiquette as having no implication for an agent's reasons—most speakers

---

[36] Another example of Williams' (from "'Ought', 'Must', and the Needs of Morality," an unpublished lecture).

[37] As Harman notes elsewhere, understanding the moral "ought"-claims as claims about agents' reasons also helps makes sense of the fact, emphasized by W.D. Ross, that we use "ought" in two ways—to express what Ross calls *prima facie* "oughts" (as we do, e.g., when we say "One ought to keep one's promises"), and to express all-things-considered "oughts." The *prima facie* "ought" signifies the presence of a reason to act in a certain way (a reason pointed toward, for example, by the true moral principle about promise-keeping), whereas the all-things-considered use of "ought" indicates the direction the balance of all reasons tips. (Harman, "Reasons," pp. 8–10.)

who would say something like "you ought to begin eating with the out-ermost fork" assume that conforming with the rules of etiquette *is* some-thing you have reason to do. It may be possible for a speaker, by means of the right set-up and intonation, to cancel the implication: "you're *supposed* to use the outside fork first, but you should *really* use which-ever fork you like." But such uses of "ought" and "are supposed to" seem more *descriptive* than normative—they merely report the require-ments spelled out by certain rules, without taking those requirements to be considerations actually counting in favor of anything. Indeed, the switch from "you ought to" or "you should" to the (to me) much more comfortable-sounding "you're *supposed* to" in cases like this is a telltale sign that we've moved away from normative talk here. "You're supposed to" is a passive formulation: it feels more comfortable, when the speaker is communicating the verdict of norms she doesn't embrace, because it allows her to report the verdict of those norms descriptively, as endorsed by others, without endorsing them herself.

Clearly, moral judgments aren't like this: when we say, of Williams' cruel husband, that he *ought* to be kinder to his wife, we aren't just reporting that some widely accepted standard of behavior requires it; we are condemning him. In any case, reducing the force of moral-ought claims to the kind of descriptive force evinced by etiquette-judgments seems a terribly unsatisfactory way for anyone with anti-relativist moral intuitions to avoid Harman's relativist conclusions.

This brings us back to Williams' question, asked rhetorically, per-haps, but deserving of an answer nonetheless:

> [W]hat is the difference supposed to be between saying that the [cruel husband] has a reason to act more considerately, and saying one of the many other things we can say to people whose behaviour does not accord with what you think it should be?

What gets lost if we concede that our moral language does not imply anything about the reasons of the agents we judge?

The first answer to this question is one that Williams himself pro-vides. Williams is certainly right that it would be better if the cruel hus-band acted otherwise, just as it would be better if cancer killed fewer people, and better, too, if Hitler had killed fewer people. But as I've said, we react very differently to the cancer epidemic than to the Holocaust. We deeply *regret* deaths caused by cancer; we *wish* the disease were less deadly, more susceptible to a cure. But we don't just *regret* the deaths Hitler caused; we *blame* Hitler for them.[38]

Williams offers an account of blame that is in keeping with his internalist commitments. He concedes that *blaming* someone for an action is appropriate only in cases where that person can be said to have *some reason* to act differently. But this doesn't mean, he says, that we can *only* blame people who already share our moral commitments. There are two kinds of circumstances, he argues, in which it is appropriate for us to blame people who act in ways that violate our moral commitments. First, they may have acted in ways that violate some commitment in their *own* motivational set—a commitment they share with us. These are the easy cases. But just as importantly, he argues, we often blame people who may lack the relevant commitment, provided they have, instead, a desire to avoid our disapproval. Our very act of blaming, then, *gives* them a reason not to act in this way which they would not have had, had their act not registered our disapproval.

Williams continues:

> Focused blame, then, involves treating the person who is blamed like someone who had a reason to do the right thing but did not do it. It does not typically register simply a deliberative failure at the time, but rather, in varying strengths, the kinds of proleptic mechanism I have sketched. Of course, there are some hard cases, people who lie beyond any such mechanism; and it is a support for an account on these lines, that it is precisely people who are regarded as lacking any general disposition to respect the reactions of others that we cease to blame, and regard as hopeless or dangerous characters rather than thinking that blame is appropriate to them. This represents the absence from their

---

[38] Blame is the impersonal counterpart to the "personal reactive attitude" of resentment discussed by Peter Strawson. Here I am in agreement with Strawson about the kinds of circumstances that would make such resentment (or blame) inappropriate: ignorance, compulsion, accident. Williams' "hard cases" do not act in ignorance, or under compulsion, or accidentally. See Strawson, "Freedom and Resentment."

[motivational set] of anything that can be reached by these mecha-
nisms, anything it might even be hoped could yield recognition.[39]

But this pragmatic account seems to me to not to capture our practice
of blaming. Unless we consider these "unreachable" people—the "hard
cases"—to be fundamentally *irrational* (in essence, not guilty by reason of insanity)—and it is precisely this characterization of such people that Williams wants to reject—we think them just as deserving of
blame, if not more so, as people who are more responsive to our opinions.[40] If Williams is right, and such people really have no *reason* to act
differently, then blaming them becomes inappropriate. So here, then,
is one thing we seem to lose by giving up on the link between moral
judgments and reasons-ascriptions: the tie between wrongdoing and
blameworthiness seems severed, too.

The discussion of etiquette-judgments, above, suggests an additional answer to Williams' question: what gets lost when we cut the
tie between moral judgments and reasons-ascriptions is the objective
normativity we intend our moral judgments to have.

Williams claims that even the internalist can say of the cruel husband
that he is "ungrateful, inconsiderate, hard, sexist, nasty, selfish, brutal."
But these words, as Williams of course recognized, have normative as
well as descriptive components. In calling the man cruel, I mean more
than that he is willing to cause his wife to suffer to no purpose. I mean
that his doing so is *unjustified*. On Williams' view, as on Foot's, this
further, supposedly normative element of my judgment simply reports
the fact that the man's actions conflict with my own commitments—
that, for example, *I* would have reason to be nicer to his wife, were I in
his shoes (given the elements in *my* motivational set), and that I *do* have
reason to wish he'd be nicer. The Williams-internalist makes no claim,
of course, to the universal authority of those commitments. Williams'

---

[39] Williams, "Internal Reasons and the Obscurity of Blame," pp. 42–43.
[40] Note that on Williams' view, blame becomes inappropriate as soon as the proleptic mecha-
nism fails—that is, as soon as *our* bad judgment would fail to motivate the agent in question. We
needn't imagine this recalcitrant agent as someone who is totally immune to the judgments of *all*
others—just as someone immune to *our* negative judgment. It seems to me that we blame *a lot* of
people who don't care what *we* think of them.

account seems to avoid the threat of a Harman-style agent-relativism only by falling into a kind of *appraiser-relativism* instead: the judgment that the cruel husband acts wrongly is true, on this reading, when his actions conflict with the (contingent) moral commitments of the person making the judgment.

Williams' internalist account of reasons is, of course, inspired by Hume. But Hume is more open-eyed than Williams about the extent to which limiting reason to a procedural role threatens to constrain our ability to make *moral* judgments. Moral judgments, Hume says, unlike, for example, judgments about what had better, from my perspective, occur, purport to have objective, or at least *intersubjective*, validity. He draws the contrast this way:

> When a man denominates another as his *enemy*, his *rival*, his *antagonist*, his *adversary*, he is understood to speak the language of self-love, and to express sentiments, peculiar to himself, and arising from his particular circumstances and situation. But when he bestows on any man the epithets of *vicious* or *odious* or *depraved*, he then speaks another language, and expresses sentiments, in which he expects all his audience are to concur with him. He must here, therefore, depart from his private and particular situation, and must choose a point of view, common to him with others; he must move some universal principle of the human frame, and touch a string to which all mankind have an accord and sympathy.[41]

Making a moral judgment in the absence of a true internal-reason ascription is not an option, according to Hume. Indeed, moral judgments, on Hume's view, implicitly appeal to *universally shared* internal reasons.

Hume, of course, does not succumb, as a result, to total skepticism about morality. He argues instead that there is (at least, as he puts it, "while the human heart is compounded of the same elements as at present") an item that is common to the motivational sets of all people, which can therefore serve as the foundation of an intersubjectively valid moral code. All people, Hume says, in fact care about social stability and the public good, at least to some extent; since this, he says, is

---

[41] Hume, *Enquiry*, p. 272 (Second Enquiry, IX, i), emphasis in the original.

the only thing *all* people care about, any *moral* judgment, or expression of moral approval or disapproval, must be built on this foundation—must attach to actions which promote or undermine the public good: "this affection of humanity,... being common to all men,... can alone be the foundation of morals, or of any general system of blame or praise."[42] This is why Hume leans towards utilitarianism.

While Hume is optimistic that there is something—the public good—we all in fact value, which can underwrite some universally prescriptive moral judgment, he seems to take this to be largely a contingent matter. He certainly doesn't think, as we've seen, that we're *rationally required* to value the public good. (Recall his earlier admonition: " 'Tis not contrary to reason to prefer the destruction of the whole world to the scratching of my finger.") If someone does not value the public good (and not because of a failure of information or means-end reasoning), then, it seems to follow from Hume's view, we cannot claim that promoting the public good is something we ought, morally, to do. Hume takes moral relativism to be an untenable position—morality is, on his view, *conceptually universalistic*. If he is right, then internalism seems to threaten to lead not to moral *relativism* but to moral *nihilism*.

Unfortunately, Hume's optimism seems unwarranted: it appears that there are people who do not value the public good, and not because of any obvious ignorance or instrumental irrationality. But Hume is, I think, on the right track. The compatibility of internalism about reasons with universal moral truths hinges not on the rejection of the link between moral requirements and reasons but on the discovery of some end that all procedurally rational agents share, which can form the foundation of morality. Whether there is any such end will be the subject of the second half of this book. But first, a simpler solution must be assessed: we can avoid the threat of moral relativism and hold on to the link between what we ought to do and what we have reason to do by rejecting the internalist account of reasons. Perhaps what we have reason to do does not, after all, depend on our desires, broadly understood. Why should we accept internalism about reasons?

---

[42] Hume, *Enquiry*, p. 272 (Second Enquiry, IX, i).

2

Internalism and the Motivating Intuition

2.1 Two Arguments for Internalism

Internalist theses, of which Bernard Williams' is a leading example, describe a necessary relation between an agent's having a reason and some other, broadly-speaking motivational, fact about the agent. So, for example, internalists might claim that an agent can have a reason to perform some act only if he has a relevant desire, or only if he would be motivated to perform it in suitably idealized circumstances, such as the conditions of procedural rationality. Why should we accept internalism about reasons?

I'll begin by exploring the thought, appealed to by Williams and often cited in support of internalism, that reasons must be capable of explaining action: it must be possible for a fact that is a reason for an agent to act to be the reason he acts—the reason that motivates him. I'll call this the Motivating Intuition. As I will argue, it represents a key step in Williams' argument for internalism. And indeed (as I will try to show), the Motivating Intuition has much to be said for it. The problem is that versions of internalism that reflect the Motivating Intuition are vulnerable to numerous counterexamples, and that attempts to revise the internalist thesis to avoid these counterexamples introduce a divide between normative reasons and possible explanations of action. The result is that workable versions of internalist theses lose the support of the Motivating Intuition, and so begin to appear unmotivated. But the same counterexamples that forced the modification of internalist theses, and others, should also lead us to reconsider the Motivating Intuition itself. Indeed, I will argue in this chapter that we should reject the Motivating Intuition, and that examples of reasons we have to act which cannot, or should not, be the reasons why we act are in fact quite common.

Where does this leave internalism? If the Motivating Intuition is misguided, should we reject the internalist thesis? Are there any other grounds for thinking there is a necessary connection between facts about our reasons and facts about our current motivational profile? In the next chapter, I will argue that there are.

The first argument. Williams' argument for internalism about reasons in his seminal article "Internal and External Reasons" seems to *begin* from the assumption that the concept of a reason *is* the concept of a consideration that could explain the actions of a rational agent. Williams thinks that when we say someone has a reason to φ, what we *mean* is that he would be motivated to φ if he were rational. Though this claim is sometimes presented as the internalists' *conclusion*, it is in fact the *starting point* of Williams' argument. (For example, Williams claims that an *external* reasons statement (not just an internal reasons statement) "implies that a rational agent would be motivated to act appropriately."[1]) He then points out that it's easy enough to see what it would take for an *internal* reasons statement to be true of an agent. If A has an *internal* reason to φ, this means that A would be motivated to φ if he deliberated *in a procedurally rational way from his existing ends and motivations* (that's the internalist part), and it's easy enough to see why such procedurally rational deliberation might give rise to a new motivation, derived from one of the old ones. It's no mystery, Williams suggests, to see how an internal reason might serve to explain the actions of an agent who deliberates rationally.

It's much harder, Williams argues, to understand what it would take for an *external* reasons statement to be true of an agent. Because if claiming that an agent has a reason to φ amounts to claiming that he would be motivated to φ if he were rational, and if claiming the

---

[1] Williams, "Internal and External Reasons," p. 109.

reason is *external* amounts to claiming that it does not apply to the agent in virtue of any of his existing motivations, then the external reasons theorist must explain *how* it could be true of the agent that a process of rational deliberation would motivate him to φ, despite the fact that, by hypothesis, he need have no existing motivations from which the new motivation to φ could be derived. And Williams finds it hard to imagine a process of rational deliberation that could give rise to a motivation to act, but not by taking any existing motivations as a starting point.

Williams considers the possibility that an external reason could explain the action of the agent whose reason it is, provided the agent is rational, by means of the agent's *coming to believe* he has the reason to act. Rational agents, after all, will form true beliefs about their reasons, and will be motivated to do as they believe they have reason to do, so if an agent comes to believe an external reason to φ applies to him, then if he is rational he will be motivated to φ, regardless of his former motivations. And this, the thought is, is enough to establish the truth of the external reasons claim.

An example might make this possibility clearer. The external reasons theorist will want to claim that Jim has a reason to give to charity, say, regardless of whether he has any desire, broadly understood, which might give rise, after procedurally rational deliberation, to a motivation to give to charity. That is to say, Jim has an external reason to give to charity. But if Williams is right about what all reasons claims (including external reasons claims) must mean, then this statement amounts to the claim that Jim would be motivated to give to charity if he were rational, regardless of his actual motivations. How could that be true? The suggestion under consideration is that the external reasons claim is true because, if Jim were rational, he would recognize that he has reason to give to charity, and (because he is rational) this recognition would motivate him to do so (regardless of his prior motivations).

But, Williams asks, what would Jim's "recognition" amount to? If, again, Williams is right about our concept of a reason, it would have to amount to the recognition, on Jim's part, that he would be motivated to give to charity if he were rational (regardless of his existing motivations). It is a *true* belief in this proposition that is supposed to trigger in the rational Jim a motivation to give to charity. But now we do seem to have put the cart before the horse. After all, we were trying to determine how *that* proposition could be true. It doesn't seem to help to say that it can be true, because if it were true, and rational Jim therefore believed it and was motivated accordingly, then it would be true. So, Williams concludes, we can make sense of the idea of a normative reason, which Williams says, just *is* the idea of a consideration that would motivate a rational agent, only if we accept his version of the internalist thesis: that an agent can have a reason to perform some action only if he could be motivated to perform it by following a sound deliberative route from his existing ends and motivations.

The second argument. Some of the central claims of Williams' defense of internalism sow the seeds of another argument Williams himself does not make, but that is often attributed to internalists.[2] This argument begins from something like Williams' conceptual claim about reasons: "It must be a mistake," Williams writes, "to simply separate explanatory and normative reasons. If it is true that A has a reason to f, then it must be possible that he should f for that reason; and if he does act for that reason, then that reason will be the explanation of his acting." Similarly, the first premise of this second argument claims:

(1) It must be possible for me to be motivated by the reasons that apply to me. So a consideration can be a reason for me to φ only if it can motivate me to φ.

A second premise also looks familiar:

(2) A consideration can motivate me to φ only if it is relevantly connected to my "motivational set"—that is, only if it would motivate me to φ if I were deliberating in a procedurally rational way from my existing ends and motivations.

---

[2] Thomas Nagel offers it on behalf of internalism in *The Possibility of Altruism* (p. 27), although he rejects one of the premises.

The internalist conclusion follows from these premises:

(3) Therefore, a consideration can be a reason for me to φ only if it
would motivate me to φ if I were deliberating in a procedurally
rational way from my existing ends and motivations.

What should we make of this argument? One question it raises immediately is whether the notion of possibility at work in premise (1) is
plausibly the same as the notion of possibility at work in premise (2), as
it must be if the argument is to go through. The "can" in premise (2) suggests psychological possibility: it identifies the conditions under which
an agent who begins with a particular psychological profile might be
motivated to perform some action. Is this also a plausible interpretation of the "can" at work in premise (1)? Is it plausibly a conceptual
constraint on when a consideration can count as a reason for an agent
that there are circumstances in which that agent, burdened, at least at
the outset, with his actual psychological profile, might be motivated by
that consideration to act? If we take seriously Williams' claim that our
concept of a reason is the concept of a conditional explanation of the
actions of the agent for whom it is a reason, then this does strike me as
a reasonable way of interpreting the argument's first premise. And the
premise seems to gain some support from the *ought-implies-can* principle: it's very plausible that we *ought* to be motivated by the reasons
that apply to us, so it's also plausible that it must be psychologically
possible for us to be motivated by those reasons.

The second premise raises some additional worries. It looks like a
version of what is sometimes called the Humean Theory of Motivation.
Recall Hume's contention:

> Where...objects themselves do not affect us, their connexion [of effect
> to cause, which reason makes evident to us] can never give them any
> influence; and 'tis plain, that as reason is nothing but the discovery of this
> connexion, it cannot be by its means that the objects are able to affect us.

He continues:

> ...[R]eason alone can never produce any action, or give rise to voli-
> tion...Nothing can oppose or retard the influence of passion, but a

contrary impulse....Reason is, and ought only to be the slave of the passions, and can never pretend to any other office than to serve and obey them.[3]

In its crudest form, the Humean Theory of Motivation claims that all motivation depends on a relevant antecedent desire. The argument I've outlined refines this thesis in one important respect: it expands the set of attitudes that can ground motivation to include more that just desires (narrowly understood). Williams, recall, makes clear that he takes agents' "motivational sets" to include, in addition to straightforward desires, "such things as dispositions of evaluation, patterns of emotional reaction, personal loyalties, and various projects, as they may be abstractly called, embodying commitments of the agent."[4]

Even so, the second premise of the argument is controversial at best. It looks to be making an empirical assertion about psychology—an assertion about what kinds of mental events can trigger the formation of new motivations—without backing it up with empirical research (never a promising strategy in philosophical argument). Why should we believe that the formation of a belief *never* triggers the formation of a new motivation?[5] After all, even a knock on the head could do that.

But we might again revise the premise to make it more plausible. Alfred Mele, for example, defends a view he calls the "antecedent motivation theory" and attributes to Hume. He writes:

> in actual human beings, all motivation nonaccidentally produced by practical reasoning issuing in a belief favoring a course of action derives at least partly from motivation-encompassing attitudes already present in the agent before he acquires the belief.[6]

Mele allows that beliefs might sometimes motivate, but claims that *reasoning* can motivate us *nonaccidentally* only on the back of an antecedent motivation.[7]

---

[3] Hume, *A Treatise of Human Nature*, pp. 414–415 (II, 3, iii).

[4] Williams, "Internal and External Reasons," p. 105.

[5] That is, one not derived from our existing motivations.

[6] Mele, *Motivation and Agency*, p. 89.

[7] Mele contrasts this view with the "cognitive engine theory," which asserts:

> in actual human beings, some instances of practical evaluative reasoning, in or by issuing in a belief favoring a course of action, nonaccidentally produce motivation that does not derive at all from antecedent motivation. (p. 89).

It is not obvious how we are to understand the notion of nonacci-dental motivation, but it is possible that if we spell that notion out, and adjust our first premise accordingly, a version of the above argument for internalism may still go through. We might interpret the idea of practical reasoning non-accidentally producing motivation in terms of *rational motivation*—motivation that drives us when and because we are rational. If we amend the premises of the internalist argument accordingly, it reads:

(1*) It must be possible for me to be *rationally* motivated by the rea-sons that apply to me. So a consideration can be a reason for me to φ only if it can *rationally* motivate me to φ: that is, motivate me to φ *when and because I am rational.*

(2*) A consideration can *rationally* motivate me to φ only if it is rel-evantly connected to my "motivational set"—that is, only if it would motivate me to φ if I were deliberating in a procedurally rational way from my existing ends and motivations.

(3*) Therefore, a consideration can be a reason for me to φ only if it would motivate me to φ if I were deliberating in a procedurally rational way from my existing ends and motivations.

Our new premise (1*) stays true to the intuition from which we began—that a reasons statement—even a normative reasons state-ment—must still be able to serve as an explanation. After all, it was never the internalist's claim that any normative reason will serve as the actual explanation of the actions of the agent to whom it applies, since agents frequently fail to act as they have reason to act, whether because of ignorance or poor judgment or weakness of will. Rather, internalists appeal to the intuition that reasons should explain our actions when things go well—when we're not subject to such irration-alities. Reasons must be able to explain how we act when and because we are rational.

And consider the support the premise got from the *ought-implies-can* principle. I suggested earlier that premise (1) was plausible because it is entailed by *ought-implies-can* and another plausible claim: that we ought to be motivated by the reasons that apply to us. But it seems that we can plausibly claim more than this: it's better to be rationally responsive to our reasons than to be merely accidentally motivated by them. In other words, we ought to be not just motivated by our reasons, but *rationally* motivated by them.

Our new premise (2*) also improves upon the old premise (2). It no longer makes overreaching empirical claims about the conditions under which motivation *of any kind* is possible. And it sticks closer to its Humean origins in its focus on the role *Reason* can play in generating motivation. (3*) is identical to (3): our two new premises issue in the internalist conclusion as surely as the original ones did.

2.2 Motivating Intuitions

Fleshing out the second argument for internalism along these lines brings out a striking similarity between this argument and the argument for internalism that Bernard Williams actually makes in "Internal and External Reasons." For it is now clear that the central premises driving both arguments are the same: both rely, first, on the claim that a consideration could be a reason for me to act only if it would motivate me to act if I was rational, and second on the claim that no process of rational deliberation could produce in me a new motivation to act except by taking my existing motivations as a starting point. Nonetheless, the arguments—at least their first central premises—are powered by different intuitions. Williams takes his first premise to be supported by intuitions about what our reasons statements *mean*. The second argument's first premise is supported by appeal to a conceptual connection between reasons (even normative reasons) and action-explanations, and also, I have suggested, by a plausible assumption about how we ought to be motivated, taken together with the *ought-implies-can* principle.

The arguments' second central premise—the Humean one—has been the chief focus of the philosophical disagreement about the nature of reasons for action. Defenders of internalism about reasons have touted their theory's ability to reflect the myriad intuitions captured by the arguments' first premise: that practical reasons must be capable of motivating rational agents. Externalists have defended their view by attempting to block the implication from that first premise to the internalists' conclusion, largely by attacking the Humean Theory of Motivation in its various forms. But the first premise itself, and the intuitions underlying it, have received less scrutiny.

In this chapter, I will describe in detail some of the varied intuitions that might be taken to support the claim that it must be possible for us to be motivated by the reasons that apply to us, at least if we are rational. Then I will describe a series of counterexamples intended to undermine our confidence in that premise: reasons to act that cannot, or should not, motivate us to act are, I will argue, quite common. But, I will argue in the next chapter, this should not lead us to abandon internalism. Some of the intuitions that were taken to support the internalists' first premise might nonetheless provide some direct support for a version of internalism that does not rely on that premise. And this version of internalism has more to be said for it. Because this version of internalism does not rely on the Humean Theory of Motivation, it may also be better placed to withstand the externalist attack.

So: why might one think that some consideration cannot be a reason for us to act unless it could motivate us to act, and would do so if we were rational? I touched on some of the reasons for thinking this in setting out the two arguments for internalism above. I'll begin with the intuition about the *meaning* of our reasons statements that, I have suggested, is the driving force behind the first argument for internalism—the one Williams actually makes explicitly. Why does Williams think that the conception of reasons as facts that would motivate us if we were rational is one that internalists and externalists *share*? Williams writes:

> There are of course many things that a speaker may say to one who is not disposed to φ when the speaker thinks that he should be, as that he is inconsiderate, or cruel, or selfish, or imprudent; or that things, and he, would be a lot nicer if he were so motivated. Any of these can be sensible things to say. But one who makes a great deal out of putting the criticism in the form of an external reason statement seems concerned to say that what is particularly wrong with the agent is that he is *irrational*. It is this theorist who particularly needs to make this charge

precise: in particular, because he wants any rational agent, as such, to acknowledge the requirement to do the thing in question.[8]

The whole point of ascribing a reason to someone, either internal or external, Williams thinks, is to make clear to them that if they fail to act accordingly, they are failing *by their own lights*—they are failing to live up to a standard whose bindingness on them they must themselves, as rational agents, acknowledge: the standard of rationality. This is what makes such a charge different from saying merely that it would be better if they acted this way, or that we would wish them to do so, or would do so in their place. The shared etymology of *reason* and *rationality* is no accident. (Williams' claim is that on this understanding of what reasons statements mean, only internal reasons statements can be *true*.) As I argued in the last chapter, reasons statements aim at objectivity, or at least intersubjectivity, and they add something to our arsenal only if we can use them, in this way, to appeal to the requirements of this shared standard.[9]

Williams' claim about what our reasons statements mean is backed up by an additional claim about the conceptual link between reasons and explanation. It is no accident of etymology that we use the same word, "reason," to describe both the grounds on which we act (sometimes called motivating reasons), and the reasons *for us* to act (sometimes call normative reasons). In both cases, Williams suggests, reasons statements explain action: motivating reasons statements explain why we actually act the way we do, and normative reasons statements explain how we would act if all went well—if we did not succumb to weakness of will, or confusion, or ignorance, or poor judgment: if, in other words, we were rational.

So, Williams takes it to be a conceptual truth about reasons that they are the considerations that would move good practical reasoners. This certainly seems plausible, and it is reinforced by a claim that is

---

[8] Williams, "Internal and External Reasons," p. 110.

[9] As I argue in Chapter 1 (§1.4), my own view is that thick moral concepts like *cruel* or *selfish* also aim at objectivity—and so can be appropriately applied only when a reason-ascription is also appropriate. The charge of selfishness, for example, does not merely imply that the selfish person is more protective of her own interests that we would like her to be, say, or than is normal, but rather that she is more protective of her own interests than she has *reason* to be.

often made about practical reasons: that they must be *action-guiding*. Reasons, the thought is, are not purposeless: they guide us in how to behave. But a reason that could not motivate us, even if we were perfect practical reasoners, could not play this action-guiding role. So all reasons must be capable of motivating us insofar as we are reasoning well.

Michael Smith has called the claim that "what we have normative reason to do is what we would desire to do if we were fully rational" a "platitude" about practical reasons. He argues that it follows naturally from considering what is involved in identifying our reasons: from how we should go about deciding what to do. When we deliberate about how to act, he says, we ask for *advice*. But we don't ask just anyone for advice; we look for advice from people who are better situated than we are to know what we should do—who are better informed, and more rational, and less subject to our weaknesses of will—but who know us, and what drives us, well. In other words, Smith suggests, suitably idealized, we are *ourselves* best placed to give ourselves advice. When we look for our reasons, what we want to know is how *we* would act if we were better placed than we actually are: if we were fully rational.[10]

Then there is the claim that I appealed to in support of the second argument for internalism, above. Surely, we *ought* to be motivated by any reason that applies to us—indeed, we ought to be so motivated when and because we are rational. Since *ought* implies *can*, it must follow that we *can* be motivated by any reason that applies to us, when we are rational. This thought becomes all the more forceful if we accept the very plausible claim that *virtue* is a matter of motivational responsiveness to practical reasons.[11] For if we accept that thought, but deny that we ought always to be responsive to our reasons, then we are denying that we ought always to be virtuous.

The power of reasons to motivate rational agents might also help explain another fact that often comes up in the literature on internalism about reasons: that rational agents are reliably motivated to act

[10] Smith, *The Moral Problem*, pp. 150–151.
[11] For defenses of this claim, see, e.g., my "Acting for the Right Reasons" and Nomy Arpaly's *Unprincipled Virtue*.

as they judge they have reason to act. If considerations that provide reasons themselves have the power to motivate rational agents, this fact is neatly explained: rational agents are motivated to act by their judgment that they have reason to act because rational agents' judgments about their reasons are true, and are the discovery of facts that themselves have the power to motivate those agents when they are rational.

Finally, some philosophers have appealed to a somewhat more nebulous idea in support of the claim that our normative reasons must be capable of motivating us, at least when we are rational. They have suggested that a conception of reasons that allows that we might have reasons that could get no motivational grip on us, even when we're reasoning as we should, would unacceptably *alienate* us from our reasons. Peter Railton has made a point like this as part of a defense of an internalist account of an agent's *good*: "it would be an intolerably alienated conception of someone's good," he writes, "to imagine that it may fail in any way to engage him."[12] It's appealing to think something similar may be true of our reasons more generally. As Williams and others have argued, it may be a limiting condition on our moral obligations that they somehow reflect what *drives* us.[13] And there must be something about the reasons for me to act that makes them *mine*. Shouldn't it be a requirement on some consideration's providing *me* with a reason to φ that *I* can appeal to it to justify myself when I do φ? But I can appeal to such a consideration honestly only if it was one of the (motivating) reasons I *did* φ. If a consideration can't motivate me to φ, than how can I point to it to justify myself for having done so?

Taken together, these considerations provide compelling support for the claim that reasons must be capable of motivating the agents whose reasons they are, and will motivate them if they are rational.

---

[12] Railton, "Facts and Values," p. 9.

[13] As Williams puts it, "[t]here can come a point at which it is quite unreasonable for a man to give up, in the name of the impartial good ordering of the world of moral agents, something which is a condition of his having any interest in being around in the world at all." (Williams, "Persons, Character, and Morality," in *Moral Luck*, p. 14.)

I will call this claim the *Motivating Intuition*. As I have argued, the Motivating Intuition plays an essential role in at least two important arguments for internalism about reasons. Unfortunately, as examples will show, the Motivating Intuition is false.

2.3   Counterexamples to the Motivating Intuition

The counterexamples to the Motivating Intuition that I will describe fall into several classes. The first, and most commonly discussed, class of counterexamples encompasses reasons we have *because* we are not perfectly rational. Some of these examples put pressure on the idea, which is reflected in part of the Motivating Intuition, that how we *should* act is determined by how we *would* act if we were more ideally rational than we are. Here are two such examples, both of which are, in some version, familiar from the literature on internalism:

> **The Student of Reasoning.** We surely have reason to take measures to improve our ability to reason: we have reason, for example, to take lessons in chess, or logic, and it is becoming increasingly common for universities to require students to take courses in "reasoning and critical thinking." But if we were fully rational, we would not be motivated to take any such measures.

Even if our reasoning ability itself is unexceptionable, lack of self-control or weakness of will can also present us with obstacles that we ought to take into account:

> **The Sore Loser.** A squash player, who, after suffering an embarrassing defeat, rightly believes he will hit his opponent out of anger if he does not leave the court immediately, surely has reason to leave, although if he were fully rational, and so not weak-willed, he would be motivated instead to shake his opponent's hand.[14]

As these examples bring out, facts about how we would act if we were ideally rational can seem irrelevant to our actual, non-ideal

---

[14]   The example is due to Michael Smith ("Internal Reasons," p. 111), who is elaborating on a character introduced by Gary Watson.

circumstances, in which we face impediments that our perfectly rational counterparts do not. And we might wonder, more generally, why we should care about the motivations of people who are, after all, quite fundamentally different from us: what makes sense for Spock may make no sense for Captain Kirk.

What can we learn from these examples? They suggest that the Motivating Intuition, as I've stated it, is false; that (*contra* Smith) it is not, after all, a "platitude" about practical reasons that what we have reason to do is what we would be motivated to do if fully practically rational; and certainly that Williams' claim about what our reasons statements *mean* is mistaken: if we think someone has reason to improve his reasoning skills, despite acknowledging that he would not be motivated to do so if he were fully rational, we cannot plausibly *mean* by our reasons claim that he would be motivated to improve his reasoning skills if he were fully rational.

Where does this leave internalism? Examples such as these show that a simple version of the internalist formula, like the one that emerges as the conclusion of the two influential internalist arguments I set out above, is guilty of the "conditional fallacy." Our reasons can't be restricted to what we would be motivated to do if we were perfectly procedurally rational—rational relative our existing ends and motivations. If we were fully rational relative to our existing ends and motivations, we would not be motivated to do things like take chess or reasoning lessons, or abruptly walk off the squash court to avoid instigating a fight. So many internalists, Smith included, have replaced the simple internalist thesis with a more complicated thesis that avoids the conditional fallacy: they have suggested, for example, that we have reason to do what our fully procedurally rational *counterparts* would *desire or advise* us to do *in our actual situation*.[15]

Responses of this kind have some virtues. They allow internalism to retain the appeal to the shared standard of rationality that Williams considered so central to understanding reasons claims. And they also

---

[15] See, for example, Smith, *The Moral Problem*, p. 151.

retain the tie between reasons and *advice* from a well-placed advisor that Smith appealed to in support of the supposed "platitude" about practical reasons. But Robert Johnson has argued that revisions like this sacrifice the most appealing feature of internalism about reasons—its accommodation of the intuition that a reason for an agent to act must be capable of serving also as an explanation of how the agent acts, in the right circumstances:

> Once one moves away from [simple internalism about reasons] in such ways in order to avoid the conditional fallacy, an explanatory gap opens up—in this case, between your better self desiring that you should do something and you yourself being motivated to do it. The gap opens because it may be impossible for the desire had by your rationally ideal self to play any role in the explanation of your actions.[16]

Johnson suggests that if internalists are to retain their advantage over externalists, they must find a way of avoiding the conditional fallacy while continuing to satisfy the "explanatory requirement"—the requirement that an agent's normative reasons be capable of explaining his actions, by serving as his motivating reasons for acting. The two examples I've discussed so far do nothing to undermine the force of that requirement: *we* can be motivated by the reasons we have not to harm people to walk away instead of instigating a fight, and *we* can be motivated by the reasons we have to improve our reasoning skills to take chess lessons or courses in critical thinking, even if our ideally rational counterparts would not be so motivated, and even though the desires they might have on our behalf seem explanatorily irrelevant to how we act.

But as other counterexamples to the Motivating Intuition, including the example on which Johnson himself focuses, show, the case for internalism about reasons would not be strengthened by its satisfying the explanatory requirement, because reasons need not be capable of motivating us, after all.

---

[16] Johnson, "Internal Reasons: Reply to Brady, Van Roojen and Gert," p. 574. See also Johnson, "Internal Reasons and the Conditional Fallacy."

Let's start with Johnson's own example[17] :

> **"James Bond".** Let's say I become convinced I am James Bond. The fact that I am suffering from such a delusion may give me an excellent reason to see a psychiatrist for treatment. But it cannot motivate me to see the psychiatrist. For if this fact could motivate me to seek help, I would no longer be convinced I was James Bond. Someone who firmly believes he is James Bond cannot be motivated to seek a psychiatrist by the fact that his belief is a delusion.

Johnson is right that the versions of internalism about reasons that are revised to avoid the conditional fallacy must allow that "James Bond" has such a reason, since it seems hard to deny that "James's" perfectly rational counterpart would advise him to seek psychiatric help, or would wish that he'd (fortuitously) seek help, were he to suddenly find himself in "James's" less-than-ideal position. And he is right that this shows that such revised versions of internalism do not satisfy the explanatory requirement. But the "James Bond" example is as much a counterexample to the explanatory requirement itself as it is to simple, unrevised internalism. It suggests that internalists should perhaps not be trying to accommodate the explanatory requirement in the first place.

The story of "James Bond" has the characteristic neatness and outlandishness of a philosopher's example. But I hope to demonstrate that cases of normative reasons that cannot motivate the agents whose reasons they are are in fact quite common and familiar. I'll begin with an example from theoretical reasoning:

> **My Fallibility.** I currently have some unjustified beliefs. Let's call this plausible proposition *my fallibility*. My current unjustified beliefs are reasons for me to believe that I have some unjustified beliefs. But they can't be the reasons *why* I believe in *my fallibility*. Because if I were convinced of *my fallibility* by the fact that I have those beliefs, then I would no longer count as having them. For example, imagine that I believe that Elvis is still alive, despite overwhelming good evidence to the contrary. Call the fact that I believe Elvis lives *BEL*. I'm aware of *BEL*, and *BEL* provides good evidence of *my fallibility*. But I can't be convinced of *my fallibility* by *BEL*. If I were, I wouldn't really count as believing that

---

Elvis lives, and so *BEL* would not obtain (and, of course, could no longer provide support for *my fallibility*).

Similarly (given that I believe Elvis lives), the fact that Elvis is dead and this has been well-documented (call this fact *ED*) provides me with a good reason to believe in *my fallibility*. And I undoubtedly ought to believe in *my fallibility*. But I can't be justified in believing in it by *ED*, because if I believed *ED*, I couldn't really believe Elvis lives. In which case *ED* would no longer provide support for *my fallibility*.

We might respond to this case by questioning whether the fact that I believe that Elvis lives really gives *me* a reason to believe in *my fallibility*. But it clearly gives *you* a reason to believe in *my fallibility*, if you have access to exactly the same information as I have, both about Elvis and about my beliefs. And it would be strange if a fact that provided you with a reason didn't also provide me with a reason, when you and I have access to the same evidence. Similarly, I'm not tempted to conclude that, since I believe Elvis lives, *ED* isn't really evidence *I* have for *my fallibility*, and so isn't a reason for me to believe in *my fallibility*. It seems indisputable that I have reason to believe *ED*, and *ED* clearly establishes *my fallibility*.

The examples I've discussed so far all involve reasons we have because we are not perfectly rational. These reasons could not motivate us if we were fully rational, because they would not *apply* to us if we were fully rational. But there are other circumstances in which our reasons might not be capable of motivating us. One interesting class of counterexamples to the Motivating Intuition concerns things we have reason to do (and can do), but which we cannot *do for those reasons*. In a paper investigating some apparent paradoxes of deterrence, Gregory Kavka describes circumstances, which he calls "Special Deterrent Situations" (or SDSs), in which agents would find themselves faced with reasons of this sort. An SDS arises when we have reason to *intend* to apply a very harmful sanction, affecting many innocent people, in retaliation for what would be a similarly extremely harmful and unjust offense, because *intending* to apply such a sanction is the likeliest means of deterring the offense. But, because the sanction is so harmful and its victims innocent, we have no reason to *actually apply* the sanction should the offense occur.[18] Such

---

[18] See Kavfa, "Some Paradoxes of Deterrence."

circumstances are likely not just the stuff of philosophy papers: a plausible real-life SDS (which Kavka discusses) is provided by:

Nuclear Deterrence. Perhaps the most likely way to deter a nuclear attack is to intend to retaliate against any attacking nation by responding in kind.[19] But if an attack should occur, no good could come of actually retaliating. So if I am responsible for the defense strategy of a nation threatened by nuclear attack, I have reason to *intend* to retaliate against any such attack with a nuclear attack targeting the aggressor. But I have no reason to actually retaliate. Because of this I cannot be motivated to form the intention to retaliate if I am fully rational: rational agents do not form intentions to act against their own (correct) assessment of the balance of reasons. And what's more, they cannot intend to perform actions they know they will not perform when the time for performance comes: if the nuclear attack occurs, and I know I have conclusive reason not to retaliate, I won't retaliate. And since I know, now, that I won't retaliate were an attack to occur, I cannot intend to retaliate.

Kavka's familiar *Toxin Puzzle* provides a similar, if more fanciful, example:

Toxin Puzzle. If I am offered a million dollars today to simply *form the intention* tonight to drink a (non-lethal, but ill-making) toxin tomorrow, I cannot (certainly not if I am rational) be motivated to form the intention to drink the toxin by the reason (the million-dollar prize) I have to form it, since I know now that I will not need to drink the toxin to win the prize, and so have no reason to drink the toxin, and conclusive reason not to. When tomorrow rolls around, drinking the toxin can make me no richer, and will make me considerably sicker. So I would have to be very *ir*rational to drink it. If I'm resourceful, I may succeed in finding another way to motivate myself to intend to drink the toxin (and to drink it)—for example, by betting a friend a substantial sum of money that I will drink it; but in this case I will not be motivated to form the intention by the original reason I had to form it—that is, by the million-dollar prize (though the prize will have motivated me to make the bet).[20]

---

[19] Kavka notes (citing Herman Kahn, *On Thermonuclear Warfare*, p. 185, and Anthony Kenny, "Counterforce and Countervalue," pp. 162–164), that "writers on strategic policy frequently assert that nuclear deterrence will be effective only if the defending nation really intends to retaliate." (Kavka, p. 278).

[20] See Kavka, "The Toxin Puzzle," pp. 33–34.

The *Toxin Puzzle* and the problem of *Nuclear Deterrence* differ from the cases I've already discussed: they do not turn on reasons that I have *because* I am not fully rational. (If anything, the problems of motivation they bring to light afflict us because we are, in a sense, prisoners of our own rationality.) And the reasons I have to intend to drink the toxin, or to intend to initiate a retaliatory attack, might not be capable of motivating me even when I'm not fully rational. This is simply not how the process of intention-formation works. The forming of intentions to act is driven by our motivations to perform the intended act. I cannot, through sheer force of will, form an intention to do something I believe I have no reason to do, and conclusive reason not to do, even if I believe I have reason to form the intention.

In being non-voluntary in this way, intention-formation resembles belief-formation. We cannot believe at will, simply because doing so would benefit us in some way, when our perception of the balance of epistemic reasons tips the other way. So here is another counterexample to the Motivating Intuition from the realm of reasons for belief:

> **Pragmatic Belief.** I may have overwhelming pragmatic reasons to believe some proposition—perhaps that my disease is curable, if optimism would make me more likely to recover. But I cannot believe my disease is curable for that reason—I cannot be motivated to believe this by the fact that believing it will increase my chances of survival. Again, I may be able to bring myself to believe it by some other means; but I cannot believe it for the only genuine reason I have to believe it: my pragmatic reason.

Should we perhaps conclude that reasons such as these—reasons for believing that are not generated by the believed proposition's truth, or reasons for intending that are not generated by the intended action's value—are not genuine reasons after all? I don't think so. After all, it may be possible for me to get myself to form the relevant intention or belief by other means: I might, in *Toxin Puzzle* (as I suggested), make a bet with a friend that gives me reason to actually drink the toxin, and so motivates me to form the intention to drink it; or I might, in *Nuclear Deterrence*, encourage in myself the kind of jingoistic fervor that I know will reduce my level of concern for the potential victims of a retaliatory attack to the point where I could intend to retaliate; or I might, in *Pragmatic Belief*, purposefully seek out medical opinions only from doctors with a reputation for optimism. If any of these methods of manipulating my own beliefs and intentions have a chance of success, I may have reason to undertake them. The very facts that could not motivate me to form the relevant beliefs and intentions give me reasons to try to bring it about that I form them in some other way. But it would be very strange if I had a reason to bring it about that I believe or intend something I have no reason to believe or intend. If I have no reason to believe or intend something, why trick myself into doing so? In order to explain why we might sometimes have reasons to manipulate ourselves in this way, we need to acknowledge that we can have reasons to believe or intend something that cannot motivate us to believe or intend it.[21]

As Kavka notes, SDSs also bring out the somewhat surprising conclusion that we might sometimes have reason to corrupt ourselves—to bring about in ourselves dispositions to act against the balance of moral reasons, or to fail to be properly motivationally sensitive to some moral reasons. An agent faced with a genuine SDS, like *Nuclear Deterrence*,

---

[21] Might I be misdescribing these cases? Are they really cases where our reasons to believe or intend something *can* motivate us to believe or intend it, just *indirectly*? Maybe, for example, I count as being motivated to intend to drink the toxin by the promise of the million-dollar prize in virtue of the promise of the prize's serving as a *second-order* motivation for me to be (first-order) motivated by something else—my bet with my friend, say—to intend to drink the toxin. If that's right, this might not be a counterexample to the Motivating Intuition after all.

But higher-order motives don't co-motivate the acts motivated by the first-order motives that they target—at least not simply in virtue of functioning as higher-order motives. Other cases help bring this out. Consider, for example, a religious believer, who, from self-interested motives (she fears divine retribution) manages to turn herself (perhaps through particularly effective counseling—let's not worry too much about the details) into someone who is genuinely (and noninstrumentally) motivated by the needs of others. Or consider a violent heavy drinker whose wife threatens to leave him unless he starts acting out of (noninstrumental) concern for her wellbeing, and who is motivated to stop drinking, not out of concern for his wife, but simply, and selfishly, because he fears loneliness—knowing that getting sober will result in his becoming more concerned for his wife for her own sake. It seems right to say, of both these people, that they are morally better after their reformations than before, despite the self-interested motives driving those reformations. Though they may be motivated to develop good motives by selfish reasons, their actions after their reformation do not seem to be motivated by self-interest. And just as their higher-order selfish motivating reasons should not be seen as co-motivating the actions motivated by the first-order motives the selfish ones targeted, so my higher-order motivating reasons to acquire a motivation to intend to drink the toxin should not be seen as co-motivating that intention.

ought (if she can) to bring it about that she forms the deterrent intention—in this case, to retaliate—even though this means she'll have reduced her sensitivity to genuine moral reasons. This has important implications for our consideration of the Motivating Intuition. In particular, it seems to run counter to a thought which played an important role in our defense of the Motivating Intuition: that we *ought* always to be as virtuous as we can be, and therefore, since it's plausible that being virtuous is a matter of being appropriately motivationally sensitive to our moral reasons, that we ought always to be motivated by the reasons that apply to us. This thought, I argued, underlies the crucial first premise of the second argument for internalism I set out in §2.1. But as Kavka's SDSs show, we sometimes have reasons to lessen our own sensitivity to reasons.

In *Nuclear Deterrence* and *Pragmatic Belief* we may have reason to corrupt ourselves because unless we do, we will not be able to form intentions or beliefs we have good reason to form. In *Nuclear Deterrence*, the problem arises because of the partly involuntary nature of intention-formation: we cannot, at will, form the intention to do something we believe we have no reason to do. And cases where we have reason to intend to do something we have no reason to do may be quite rare. But the problem for the Motivating Intuition is in fact much broader than the example of SDSs suggests. It is in fact surprisingly often true that we ought not to be motivated by reasons that apply to us.

Usually, when it is true that we ought not be motivated by our reasons, this is because we are more likely to succeed at doing what we have reason to do if we aren't motivated by those reasons.[22] A particularly grim version of this problem is faced by soldiers fighting in a justifiable war. The military historian Richard Holmes, who interviewed

---

[22] We can design science-fiction-y cases to show that it might be possible for an agent to find herself in a situations where she cannot successfully do what she has reason to do if she is motivated by that reason. Philip Stratton-Lake describes such an example: he imagines an evil-demon world, in which we cannot do what we have reason to do *for that reason*, because the demon will ensure that the actions of well-motivated people bring about horrific consequences. In this world, we can't act for the reasons we have to act. But it doesn't follow that we can't do what we have reason to do. (See Stratton-Lake, *Kant, Duty, and Moral Worth*, p. 18.)

veterans of many wars, describes the problem faced by the soldier this way:

> [a] soldier who constantly reflected upon the knee-smashing, widow-making characteristics of his weapon, or who always thought of the enemy as a man exactly like himself, doing much the same task and subjected to exactly the same stresses and strains, would find it difficult to operate effectively in battle.... Without the creation of abstract images of the enemy, and without the depersonalization of the enemy during training, battle would become impossible to sustain.... If ... men reflect too deeply upon their enemy's common humanity, then they risk being unable to proceed with a task whose aims may be eminently just and legitimate.[23]

This might be so even if the "enemy's common humanity" underlies the justification for the war itself, and so provides a fundamental reason for fighting. That is:

> **Soldier in a Just War.** In a war fought on humanitarian grounds, soldiers may have reason to desensitize themselves to the common humanity of the inhabitants of an enemy state so that they can more effectively fight a war whose very justification is provided by that common humanity. If they have reason to fight in the war, and fight effectively, then they ought not be motivated to fight by that reason.[24]

Pragmatic grounds not to be motivated by the reasons that apply to us are often generated when we are forced to act in emergency situations and against great odds, a fact that was strikingly demonstrated by post-crash interviews of Captain Chelsey Sullenberger, the US Airways pilot who miraculously succeeded in landing a commercial

---

[23] Holmes, *Acts of War: The Behaviour of Men in Battle*, p. 361.

[24] I don't want to suggest that such desensitization is easy to justify or usually justified. Indeed, the fact, described by Holmes, that soldiers often must be desensitized in this way to be effective soldiers is, I believe, one of the reasons why wars are hard to justify. Not only do wars require participants to "corrupt" themselves to be effective soldiers (a cost with immediate and long-term effects, for the soldier as well as for others, that should not be underestimated), but the need for such self-corruption also creates a significant risk that soldiers will prosecute a potentially justifiable war in a manner that makes it unjustified; as Holmes says, "if the abstract image [of the enemy, internalized by soldiers in training] is overdrawn or depersonalization is stretched into hatred, the restraints on human behavior in war are easily swept aside" (p. 361).

jetliner with no working engines on New York's Hudson River, improbably saving the lives of all 155 passengers and crew on board:

> **Emergency Landing.** On January 15th, 2009, Captain Sullenberger successfully emergency-landed an Airbus A320, which had lost all thrust in both engines due to a double bird strike, in the icy waters of the Hudson River, with no loss of life. Asked, in a *60 Minutes* interview by Katie Couric, whether he had been thinking about the passengers as his plane was descending rapidly towards the Hudson, Captain Sullenberger replied, "Not specifically.... I mean, I *knew* I had to solve this problem. I knew I had to find a way out of this box I found myself in.... My focus at that point was so intensely on the landing... I thought of nothing else."[25]

While the fact that many lives depended on his successfully landing the aircraft undoubtedly provided Captain Sullenberger with a reason to do so, it is also clear that it was a very good thing that the Captain was not in fact motivated by this reason as he guided the plane onto the water. Indeed, it seems likely that years of training in emergency preparedness coached the Captain, with good reason, not to think about the ultimate reasons for successfully handling a crisis situation when faced with the need to do so.

The lessons of *Soldier in a Just War* and *Emergency Landing* generalize. A specialist in a rarely curable disease may be able to cure more patients if she's in it for the social prestige than if she's in it chiefly to save lives, since her low success rate might otherwise drive her to quit. A surgeon may operate more successfully if she learns to suppress some normal sympathy for patients in unavoidable pain[26], and she may be less likely to make nervous mistakes in delicate procedures if she is not thinking of the life that is at stake. In fact, many of us have found ourselves in situations in which we were fortunate that we were driven by ulterior motives, habit, instinct, or "auto-pilot" rule-following to make decisions or react to threats which we would have likely reacted to less well if we had been responding motivationally to our reasons for doing

---

[25]   Couric interviewed Captain Sullenberger on *60 Minutes*, airdate February 8th, 2009.

[26]   As Kavka also suggests—see "Some Paradoxes of Deterrence," note 20, p. 278.

so. If a child runs into the street right in front of my car, I hit the brakes automatically—I am not motivated by a concern for the well-being of the child. In a surprising number of cases, there is much to be said for *not* being motivated by our reasons.

2.4 What These Counterexamples Can Teach Us

What can we learn from these counterexamples? Has anything survived of the intuitions that supported the Motivating Intuition?

The examples of the *Student of Reasoning* and the *Sore Loser* show us that "A has a reason to φ" cannot *mean* "A would be motivated to φ if she were rational," as Williams suggested, and that the Motivating Intuition does not state a "platitude" about practical reason, as Smith suggested. We readily ascribe reasons to the *Student of Reasoning* and the *Sore Loser* despite the fact that we are perfectly aware that they would not be motivated to act on those reasons if they were perfectly rational (because they would not have those reasons).

While the *Student of Reasoning* and the *Sore Loser* would not be motivated by their reasons if they were perfectly rational (because the reasons would, in that case, no longer apply), their reasons could nonetheless serve as explanations of their actions in their *actual* circumstances—the circumstance in which they do apply. So does the conceptual link between normative reasons and possible *explanations* of actions, to which Williams also appeals, hold up? No: the examples of the deluded *"James Bond"* and of *My Fallibility* show that we can have reasons for both action and belief that could not possibly serve as explanations of our actions or beliefs, even in the circumstances in which they do apply to us.

Moreover, the problem is not just a result of our imperfect rationality, as the cases of the *Student of Reasoning*, the *Sore Loser*, *"James Bond,"* and *My Fallibility* might suggest. The predicaments presented by *Nuclear Deterrence*, the *Toxin Puzzle*, and the problem of *Pragmatic Belief* show that even if we're fully rational, we might have reasons to act or believe that could not motivate us to act or believe accordingly. It won't always be possible for us to do as we have reason to do, *for* the reason we have to do it.

And finally, as the cases of the *Soldier in a Just War* and the *Emergency Landing* show, and as our own experience will confirm, even when we *can* be motivated to do something by the reason we have for doing it, it's not always true that we *ought* to be motivated by that reason. Sometimes, we are significantly more effective in doing what we have reason to do if we train ourselves to be motivated differently. If it's not always true that we *ought* to be (rationally) motivated by the reasons that apply to us, we cannot appeal to the *ought-implies-can* principle to derive the conclusion that we *can* always be (rationally) motivated by the reasons that apply to us.

Remember that the *First Argument* for internalism about reasons, the one explicitly made by Williams in "Internal and External Reasons," depended on the claim that the Motivating Intuition captures what our reasons-statements *mean*: that what we *mean* when we ascribe a reason to φ to someone is that they would be motivated to φ if they were rational. And remember my suggestion that the *Second Argument* for internalism about reasons, which also includes the Motivating Intuition as a premise, gained support from the *ought-implies-can* principle. As the counterexamples to the Motivating Intuition show, both of these influential arguments for internalism about reasons fail before we've even considered their controversial Humean premises. If, as Williams and Johnson have suggested and as the structure of the debate about internalism implies, internalism's ability to accommodate the Motivating Intuition was its chief virtue, then considering the counterexamples I've described should lead us to abandon internalism about reasons.

But I don't think we should abandon internalism. I believe internalism still receives some direct support from some of the considerations to which I appealed in defense of the Motivating Intuition in §2.2. And I believe we have other good grounds for taking internalism about reasons seriously.

3

Why Be An Internalist About Reasons?

3.1 Internalism without the Motivating Intuition

I've argued that Bernard Williams was wrong to present the Motivating Intuition as an account of what our reasons statements mean. But a different version of the internalist thesis may still receive some *direct* support from some of the considerations that motivated the Motivating Intuition. Nonetheless, the simple version of internalism with which I began—the version defended by Williams—must be false, since it entails the Motivating Intuition. A reason cannot be a consideration that *would motivate* me if I were deliberating in a procedurally rational way from my existing ends and motivations.

Remember that the essential feature of an internalist account of reasons is that it ties the truth of a reasons claim to the presence of a suitable element in an agent's motivational set: according to internalism, what we have reason to do depends fundamentally on what ends, broadly understood, we already have. Externalism, by contrast, holds that facts about our reasons do not fundamentally depend on facts about what we care about. The distinction is sometimes put differently: internalism embraces a *procedural* conception of practical rationality, according to which the rational requirement to hold certain ends is generated indirectly by the relation of those ends to other ends we already hold, as a result, in particular, of requirements of internal consistency and coherence. (One might compare this to the case of theoretical reason, which may require us, by means of standards of internal consistency and coherence, to hold certain beliefs in virtue of their relationship to other beliefs that we hold.) According to an externalist, *substantive* notion of rationality, reason may require us to hold some (moral and prudential) ends directly, and regardless of what else is true about us.

These ways of thinking about the disagreement between internalists and externalists make clear that the internalists' claim about the necessary motivating or explanatory power of reasons is not an essential feature of the view. Our reasons may depend on our antecedent ends not because those ends are the source of the (supposed) *motivating* force of normative reasons, but rather because those ends are the source of the *justifying* force of those reasons. As the example of a non-motivating theoretical reason provided by *My Fallibility* shows, a consideration (in that case—the fact that I have the unsupported belief that Elvis lives) can throw its *justificatory* weight behind my performing or believing some action or proposition (in that case, the proposition that I have some unjustified beliefs), even if it cannot *move* me to perform the action, or *convince* me of the proposition.

According to the version of internalism about reasons for action that I am most interested in defending,

> a reason for an agent to φ is a consideration that counts in favor of φ-ing—that throws its justificatory weight behind φ-ing—in virtue of the relation it shows φ-ing to stand in to the agent's existing ends (for example, by showing that φ-ing is a means to one of those ends, or constitutive of it, or valuable in consequence of the value of that end).

This thesis is internalist, because it takes what we have reason to do to depend fundamentally on what ends we already have. But unlike many internalist accounts of reasons, my account does not rely on the claim that reasons must be capable of motivating rational agents, or necessarily motivate agents who recognize them: on this view, facts give us reasons when they are the source of a certain kind of *evidence* (given our other ends), not when they are the source of a possible *motivation* (given our other ends).

It may be helpful to think through how this version of internalism, unlike Williams', can recognize the reasons for action and belief I've appealed to as counterexamples to the Motivating Intuition in the cases I've discussed. Take, for example, the case of Captain Sullenberger: although the Captain should not and perhaps *could* not have been motivated to take the necessary actions to land the plane safely by the fact that over a hundred and fifty lives depended on his doing so, it is clear that the fact that his taking those actions would save those lives was evidence, relative to his antecedent value commitments, that taking the actions in question would be a valuable thing to do. The value of *that end*, in other words—of doing what was necessary to get the plane safely on the Hudson—was entailed by the value of his other ends and the consistency and coherence requirements of procedural rationality.

Similar arguments can be used to show that the soldier in my *Just War* example has an *internal reason* (as I understand it) to fight effectively (provided by the common humanity of the inhabitants of the enemy state); that the sick person in my example of *Pragmatic Belief* has a (practical) *internal reason* to believe her disease is curable (provided by the survival benefits of believing this); that I have an *internal reason* to intend to drink the toxin when faced with the *Toxin Puzzle* (provided by fact that so intending will win me the million-dollar prize); that the defense strategist in *Nuclear Deterrence* has an *internal reason* to intend to retaliate (provided by the deterrence benefits of the intention); that Johnson's *James-Bond*-delusional patient has an *internal reason* to see the psychiatrist (since, presumably, it is one of his important ends that he not be deluded); that the *Sore Loser* has an *internal reason* to leave the court without shaking hands (since this will prevent him from punching his opponent); and that the *Student of Reasoning* has an *internal reason* to take rationality-improving lessons. In each case the agents have value-commitments that, taken together with requirements of consistency and coherence and the reason-providing fact, entail the value of their taking such actions, despite the fact that they either should not, cannot, or could not if fully rational be motivated by those reason-providing facts to act.[1]

3.2 Remotivating Internalism: Epistemic Humility

This revised version of internalism about practical reasons has a lot more to be said for it. It retains some of the features of Williams' internalism about reasons that made it an attractive view—some of the features that motivated the Motivating Intuition. It avoids alienating us from our reasons: on the picture of reasons it presents, reasons are firmly rooted in facts about what matters to us. It also allows that reasons are action-guiding, though they may not guide us to the action they provide us with reason to do. So, for example, while the agents in the *Toxin Puzzle* and *Nuclear Deterrence* cases can't be motivated to form the valuable intentions by the reasons they have to form those intentions, they *can* be guided by those reasons to do what it takes to bring it about that they form the relevant intentions for *other* reasons. (The agent in the *Toxin Puzzle* might, I suggested, make a side bet with a friend that makes it worth her while to *actually drink* the toxin, thereby ensuring that she will, at the relevant time, intend to drink it.) Johnson's imagined patient in the *James Bond* case admittedly can't be guided by his reasons in this way. But here Michael Smith's suggestion that when we deliberate about our reasons, we're interested in the advice of people who share our basic commitments but are better-informed and more rational than we are may be helpful, and may provide some direct support for the internalist view of reasons. This thought may spell out one way in which reasons may be action-guiding—not irrelevant to moral deliberation—even when they can't motivate the agent whose reasons they are: an agent's reasons should at least guide *us*, when we advise her about how she should act.

---

[1] I omit the case of *My Fallibility* because it concerns *epistemic* reasons for belief, and I am not concerned with the possibility of internal epistemic reasons here. I return to the case of epistemic reasons in §3.3, below.

More importantly, the revised version of the internalist thesis still captures Williams' thought that when we attribute a reason to someone, we intend to appeal to a shared standard of conduct that that person must, as a rational agent, recognize as authoritative.

Remember that the notion of rationality that plays a central role in the internalist account of reasons is *procedural*, not *substantive* (that is, it concerns standards for proper relations *between* ends, but doesn't specify any end as rationally required, *per se*, regardless of its relation to things we already care about). Despite being irreducibly normative, the standards of procedural rationality may be both less controversial and, like their theoretical counterparts, significantly harder to question than the substantive standards of rationality to which externalists appeal—standards declaring us to be irrational simply in virtue of not caring about some end, like the well-being of others, regardless of that end's relation to our other ends and commitments. As Nagel had put it, in *The Last Word*, his defense of the objectivity of reason, "it is necessarily employed in every purported challenge to itself."[2]

To be sure, some substantive reasons claims (we have reason not to torture others for fun) seem decidedly uncontroversial. And we might question quite how uncontroversial the standards of procedural rationality really are. But uncontroversial cases are not the problem cases for externalists. The difficulty emerges instead in the context of *disputes* about reasons. The procedural standard of rationality, if not exactly uncontroversial, may nonetheless be one that someone who disagrees with the internalist at the outset about what her *reasons* are might agree on. So it could serve as a kind of Archimedean point against which we might brace ourselves in disputes about reasons. Externalists, by contrast, if they want to appeal to a supposedly shared standard of rationality, must appeal to a substantive standard—one that simply incorporates, as a *rational requirement*, the need to respond to the very reason whose existence their interlocutor disputes. If she disputes the existence of the reason, she'll also dispute the existence of

---

[2] Nagel, *The Last Word*, p. 233.

the corresponding rational requirement. So internalism offers important dialectical advantages over externalism.

Relatedly, internalism about reasons seems less presumptive than
externalism. We should not assume that some of us have special epistemic access to what matters, especially in the absence of any criterion
for making such a judgment. It's better—less dogmatic—to start from
the assumption, as internalism does, that everyone's ends are equally
worthy of pursuit—and correct this assumption only by appealing to
standards that are as uncontroversial as possible, or at least don't beg
the very question that is under debate.

According to externalism about reasons, what matters normatively—that is, what we *have reason* to do or pursue or protect or
respect or promote—does not depend in any fundamental way on
what in fact matters to us—that is, what we *do* do and pursue and protect and respect and promote. Some of us happen to be motivated by
what actually matters, and some of us are "wrongly" motivated. But
externalists can offer no explanation for this supposed difference
in how well we respond to reasons—no explanation of why some of
us have the right motivations and some of us the wrong ones—that
doesn't itself appeal to the views about what matters that they're trying
to justify. (They can explain why some people have the right motivations by saying, for example, that they're good people, but that assumes
the truth of the normative views that are at issue.[3])

A comparison to the epistemic case helps bring out what is unsatisfactory in the externalist position. We sometimes attribute greater
epistemic powers to some people than to others despite not being able
to explain why they're more likely to be right in their beliefs about a
certain topic. Chicken-sexing is a popular example of this among philosophers. We think some people are more likely to form true beliefs
about the sex of chickens than others even though we can't explain
why they are better at judging the sex of chickens. But in the case of

---

[3] The same problem confronts the Aristotelian view, according to which well-motivated people
have their good upbringing to thank for it. What counts as a good upbringing seems itself to be a
moral question.

chicken-sexing, we have independent means of determining the truth, and so we have independent verification that chicken-sexers usually get things right. Externalism seems to tell us that some of us are better reasons-sensors than others, but without providing the independent means of determining which of us are in fact more reliably motivated by genuine normative reasons (or even that some of us are).[4]

Internalism paints a different and more informative picture of what's going on when some people are more responsive to genuine reasons than others. According to internalism, what matters normatively depends in part on what in fact matters to us: on what we are motivated to do and pursue and protect and respect and promote. Something's mattering to me provides a *prima facie* reason to promote it, but only a *prima facie* reason. I might care about some things whose mattering is incompatible with the mattering of other things I care about—that's an inconsistency. Or I might fail to care about some things whose value is entailed by the value of other things I care about (failure to intend to take the necessary means to my ends provides one example of this). So the set of ends whose value is entailed by the standards of procedural rationality, applied to my actual ends, is very likely not identical to the set of my actual ends. The internalist picture offers an account of what goes wrong when we fail to be motivated to act as we have reason to act. And according to internalism, we're all equally good at responding to our reasons so long as we're equally procedurally rational.[5]

---

[4] What counts as an "independent means" of determining the truth? After all, the chicken-sexer and the biologist both rely on sensory experience when investigating the sex of chickens—are their means really independent? If not, then the chicken-sexing example may not provide the contrast-case to externalism that I am looking for.

It is true that both chicken-sexers and biologists rely on their senses for determining the sex of chicks. So the fact that they usually agree cannot be appealed to in support of the supposition that sensory experience is a good way to gather information about the sex of chickens. If such experience is in general illusory, that discredits the biologists as much as it does the chicken-sexers. But I am assuming here that sensory experience is a good way to gather this information. The question is whether the *particular* way in which chicken-sexers employ their senses is a good way of sexing chickens. And the fact that biologists employ their senses to do this in a different way, and yet arrive at the same result, gives us some reason to think that chicken-sexers are good at sexing chicks.

[5] It does not help to say that the person who responds well to what matters is the person who is more *substantively* rational, since the standards of substantive rationality build assumptions about what matters in from the start. To call someone substantively rational is just to say that (in addition to being procedurally rational) they respond well to what matters. So calling someone substantively rational cannot *explain* this fact.

Internalism recognizes the well-motivated agent—the person who responds well to practical reasons—the same way we recognize a talented logician. Unlike in the case of chicken-sexing, we have no independent means of verifying that the talented logician gets at the truth about logic—no means that don't employ the same procedure as the logician uses herself. But we do have a view about what makes someone good at getting at logical truths: superior reasoning skills. In other words, they're particularly good at following the relevant procedure. In fact, we think superior logical reasoning skills make people better at identifying logical truths precisely because we think it's plausible that such truths are constituted by what following the procedure produces—by the conclusions at which someone following the procedure perfectly would arrive. Similarly, internalism holds that being procedurally rational will make a person more likely to respond appropriately to her reasons because it holds that what a person's reasons are depends on what matters to her and the requirements of procedural rationality, and so is often determined by what matters to a person when she's fully procedurally rational (though not always, as the arguments of the last chapter showed). The situation resembles what Rawls called "pure procedural justice." In cases of pure procedural justice, a decision procedure is just not because it allows you to track or identify outcomes that are independently just; rather, the outcomes it produces are just *because* they result from the right procedure.[6]

3.3 Remotivating Internalism: the Analogy to Theoretical Reasons

Internalism about reasons is usually presented as a thesis about *practical* reasons. This is not surprising, since the standard arguments for internalism appeal to theories concerning what can motivate us to act, and concerning the supposed motivating force of moral judgments. But it is useful to think about what internalism about *theoretical*

---

[6] John Rawls, *A Theory of Justice*, p. 86.

reasons might look like. Doing so helps illustrate another advantage internalism offers over externalism: I will argue that while there *might* be some external reasons for belief, any plausible candidate for an external reason for belief will have special features that can have no parallel in the practical case. So considering the case of theoretical reasons should lead us to conclude that there are no external practical reasons.

Remember that an *internal practical reason* to φ is a consideration that counts in favor of φ-ing in virtue of the relation it shows φ-ing to stand in to our antecedent ends. So, according to internalism about reasons, what we have reason to intend, or what ends we ought to adopt, depends only on what ends we already have and the requirements of procedural rationality. If we're procedurally rational (rational relative to our ends), then we're rational all-things-considered.[7] (We'll be complying with our subjective reasons, and, if we're also fully informed, we'll be complying with our objective reasons.) An *external practical reason* to φ would be a consideration that counts in favor of φ-ing regardless of the relation it showed φ-ing to stand in to our antecedent ends. According to externalism about practical reasons, what we have reason to do or intend—what ends we ought to be motivated to adopt—does not depend, fundamentally, on what ends we already have. And someone who fails to act as he has conclusive reason to act need not be procedurally irrational or ignorant of any relevant facts.

What would an *internal epistemic reason* look like? Let's call an epistemic reason to believe some proposition P an internal reason if it's a consideration that counts in favor of believing P (by providing

---

[7] As the examples in Chapter 2 show, there may be circumstances in which we cannot be fully procedurally rational, because complying as well as we can with some of our reasons requires us to bring it about that we're not motivationally responsive to those reasons. We may sometimes have internal reasons to bring it about that we're *locally* procedurally irrational. Derek Parfit's discussion of what he calls "Schelling's Answer to Armed Robbery" (after the game-theorist Thomas Schelling) provides a striking example: he imagines a case where taking a drug that temporarily causes severe irrationality may be the best way to prevent a violent attacker from carrying out the threats he hopes will help him achieve his aims. (*Reasons and Persons*, pp. 12–13.) In such cases, we cannot be fully procedurally rational, since, by deciding against making ourselves *locally* procedurally irrational, we would still be behaving procedurally irrationally—we would be failing to respond to some of our internal reasons.

evidence for P) in virtue of the relation it shows P to stand in to our existing beliefs. (So, for example, the fact that shining a coherent beam of light through two parallel slits produces a certain pattern on the screen behind them may give the physicist performing the experiment an internal reason to believe that light is a wave, given her background beliefs about the behavior of waves.) According to *internalism about epistemic reasons*, what we have reason to believe depends *only* on what we already believe and the standards of procedural rationality. We believe in accordance with our evidence (that is, we respond appropriately to our subjective epistemic reasons) whenever our set of beliefs is fully *procedurally* rational— maximally internally consistent and coherent (however that's best spelled out).

As a view about epistemic reasons, internalism seems problematic. This is because it seems possible for our system of beliefs to be internally consistent, but for us nonetheless to be wildly deluded—even relative to our evidence. If we're to count as properly responsive to reasons, our beliefs must somehow be "tied to the world" (or rather, tied to the world as it appears to us to be) by means of *experience*. In other words, *experience alone* seems to give us some reasons for belief, regardless of what else we believe, and these reasons can fix certain of our beliefs, and so constrain what sets of beliefs we can have and still count as fully rational.

This thought might be put differently: it seems like, for *some* P, there are some *external* reasons to believe P—considerations that count in favor of believing P (by providing evidence for P) but *not* in virtue of the relation they show P to stand in to our antecedent beliefs. Here are some plausible examples: The fact that I feel pain seems to give me a reason to believe *I'm in pain*, regardless of what else I already believe. And the fact that I have an experience of redness gives me a reason to believe *I'm having an experience of redness* regardless of what else I believe.

It's worth stepping back a bit at this point and thinking again, quite generally, about what reasons are. Most generally, reasons are considerations that count in favor of things. Practical reasons count in favor of forming certain intentions or adopting certain ends. Epistemic reasons count in favor of forming certain beliefs, by providing evidence for them. Both kinds of reasons count in favor of things in a particular way: by providing *justification*. Normative reasons can be thought of as *justificatory forces*—they're in the business of providing justification.

Internal and external reasons differ in *how* they provide justification. Internal practical reasons, internalists claim, justify some intention or end by showing the relationship it stands in to some other end we already hold. (So, when people like Parfit, for example, say that "there are no internal reasons," they mean that no end-adoption can ever be justified fundamentally in virtue of the relation it stands in to some other end we already have; they think this would amount to a kind of boot-strapping.) Internal epistemic reasons are very similar: they justify a belief in virtue of the relationship they show it to stand in to our other beliefs. In both cases, the relationships that can transmit justification in this way are established by the standards of procedural rationality (*modus ponens*, in the epistemic case, and the instrumental principle, in the practical case, provide familiar examples).

External practical reasons (externalists claim) justify the adoption of some end differently: they purport to justify it directly, and regardless of our other ends—that is, *not* in virtue of the relationship they show it to stand in to those other ends. In this way, they are like external *epistemic* reasons, which, as I've said, provide justification for some belief directly, and not in virtue of the relation they show it to stand in to our other beliefs.

Describing the disagreement between internalists and externalists about practical reasons this way—in terms of the kind of justification they recognize as possible—makes it begin to resemble a familiar dispute about the nature of *epistemic* justification. *Coherentists* about epistemic justification might be understood as defending an internalist view of epistemic reasons: they argue that all beliefs are, ultimately, justified in virtue of the relationship they stand in to our other beliefs. In other words, all beliefs are justified by *internal* reasons. They deny the existence of external reasons for belief—of reasons that can justify a belief directly—*not* in virtue of the relationship they show it to stand in to our other beliefs.[8] *Foundationalists*, by contrast, might be thought of as externalists about at least some epistemic reasons—they think that some of our beliefs—those that are *basic*—are not justified in virtue of the relationship they stand in to our other beliefs, but rather, are justified in some other way: perhaps they are justified directly by experience, or perhaps they are self-justifying. And just as externalists like Parfit worry that internalism about practical reasons entails a kind of boot-strapping, so foundationalists in epistemology suspect coherentism of a kind of boot-strapping: if the beliefs we already have aren't justified or supported by reasons, how can new beliefs be justified in virtue of the relationship they stand in to the old ones?

As I said earlier, I'm inclined to agree that internalism doesn't tell the whole story of epistemic justification: not all our beliefs can be internally justified, and sensory experience seems to play an important role in anchoring our beliefs in the real world. But looking at the kinds of beliefs foundationalists suggest might be *basic*—that is, justified fully by external *epistemic* reasons—teaches us something about the possibility of external *practical* reasons. The first thing to note is that there is no obvious analog in the practical case to the source of justification that plays the essential anchoring role in the case of belief: sensory experience of the world. Our senses may give us access to the world as it *is*, but don't seem to give us access to the world as it *should be*.

Moreover, the beliefs that foundationalists point to as the most likely candidates for basicality—justification by external epistemic reasons—have something in common: they are not merely uncontroversial, but tend to be self-evident, incorrigible, indubitable, or in some other way plausibly immune to error. Because of this, they are the sorts of beliefs that we usually accept as true as soon as we take them to be asserted sincerely: if you tell me something hurts you, I will believe it so long as I believe your assertion is sincere, even if I did not believe you were in pain before. Beliefs that are plausibly supported by external reasons are not the sorts of beliefs we think require *further*

---

[8] At least, coherentists think that no belief is sufficiently justified externally: there are no *sufficient* external reasons.

justification, beyond their sincere avowal. The fact that these beliefs seem almost self-evident in this way is what makes them plausible candidates for support by external reasons.

Is there a *practical* counterpart to beliefs supported by external reasons? Are there ends or intentions that seem to fit the model provided by such beliefs? That is, are there any ends that are uncontroversial, largely immune to erroneous adoption, and therefore not the kinds of things we feel people must offer further justification for caring about, beyond telling us they care about them? I don't think there are any such ends. There are some ends that many of us share, and which are so widely understood, that it might not occur to us to ask for or require further justification once they're appealed to (the well-being of our children, maybe, or maybe pleasure). But this case is different—here, we don't feel the need to ask for further justification to believe the ends are supported by genuine reasons because we share the ends (or very similar ones) at the outset. In the case of beliefs supported by external reasons, by contrast, the sincere avowal of the belief was itself enough to persuade someone of its justification even if that person did not share the belief at the outset: even if I don't think that, say, hiccups can hurt, if someone says they do then, unless I think they are being insincere, that's enough to convince me. Because such beliefs have no counterpart in the practical case, thinking about the parallel to epistemic reasons should lead us to conclude that there are no external *practical* reasons, even if we think there *are* external *epistemic* reasons.

More recent versions of foundationalism, however, are more permissive with regard to what kinds of beliefs might count as basic. They don't require that beliefs be immune to error, for example, to be candidates for basicality. According to these versions of foundationalism, simple sensory beliefs—for example, the belief that there is a table over there—might be basic. And some foundationalists[9] allow that (reliable) memory can be a source of basic, non-inferentially-justified belief.

---

[9] For example, Alvin Goldman, "What Is Justified Belief?"

Foundationalists of this stripe might allow that there could be beliefs that are open to doubt, but basic nonetheless.

But even these more permissively-identified basic beliefs have no practical counterpart. Although my basic belief that there is a table over there might count as justified, on these versions of foundationalism, regardless of whether I inferred this in part from my belief that my sense-experience is veridical, or whether I also believe that I'm, say, not in a brain-in-vat world, it seems to me that we (philosophers) would accept the claim that this belief is basic only because we (philosophers) generally agree that simple sense experience is reliable in most circumstances, and that we're not in brain-in-vat worlds. There is no corollary to this agreement in the practical case; there's no consensus among philosophers on a reliable means of directly forming simple, uncontroversial, unlikely-to-be-mistaken aims and intentions.[10]

I've argued that comparing the cases of practical and epistemic reasons, and in particular, considering the dispute between foundationalists and coherentists about epistemic justification (which, I've suggested, runs parallel to the dispute between externalists and internalists in the practical case), gives us some grounds for preferring the internalist account of *practical* reasons. But does it also leave internalism about practical reasons vulnerable to the same kind of bootstrapping objections faced by defenders of coherentism (as some externalists have suggested)? I don't think so. Our beliefs, even when we're fully procedurally rational, play no (non-trivial[11]) role in determining the way the world is. But the same may not be true of our ends. It may be that what *makes* some end valuable—one that we have reason to pursue—*is* that it stands in the right relation to what already matters to us. What we care about, in other words, *does* play a non-trivial

---

[10] Moral intuitions certainly could not play this role—they are at best a *starting point* in moral reasoning.

[11] Of course, since what we believe is part of the way the world is (it is a fact about the world that I believe Michael Jordan was the greatest basketball player ever to play the game), our beliefs do affect the way the world is in trivial ways.

role in determining what matters, and what we have reason to do. This is, in fact, the picture of normative practical reasons that I sketched a moment ago. I suggested then that responding to practical reasons is like a case of what Rawls termed "pure procedural justice"—that in those cases where reasoning well ensures willing in accord with our reasons, it ensures this because what we have reason to do is *determined* by how we would will if we were reasoning well.

3.4 Remotivating Internalism: the Motivating Force of Moral Judgments

The intuitions to which I have been appealing in defense of internalism have been largely epistemic; they haven't concerned motivation. But the version of internalism I've defended here may still lay partial claim to a virtue that drew many philosophers to the Motivating Intuition and, via it, to Williams' internalist thesis: its ability to explain the apparent motivating force of moral judgments. If, as the Motivating Intuition claims, considerations that provide reasons must be such as to motivate rational agents, we should expect rational agents to be reliably motivated to act as they have reason to act: rational agents' judgments about their reasons are true, and are the discovery of facts that themselves have the power to motivate those agents when they are rational. Even on the account of reasons I've defended here, which rejects the Motivating Intuition, this will often be the case. But counterexamples to the Motivating Intuition like those presented by the *Nuclear Deterrence, Just War*, and *Emergency Landing* show that even when we are motivated to act as we judge we have reasons to act, it may not be *those reasons* doing the motivating. The Motivating Intuition cannot explain the motivating force of such moral judgments. However, the version of internalism I have sketched, which does not rely on the Motivating Intuition, should lead us to expect that the agents in these examples will be motivated to act as they judge they ought: after all, they have such reasons, on my account, because they each have ends that will be furthered by acting in this way, and (we've assumed) have the means to bring it about that they act as they ought—just for *other* reasons.

3.5 Categorical *Internal* Reasons?

I've argued that internalism has important advantages as a theory of what practical reasons are, despite the failure of the standard arguments for internalism. Internalism avoids alienating us from our reasons, by rooting reasons in facts about what we care about, and it captures the fact that when we attribute a reason to someone, we intend to appeal to a shared standard of conduct that that person must, as a rational agent, recognize as authoritative. It offers a nonreductive analysis of what it is for some fact to be a reason for acting which is attractive, in part because it helps bring out one important way in which we're all equally sources of claims on others. The analysis appeals to the relatively uncontroversial normative standard provided by the procedural conception of rationality—or at least to standards the bindingness of which is not the controversy at issue in disputes about what we have reason to do. So it may also act as a kind of Archimedean point against which we can brace ourselves in such disputes. Internalism, unlike externalism, gives an explanation of what makes some people better at responding to reasons than others. And thinking about what internalism and externalism about *epistemic* reasons might look like gives us some reason to doubt that there could be external *practical* reasons. Internalism can also help us make sense of the action-guidingness of reasons and the motivating force of reasons-judgments.

Each of these considerations gives us reason to embrace an internalist account of reasons, even if we aren't persuaded by reductive naturalist accounts of normativity, the Humean Theory of Motivation, or the Motivating Intuition. But what does all this entail for our substantive question? If my internalist account of *what reasons are* is right, *what reasons are there*? What do we have reason to do? In particular, if we accept internalism about reasons, can the threat of relativism—or worse: nihilism—be avoided?

To sum up the argument of the preceding chapters: Philosophers have generally responded to worry that the internalist conception of reasons leads to moral relativism in one of three ways. Some (notably Gilbert Harman) have embraced moral relativism, arguing that the plausibility of the internalist conception of reasons confirms the truth of relativism. According to these philosophers, some agents—agents whose moral commitments differ sufficiently from our own—may not be acting wrongly when they cause others to suffer unnecessarily and undeservedly. I find this solution intuitively unacceptable.

A second class of philosophers has responded to the threat of relativism by divorcing claims about what we ought morally to do from claims about what we have reason to do. (Philippa Foot, Bernard Williams, and Harman himself have all made suggestions along these lines.) These philosophers might agree that the same moral rules apply to all of us, but must allow that we may not all have reason to comply with them. I've rejected this solution as well, because it too seems to me inadequate as an escape from moral relativism. It assimilates moral rules with other only conditionally binding rules, like the rules of a game, or rules of etiquette—rules governing practices participation in which is merely optional. Maintaining the tie between what we *ought* to do and what we have *reason* to do emphasizes the categorical force of moral rules, gains support from the relation between our practice of moral judgment and our practice of blaming, and also seems to me independently plausible.

An alternative is to respond to the threat of moral relativism by rejecting internalism about reasons, and with it the procedural account of rationality. This, I've argued, is not an appealing option: internalism has much to be said for it. What's more, externalism provides only a very unsatisfactory response to the threat of moral relativism. Externalist accounts of reason seem to merely insist that we have reason to be moral, rather than to argue for the conclusion from premises moral skeptics or relativists might accept. This is not the response to the amoralist's challenge—*why should I be moral?*—that we may have hoped for.

In a way, the unsatisfactoriness of the externalist response to the threat of relativism, amoralism, or nihilism mirrors that of the anti-moral-rationalist response favored by Foot, Williams, and (at times) Harman. I argued (in §1.4) that attempting to preserve the universal bindingness of moral-*ought*-judgments by divorcing such judgments from reasons-ascriptions threatened to demote morality to the status of, say, rules of etiquette. These rules may have universal or "categorical" application, in that they are about, or refer to, all of us, regardless of our desires; but they seem to lack universal *normative force*. It seems entirely open to us to declare that we don't care about such nonsense, and if we do declare this, then while our table manners may continue to be *gauche*, this will, it seems, be a fact of little practical import. Is insisting, with the externalist, that moral rules have universal-*external-reason*-giving status, regardless of what we happen to care about—that failing to comply with moral rules *is substantively irrational*—any more satisfying?

I'm not sure that it is. Faced with such insistence, the amoralist may well respond, "*whose* reasons? *Which* rationality?"[12] An assertion that rules of some old-fashioned religion—a religion that in no way reflects what I care about—belong to the requirements of (substantive) rationality and are reason-giving for me would do little to convince me of the normative import of those rules. What makes the externalist response to the amoralist any better?

Hume sought to avoid skepticism about universal moral requirements by identifying an end that everyone cares about, at least to the extent that they are rational, and that could therefore serve as the foundation for universal moral *internal* reasons. Hume thought that the general good could play this role (if only contingently). I doubt that it can, though I'll come back to this suggestion in the chapters that follow. Still, I believe Hume was on the right path. I think internalists and externalists alike have been too quick to assume that there is no end we're all required to care

---

[12] *À la* Alasdair MacIntyre (*cf.* MacIntyre's *Whose Justice? Which Rationality?*).

about, on pain of *procedural* irrationality. If there is such an end, then, as Williams puts it:

> it might turn out that when we properly think about it, we shall find that we are committed to an ethical life, merely because we are rational agents. Some philosophers believe that this is true. If they are right, then there is…something to which even the amoralist or the skeptic is committed but which, properly thought through, will show us that he is irrational, or unreasonable, or at any rate mistaken [in his amoralism].[13]

Williams, of course, isn't optimistic. But I think there are grounds for optimism that internalism needn't force us into relativism, especially once we realize that being procedurally rational involves much more than mere instrumental rationality. And as in the case of beliefs, sets of ends can exhibit looser procedural "virtues" than mere consistency: considerations of coherence and systematic justifiability, as well as inference to the best explanation, can make it more rational for us to abandon certain ends and adopt others. The example of mathematics in the theoretical case should give us some hope about the possibility of building up complex, substantive-seeming practical principles on a foundation provided by a relatively thin and hard-to-question set of axioms.

Kant's ethical theory provides a model for arguments for the existence of categorical moral reasons that proceed from within a procedural conception of rationality. He thought that a commitment to the value of any ends whatsoever also committed us to the value of humanity. In the next chapter, I'll explore the Kantian argument, and try to bring out its internalist form. Kant's argument, as he makes it, does not, I believe, succeed in establishing the existence of categorical internal reasons. But it can serve as the skeleton of a more promising argument. I develop that argument in Chapters 5 and 6. Because it is internalist in form, building its defense of categorical moral reasons from things we're all committed to, even the amoralist, given what we antecedently care about and on pain

---

[13] Williams, *Ethics and the Limits of Philosophy*, p. 29.

of procedural irrationality, this argument provides a more satisfying answer to the amoralist's question and the relativist's challenge.[14] Finally, in Chapter 7, I turn to our *substantive* question about reasons: if the internalist argument for categorical moral reasons works, *what is it we have reason to do?*

---

[14] The answer is more satisfying, because it connects the rational requirement to be moral to the amoralist's own commitments. But I do not intend to claim too much for it, or for the power of philosophy. As Bernard Williams points out, even after we have come up with our justification for morality—even one that builds from the amoralist's own commitments—"why should we expect him to stay where we have put it?" He continues, with characteristic drama:

> ...The amoralist, or even his more theoretical associate the relativist, is represented in these writings as an alarming figure, a threat. Why should it make any difference to such a person whether there is a philosophical justification of the ethical life?...
> —That is not the point. The question is not whether he will be convinced, but whether he ought to be convinced.
> —But is it? The writers' note of urgency suggests something else, that what will happen could turn on the outcome of these arguments, that the justification of the ethical life could be a force. If we are to take this seriously, then it is a real question, who is supposed to be listening? Why are they supposed to be listening? What will the professor's justification do, when they break down the door, smash his spectacles, take him away?

(Williams, *Ethics and the Limits of Philosophy*, pp. 22–23.) I concede the point. Philosophical argument is only one possible force for moral change in the world, and by no means always the most effective.

4

Kant's Argument

4.1 The Problem of Obligations

In his "Prize Essay" (1764), written long before the *Groundwork of the Metaphysics of Morals*, Kant identifies obligation as the fundamental concept of moral philosophy. There, Kant notes that while we express obligations in terms of "oughts," "ought" itself is capable of two meanings:

> Either I ought to do something (as a *means*) if I want something else (as an *end*), or I *ought immediately* to do something else (as an *end*) and make it actual. The former may be called the necessity of the means, and the latter the necessity of the ends. The first kind of necessity does not indicate any obligation at all. It merely specifies a prescription as the solution to the problem concerning the means I must employ if I am to attain a certain end.... Now since no other necessity attaches to the employment of means than that which belongs to the end, all the actions which are prescribed by morality under the condition of certain ends are contingent. They cannot be called obligations as long as they are not subordinated to an end which is necessary in itself.[1]

For Kant, the project of moral philosophy is to clarify the concept of obligations, understood as *unconditional* "oughts," and to explain how (given the apparent contingency of our ends) obligations are possible.

For externalists, this of course poses no great puzzle. Whether we *have* some end may be a contingent matter. But that contingency in no way undermines the possibility that there are ends we're rationally *required* to have. And moral *oughts—obligations—*simply reflect the

---

[1] Kant, *An Inquiry Concerning the Distinctness of the Principles of Natural Theology and Ethics* (the so-called "Prize Essay"), p. 272 (2:298), emphasis in the original.

ends we're required to have, regardless of whether we in fact do have them, or any related end.

Kant's internalist vision of the nature of moral obligation comes through more clearly in a famous passage from the *Groundwork*, in which Kant diagnoses what he thinks has gone wrong with past attempts to identify a universally binding moral principle. He writes:

> If we look back upon all previous efforts that have ever been made to discover the principle of morality, we need not wonder now why all of them had to fail. It was seen that the human being is bound to laws by his duty, but it never occurred to them that he is subject *only to laws given by himself but still universal* and that he is bound only to act in conformity with his own will, which, however, in accordance with nature's end is a will giving universal law. For, if one thought of him only as subject to a law (whatever it may be), this law had to carry with it some interest by way of attraction or constraint, since it did not as a law arise from *his* will; in order to conform with the law, his will had instead to be constrained by *something else* to act a certain way. By this quite necessary consequence, however, all the labor to find a supreme ground of duty was irretrievably lost. For, one never arrived at duty but instead at the necessity of an action from a certain interest. But then the imperative had to turn out always conditional and could not be fit for a moral command.[2]

This (rather grandiose) appraisal has provoked considerable frustration in some of Kant's less sympathetic readers. Parfit, for example, says of it:

> [S]ince I knew that Kant believed in a Categorical Imperative, I was surprised by Kant's second sentence. I asked a Kantian, 'Does this mean that, if I don't give myself Kant's Imperative as a law, I am not subject to it?' 'No,' I was told, 'you have to give yourself a law, and there's only one law.' This reply was maddening, like the propaganda of the so-called 'People's Democracies' of the old Soviet bloc, in which voting was compulsory and there was only one candidate. And when I said 'But I haven't given myself Kant's Imperative as a law', I was told 'Yes you have'. This reply was even worse.[3]

---

[2] Kant, *The Groundwork for the Metaphysics of Morals* (hereafter, *Groundwork*), pp. 40–41, (4: 432–433), emphasis in the original.

[3] Parfit, *On What Matters*, Volume One, xlii-xliii.

Parfit's irritation, is, I think, understandable, if we take Kant to be claiming both that the law is *up to us*, and that we all, by some sort of necessity, *choose the same law*.

But there is, I think, another, less maddening, way to read Kant's claims. I read the passage, instead, as an expression of Kant's nonreductive internalist way of thinking about reasons and obligations: his view that what we are morally obligated to do cannot be totally divorced from facts about what motivates us. Kant, as I read him, thought that for a law to be binding on us, it must reflect our motivational set—it must connect to what we care about. To put the point in the language of the last chapter, we have reason to do as the moral law requires only if there are considerations that count in favor of our doing so—that throw their justificatory weight behind our complying with the law—in virtue of the relation they show doing so to stand in to our antecedent ends (for example, by showing that doing as the law requires is a means to one of those ends, or constitutive of it, or valuable in consequence of the value of that end). *This* is the sense in which the law must have its source in us—the sense in which it must "arise from [*our*] will"—if we're to be obligated to obey it.[4]

Now, as Kant points out in the quoted passage, there are two ways in which we can have *internal reasons*, in the sense just described, to comply with the law. The first applies when the content of the law itself *does not* arise from our will—from what we care about. In that case, Kant says, the law can bind us—we can have reason to comply with it—only if we have some *incentive*, external to the law, to do so: perhaps a threat of punishment for non-compliance or promise of reward for compliance.[5] But the *moral* law can't be binding on us in this way, for two

---

[4] Note that it does not follow from this that we "give the law to ourselves" or are the source of its normativity. We aren't, on the view I defend and the reading of Kant I am exploring, the authors of the law or source of its normativity, because we are in no way the authors of the requirements of procedural rationality, or the sources of their normativity. This is the sense in which the internalist view I defend, and (tentatively) attribute to Kant, is *non-reductive*. (See Chapter 1, §1.2, above.) This makes my project less ambitious, in a way, than some Kantian constructivist projects, such as Korsgaard's: unlike Korsgaard, I am not trying to identify the "sources of normativity."

[5] Some Hobbes-inspired moral theories may take this form.

reasons. First, if this was the source of our reason to comply with the law, it would bind us only *conditionally*, depending on whether we had the relevant external end—the aim of avoiding the threatened punishment or winning the offered reward. But the moral law, if there is one, must bind *unconditionally and categorically*. Hence Kant's claim that, on this way of conceiving of the bindingness of the law, "all the labor to find a supreme ground of duty was irretrievably lost."

A second consideration weighing against conceiving of the moral law this way—as binding us by means of providing an external incentive to comply—is not one Kant fully explains here, though it is in keeping with views he defends elsewhere in the *Groundwork*. We might wonder, in response to Kant's first worry about this conception of the moral law, whether there could be such an incentive that does bind *everyone*, because everyone shares the incentive-providing end (say, a desire for heavenly rewards or a fear of eternal damnation). If there is such an end shared by everyone, might such a law bind categorically after all, by giving us *all* (internal) reason to comply with it?

On reflection, however, we should reject this possibility. Even if the incentive-providing end *were* universally shared, it would establish, as Kant puts it, no "duty" to act in conformity to law, but rather only "the necessity of an action from a certain interest." That is, the universal reason to be moral would, in such a case, still be a kind of *ulterior motive*—a reason external to morality—not a genuine *moral* reason.[6] The reason I'd have to keep a promise, for example, wouldn't be that it's the moral thing to do. Nor would my reason be the fact that not keeping the promise will disappoint someone who is relying on me, or fail to show proper respect for that person, or improperly make an exception of myself, or cause unhappiness, or any of the other plausible reasons *why* keeping the promise is the moral thing to do.[7] My reason to keep the promise would be that if I do, I'll be rewarded, or if I don't,

---

[6] The same might be said for the desire to avoid blame—the reason Bernard Williams suggests might motivate many otherwise recalcitrant agents to act morally.

[7] Unless I happen, contingently, to care about these things.

I'll be punished. Of course, many people are *motivated* to do the right thing by such considerations. But surely these aren't the *normative moral reasons why* we should keep our promises. Surely the reason we have to do as morality requires isn't ulterior in this way. If it were, the moral law would look no different from the bad laws of an illegitimate and violent dictator, which we might have reasons to follow, but only self-interested reasons. Or like some set of in themselves arbitrary— perhaps even absurd—rules of etiquette, which a fear of ostracism may give us instrumental reasons to obey, but which have no value in themselves. When we asked, with Kant, whether there can be genuine *moral* obligations if something like the internalist picture of reasons is the right one, this is surely not what we had in mind![8]

What about the second way in which we might have internal reasons to comply with the moral law? We might have such reasons if the *content of the law itself* reflected a universally-shared end. If there was some end all rational beings had to adopt, *on pain of procedural irrationality*—in virtue of the relation that end stands in to our existing ends and motivations—then it could provide, as Kant might put it, the *matter* of a moral law that is universally binding in *form*, without needing to provide *ulterior* motives to act rightly. The search for this end is one of the central tasks of Kant's *Groundwork*. The need to identify such an end is suggested, I have argued, by the categorical form of the moral law, coupled with Kant's internalist conception of practical reason.

---

[8] It's worth noting that if our reason to be moral were ulterior in this way, then *even if we were motivated to do the moral thing by the reasons we have to do it*, our action would have no moral worth. It would have no moral worth on Kant's view, since Kant thinks that actions have moral worth only if they are performed "from the motive of duty"—that is, for the sake of doing as the moral law requires. It would also have no moral worth on what I think is a more plausible view, according to which morally worthy actions are performed for the reasons that morally-justify their performance (since, as I said, the fact that I'll be rewarded in heaven if I keep my promises isn't what makes keeping promises the morally-right thing to do). Since it seems very implausible that actions performed for all and only the reasons that justify them wouldn't have moral worth, this, too, counts against the possibility that our reason to obey the moral law could be ulterior in the sense described. For more on the criteria for morally worthy action, see my "Acting for the Right Reasons."

4.2   Kant's "Formula of Universal Law"

So: if there is to be a universally binding moral law, it must be universally binding in virtue of its content. That is, it must tell us to pursue an end to whose value all procedurally rational beings are committed. But how are we to determine if there is such an end, and what such a law might say? Can we discover anything from the very little we have to go on: that if there is indeed a moral law, it will be categorical in form—that is, universally and unconditionally binding—and that it will be so in virtue of the universality of the end it tells us to pursue?

In Section II of the *Groundwork*, Kant asks what we can figure out about the content of the moral law by considering merely its *formal* properties, namely, the fact that moral principles, if there are any, must be categorical in form. "[W]e first want to inquire," he says, "whether the mere concept of a categorical imperative may not also provide its formula containing the proposition which alone can be a categorical imperative."[9] We want to consider whether we can learn anything about *what the moral law* (if there is one) *says* by considering the fact that the moral law (if there is one) must be universally binding, regardless of people's contingent ends and commitments.

Kant notes that identifying the *content* of an imperative by means of an analysis of the general *concept* of that imperative is impossible in the case of "hypothetical imperatives"—imperatives that tell us what to do in order to achieve a certain optional end—because they operate only within particular "conditions."[10] Hypothetical imperatives generally take the form of if-then statements of means-to-end relations, such as "if you want to quench your thirst, drink." They aim at the attainment of particular ends and hold only if the agent in question wills those ends. So no claim can be made about the content of a *hypothetical* imperative without first knowing the specific end at which it is aimed. But since categorical imperatives apply to any person's actions *unconditionally*, Kant seems, in pursuing his first attempt to identify

---

[9] Kant, *Groundwork*, pp. 30–31 (4:420).
[10] Kant, *Groundwork*, p. 31 (4:420).

the content of the moral law, to hope he can proceed without considering the end at which it aims.

Kant continues:

> Since the imperative contains, beyond the law, only the necessity that
> the maxim be in conformity with this law, while the law contains no
> condition to which it is limited, nothing is left with which the maxim of
> action is to conform but the universality of the law as such; and this con-
> formity alone is what the imperative properly represents as necessary.[11]

This is a somewhat difficult passage to unpack. It is clear, however, that
we can get from this analysis of the concept of a categorical imperative
no picture of what the moral law actually says (in a positive sense)—
that is why Kant writes only of what the imperative contains "beyond
the law," without attempting to indicate what the content of the law
itself is. Kant does tell us what the law does *not* contain—namely, it
contains "no condition to which it is limited"—that is, it holds regardless of what particular ends an agent has. This points to the only fact
we know about the categorical imperative from an analysis of its concept: it is universally valid for all rational agents, and hence any maxim
for action—any fully-spelled-out intention of the form "I will φ in
order that p"—that an agent has must conform with it if that maxim is
to be morally permissible. "[T]his conformity alone," Kant writes, "is
what the imperative properly represents as necessary."

So far, we have not learned very much. We've learned only that there's
one element in the content of a hypothetical imperative—the conditions of its applicability—that is missing from the categorical imperative, and thus that all our intentions must comply with the moral law,
whatever it says, and whatever we happen to care about or aim at.
Kant's first attempt to move beyond this rather uninformative piece of
analysis—his so-called "formula of universal law"—is famously thinly
defended and counterexample-prone. The "formula of universal law"
states: *act only in accordance with that maxim through which you can at
the same time will that is should become a universal law.*[12] In defending

---

[11] Kant, *Groundwork*, p. 31 (4:421).
[12] Kant, *Groundwork*, p. 31 (4:421).

it, Kant claims that what we know about the *form* of the categorical imperative—that it is universally binding—tells us something about the *content* of that imperative: that it tells us that our maxims must be universalizable. But why think this? It is not at all clear why the universality of the categorical imperative itself should demand that any maxim that conforms to it be universalizable.

A maxim's conformity to a universal principle does not obviously have anything to do with its own universalizability. It *may* follow from the universal bindingness of the moral law that *the law itself* must be universalizable, in that it must be possible or even desirable that everyone act on it. That is, we might think that if the moral law requires that I φ in circumstances C, then, because (given its universal bindingness) it will also require that everyone else φs when similarly placed (at least under some suitably general description of φ), it must be possible and desirable that everyone φ in such circumstances. For example, we might think that it could be a moral requirement that people keep their promises except when the consequences of doing so are very grave only if it is possible for everyone to keep their promises except when the consequences of doing so are very grave, and only if the world in which everyone does, generally, keep their promises is a morally desirable one. In fact, I have my doubts about even this inference. From the claim that it's true of each agent that that agent ought to φ, together with the principle that *"ought" implies "can,"* it may follow that its true of *each* agent that it's possible that she φ. But it does not follow that it's possible that *all* agents φ, much less that it would be *desirable* for all agents to do so.[13]

---

[13] Consider, for example, Peter Singer's famous case of the child drowning in the pond. If 100 people are standing at the pond's edge, and no one is helping, it may be true of each person that she ought to try to save the child, and that she *can* try to save the child. But it may not be possible for all the bystanders to try to save the child (if the pond is a small one), and in certainly would not be desirable for them all to do so (since they'll only get in each other's way).

Perhaps this case does not show that moral requirements needn't be universalizable. Perhaps the case instead suggests that I've misdescribed the relevant moral requirement: it should instead be "each person ought to try to save the child if no-one else is doing so," or something like that. (Singer suggests a similar amendment to the requirement that we donate a significant percentage of our income to famine relief, in response to the worry that if we all gave that much, we'd end up giving more than was needed, and resources would go to waste. See "Famine, Affluence, and Morality," p. 698.) Furthermore, we might think the claim that it must be morally desirable for everyone to do

But even if we allow that the universally binding form of the moral law entails the universalizability of that law, we should conclude from that only that moral *requirements* must be universalizable. The claim of the formula of universal law, that all morally *permissible* maxims must be universalizable, is much stronger and more contentious. Consider the example of telling a white lie in order to protect someone's feelings. Kant, of course, infamously suggested that lying even in these circumstances is forbidden.[14] It is forbidden, according to the formula of universal law, because if everyone lied in order to spare feelings in such cases, no one would believe the lie, and no comfort would be taken from it—the lie would defeat its own purpose. But telling such lies is not impermissible; and it seems irrelevant what would happen if everyone told such lies, since not everyone does tell them. The parade of counterexamples that have been offered to Kant's formula reinforces this suspicion: what could be wrong with playing tennis on Sundays to avoid crowds at the courts, or always holding the door open for others, or being the last person to leave any sinking ship?[15] *Perhaps* the dictates of the moral law must be universalizable, because it must be possible for everyone to conform to them. But my own (merely permissible) maxims need not be universalizable, since not everyone must or should act as I intend to.[16]

as they ought has independent plausibility, since surely the world in which everyone does as they ought must be a morally appealing one. My point here is that none of this follows merely from the claim that the moral law, itself, binds universally.

[14] Though elsewhere Kant may be more lenient. He seems to allow, for example, that when an author asks, "how do you like my work?," and is likely to "take the slightest hesitation in answering as an insult," one might, perhaps, "say what is expected of one." See *The Metaphysics of Morals*, p. 430 (6:431).

[15] The first example is due to Barbara Herman (*The Practice of Moral Judgment*, p. 163), the last to Derek Parfit (*On What Matters*, Volume One, p. 277).

[16] Allen Wood suggests that in making this transition Kant is in fact looking ahead to the Formula of the Realm of Ends, which maintains that the ends of all human beings should harmonize and converge into a community, thus making sense of the idea that maxims towards those ends should be universalizable, i.e., not conflict with themselves when shared by all people (Wood, *Kant's Ethical Thought*, p. 82). I'm not sure I find even this reverse argument convincing. From the perspective of a unified and mutually reinforcing system of maxims and ends, it is not just important that my maxim to act in a certain way not conflict with your identical maxim to act in the same way (i.e., that *each* of my maxims be *universalizable*) but also important that *none* of my maxims conflict with *any* of your maxims, or *any* of anyone else's. This seems to me, however, to be an impossibly restrictive criterion for moral action—it is impossible for me to act in such a way that I *never* affect or limit the opportunities for action available to others.

The formula of universal law does not, I think, present a plausible test for the permissibility of maxims for action; nor is Kant's derivation of it from the mere concept of a categorical imperative or moral law convincing.[17] But Kant's second attempt at trying to determine what the *content* of the moral law must look like if it is to be categorically binding in form is, I believe, much more promising. It begins from the insight I have already discussed: that the moral law can be categorically binding on me, in a right way, only if its content reflects an end there is rational pressure on us all to share, regardless of our contingent ends and motivations, in virtue of the relation it stands in to those ends, whatever they happen to be. Only if there is such an end can there be a *universal* internal reason to be moral that is not problematically *ulterior* to morality. Establishing the possibility of a categorically binding moral law depends, Kant concludes, on discovering an end that is itself necessary in this sense. This end, if there is one, will then provide the "matter" of the moral law—the end for the sake of which we act when we act morally, just as we act for the sake of quenching our thirst when we follow a hypothetical imperative telling us to drink. In this way, Kant eventually arrives as the content of the moral law via an analysis of its form, culminating in his second formulation of the categorical imperative, the so-called "formula of humanity," which states:

> So act that you use humanity, whether in your own person or in the person of any other, always at the same time as an end, never merely as means.[18]

In a moment, I will examine Kant's derivation of that formula, as well as its compatibility with the internalist conception of reasons. But it will be

---

[17] But for a valiant attempt to at least partially defend the formula of universal law, and a very interesting explanation of the connection between the universalizability of maxims and the law-like form of moral requirements, see Kenneth Walden's "Laws of Nature, Laws of Freedom, and the Social Construction of Normativity." Walden argues that it is a constitutive norm of agency that our actions be "interpretable," in the sense that it be possible to offer rationalizing explanations of them. He argues that (as with other sorts of naturalistic explanations, like biological explanations) our actions are amenable to rationalizing explanations only if they conform to certain patterns also exhibited by other actions subject to the same explanations.

[18] Kant, *Groundwork*, p. 38 (4:429).

helpful to begin with a closer look at Kant's conception of *imperatives* and Kant's conception of *ends*.

4.3 Three Imperatives

Kant distinguishes between three different kinds of imperatives early in Section II of the *Groundwork*. He explains that imperatives are "commands" of reason, which carry normative force, observing, "[a]ll imperatives are expressed by an *ought* and indicate by this the relation of an objective law of reason to a will that by its subjective constitution is not necessarily determined by it."[19] The Kantian imperatives, then, express standards of practical rationality for beings who are capable of rational action but who sometimes fail to act rationally. I will briefly discuss the three imperatives, because they draw distinctions that are important to understanding Kant's argument for the formula of humanity.

The first (and most narrowly binding) kind of imperative is the instrumental imperative, which Kant also calls the imperative of skill. With regard to imperatives of skill, Kant writes, "[w]hether the end is rational and good is not at all the question..., but only what one must do in order to attain it."[20] The general form of this kind of imperative is: *if you fully will an effect or end you must also will the action or means requisite to it.*[21] Kant regards this as an analytically (and therefore necessarily) true statement. That is, he thinks that contained within the idea of willing an end is the idea of also willing the means to that end.[22] The example of an internal reason discussed earlier, the reason I have

---

[19] Kant, *Groundwork*, p. 24 (4:413).

[20] Kant, *Groundwork*, p. 26 (4:415).

[21] Kant, *Groundwork*, p. 28 (4:417).

[22] In calling his imperative "analytic," Kant is not making an empirical claim about the extent to which people actually adhere to the instrumental imperative, nor is he making the non-empirical claim that it is impossible to fail to comply with it. Willing is an act of reason, and Kant believes that the imperative applies (*a priori*) to any act of reason. People must adhere to it to the extent that they are acting rationally. Kant is not claiming that people always act rationally, nor would he. He specifically states that the imperative is the proper way of expressing "the relation of an objective law of reason to a will that by its subjective constitution is not necessarily determined by it" (Kant, p. 24 (4:413)), that is, to beings who have the capacity to be fully rational, but are not always fully rational. See Thomas Hill's *Dignity and Practical Reason in Kant's Moral Theory*, pp. 18–19, for further discussion.

to leave my office now if I want to catch the 6 o'clock train home, can be restated as an instrumental imperative: *if you want to catch the 6 o'clock train home, leave your office now.* Here's another example: *if you want white teeth, brush them regularly.* Kant points out that instrumental imperatives like these are hypothetical. Their bindingness is conditional on the adoption of certain discretionary ends, in this case, that of catching the 6 o'clock train home, or of having white teeth. If I don't intend to catch the train, or don't desire to have white teeth, then, in the absence of other ends these actions serve, the imperatives "leave your office now" and "brush regularly" do not apply to me.

The instrumental imperative is, then, a law of reason that has a lot to say about how we may deliberate without saying anything about what it is we are deliberating about. In other words, it determines the proper *procedure* for our deliberation without determining its *substance.* Kant's first imperative of practical reason, the instrumental imperative, underlines the fact that Kant, like internalists Hume and Williams, believes that the scope of the normativity of a reason statement extends to include corrections of instrumental reasoning. Because it reflects a *procedural* restriction on rationality, Kant's instrumental imperative is compatible with an internalist conception of reasons.

Although Kant's characterization of the instrumental imperative suggests that his conception of rationality is procedural, his discussion of the second imperative of practical reason, the *prudential imperative*, is more ambiguous between procedural and substantive notions of rationality. The general form of this imperative is: *promote your own happiness*, or *take the means to your own greatest well-being.*[23] As with the instrumental imperative described above, Kant attributes a certain necessity to our adherence to this principle. That is, he thinks that willing one's own happiness is as necessarily true for rational beings as is willing the means to the ends one wills. There is an obvious difference between instrumental imperatives like the ones given above and imperatives of prudence. The former address discretionary

---

[23] Kant, *Groundwork*, pp. 26–27 (4:415–416).

ends, like having white teeth, which human beings may or may not set themselves according to their individual preferences or inclinations, whereas the latter refer to ends that Kant thinks that all human beings (indeed all rational beings) "necessarily" set themselves.

Nonetheless, there is a distinct similarity between Kant's argument concerning instrumental imperatives and his argument concerning prudential imperatives. When discussing instrumental imperatives, he appealed to what he considered to be analytically true about the nature of rationality: that one cannot, if one is rational, fail to will the means to a willed end. In making the case for the bindingness of the prudential imperative, Kant again appeals to an analytic truth about rational nature. He writes of happiness that it "can be presupposed [as an end] surely and *a priori* in the case of every human being, because it belongs to his essence."[24] In other words, the idea of setting one's happiness as an end is contained within the idea of a rational being itself. Kant also characterizes this imperative as hypothetical, because it also is conditional on the willing of an end, albeit an end every rational being actually—even necessarily—sets himself.

Kant's positing of a prudential imperative of reason raises some concerns for an internalist interpretation of his argument. By maintaining that all rational beings necessarily set happiness as their end, isn't Kant demonstrating a *substantive* notion of rationality?[25] Kant's

[24] Kant, *Groundwork*, p. 26 (4:415–416). This formulation makes it sound like Kant thinks the pursuit of happiness is part of the essence of *human* nature, as opposed to *rational* nature. So why interpret Kant as claiming that the bindingness of the prudential imperative is an analytic truth about *rationality*, as opposed to *humanity*? It helps to bear in mind that when Kant refers to our *humanity*, he has our *rational capacities* in mind. Our humanity, according to Kant, simply is our (distinctively human) capacity for self-directed rational behavior.

Kant is reluctant to characterize the prudential imperative as fully analytic or even as binding fully *a priori*, because, he writes, the indefinite and subjective nature of happiness makes the question of what it is to set one's happiness as an end a partially empirical one. If the idea were less "indeterminate," Kant states, then this proposition would be "just as analytic" as the previous one concerning instrumental imperatives. See p. 28 (4:417–418).

[25] Kant himself seems hesitant to describe happiness as an end that is "required by reason," in the same way that he thinks we are rationally required to treat humanity as an end. He writes of happiness that it is an end rational beings hold by a "natural necessity." The notion of natural necessity suggests at least an analogy with the laws of nature, which would seem, given Kant's picture of the natural world, to put happiness out of the realm of rational choice entirely (and into, perhaps, the realm of inclinations). But if this is the case, it's not clear why Kant believes in the existence of a prudential imperative of practical reason at all. I will return to this issue in Chapter 5 (§5.3).

discussion of prudence and happiness provokes a further question, about what kind of thing he took happiness to be, and why he associated it with prudence. Although clues may be difficult to find in Kant (they are certainly difficult to find in the *Groundwork*), thinking about how the question might be answered is useful in understanding the role the prudential imperative plays in Kant's conception of rationality. In particular, it suggests to me ways in which prudential concerns can be accommodated by a procedural conception of rationality. But happiness is not, ultimately, the end on which Kant thinks the *moral* law is built, for reasons that I will come to in a moment. So the substantive element in Kant's notion of rationality that is suggested by his discussion of happiness in the *Groundwork* does not pose a threat to my main purpose in examining his argument: to defend the compatibility of an internalist conception of reasons (and a procedural notion of rationality) with universally-shared moral reasons. For this reason, I will set the question of prudence aside for the time being, though I'll return to it briefly in the next chapter.[26]

The last kind of imperative that Kant discusses is the categorical imperative. Kant writes of this imperative that only it "declares an action to be itself objectively necessary without reference to some purpose, that is, even apart from any other end."[27] Kant uses language like this repeatedly in describing the categorical imperative. For example, at 4:414, he defines it as representing an action as "objectively necessary of itself, without reference to another end,"[28] and at 4:416, he writes that it, "without being based upon and having as its condition any other purpose to be attained by certain conduct, commands this conduct immediately."[29]

There are a couple of things which all of these descriptions have in common. First, all three descriptions suggest that the basis of a categorical imperative does not lie in a desired *effect* of some action, be it

---

[26] See especially §5.3 below. I should note that a commitment to substantive rationality is usually accompanied by a commitment to procedural rationality, the narrower of the two notions.

[27] Kant, *Groundwork*, p. 26 (4:415).

[28] Kant, *Groundwork*, p. 25 (4:414).

[29] Kant, *Groundwork*, p. 27 (4:416).

possibly desired (as in the case of instrumental imperatives) or actually desired (as with prudential imperatives), but rather has something to do with the nature of rational action itself. Secondly, all three descriptions deny the dependence of the categorical imperative on some "*other* end" or "*other* purpose." Kant's choice of phrasing leaves us asking, "other than what?"

Other than the action itself? Kant's phrasing certainly suggests this reading. And Kant does seem to think that, in a sense, morally required actions should be performed *for their own sakes*. But this certainly shouldn't be read as entailing that the moral law never tells us to perform some action for the sake of achieving something else, or for the sake of its beneficial effects—that, say, the moral law tells me to jump into the pond for the sake of jumping into the pond, not for the sake of saving the drowning child. That would be a crazy view. Kant may mean that I should *perform the morally required action* for the sake of *performing the morally required action*. Indeed, this seems, for better or for worse, to be entailed by his view of moral worth, defended in Section I of the *Groundwork*.[30] Or he may mean that when the moral law tells me to jump into the pond to save the drowning child, I have reason to do this without needing some further, external incentive (like a promised reward) to do it. This is, I think, the most plausible way of reading Kant's claims here. It ties Kant's account of the nature of the categorical imperative together with his diagnosis of where previous accounts of the bindingness of morality have gone wrong, which I discussed in the last section.

In any case, Kant's wording suggests that even categorical imperatives relate to *some* kind of end, but one which is not an *effect* of the action to which they refer. Kant has not yet explained what sort of end this might be, or in what way it is inherent in rational actions rather than a consequence or effect of them, or even what an end that is not an effect might look like. Although these intimations are unargued for

---

[30] This view of moral worth is, I think, a mistake, and in particular, should not be embraced by a Kantian, but the reasons for this are not relevant here. See my "Acting for the Right Reasons."

at this early stage, they foreshadow Kant's discussion of the formula of humanity later in Section II of the *Groundwork*.

For now, Kant simply tells us that if there is moral law, it must take the form of a *categorical* imperative. What exactly is it about the categorical imperative that gives it a better claim to universality or law-likeness than the hypothetical imperatives of skill or prudence? For to say that the former is unconditionally binding, whereas the latter two are binding only under certain conditions is, I think, misleading. Both hypothetical imperatives can, according to Kant, be shown *a priori* to apply to all rational beings. That instrumental imperatives are demonstrable *a priori* is clear because their validity is an *analytic* certainty. Kant thinks that part of the essence of (rationally) willing an end is also willing the means to that end. This therefore holds for any rational act of willing at all, *a priori*, that is, regardless of the particular end in question. Similarly, Kant states that the prudential imperative is applicable *a priori* to the actions of any rational being, because, again, it is part of the "essence" of a rational being that she desire her own happiness.

The difference in generality cannot lie in the generality of bindingness of categorical as opposed to hypothetical imperatives. It lies instead in the disparity in generality among the kinds of *ends* to which each imperative refers. Kant argues that neither the discretionary ends that underlie particular instrumental imperatives nor the "naturally necessitated" end of happiness, which underlies the prudential imperative, can serve as the foundation for the moral law. In the case of instrumental imperatives this seems clear enough. The adoption of the ends involved in these is dictated purely by the particular inclinations of the particular agent and involves no rational necessity at all. One could never, for example, establish a moral law to act in a certain way based on a desire for white teeth, because many rational beings may simply, and without irrationality, not desire to have white teeth, and therefore have no reason to adhere to the law—or at least, as Kant notes, no reason in the absence of external incentives to do so.

This line of thinking suggests, however, that the case for the failure of prudential ends to establish moral laws is much less clear. After all,

Kant explicitly states that "[t]here is...one end that can be presupposed as actual in the case of all rational beings...by a natural necessity, and that...is *happiness*."[31] Why can't the end of happiness, which seems, by Kant's own admission, to be completely universal among rational beings, be used to ground the moral law?

This is, after all, arguably what some utilitarians try to do. Utilitarians might argue, like Kant, that all rational beings necessarily set happiness as their chief end, and that therefore a universal moral principle (a categorical imperative, in fact) can be based on the notion of maximizing that happiness. So their categorical imperative states: *act so as to maximize the happiness resulting from your actions*. In other words, utilitarians might contend that since it is true that rational beings *categorically* prefer their happiness to any other end, then the *hypothetical* imperative that says "*if you value happiness above any other end, then act so as to maximize happiness*" becomes the *categorical* imperative I just stated. That is, it applies universally to all actions and all persons. Utilitarianism gains a large part of its appeal from the seemingly uncontroversial importance almost everyone attaches to the end that its categorical imperative promotes.

In fact, John Stuart Mill sets out to "prove" the principle of utility along just these lines. "[T]he sole evidence it is possible to produce that anything is desirable," Mill says, "is that people actually do desire it."[32] And then he proceeds, infamously, to argue from this premise, plus the rather dubious empirical claim that happiness is the only thing all people desire and desire for its own sake, to the conclusion that the moral law requires that we maximize happiness. The objection has often been pressed, against Mill, that the purely descriptive, psychological, fact (if it is one) that everyone desires happiness (and only happiness) for its own sake cannot establish the *normative* conclusion that only happiness *ought* to be desired for its own sake. But we could, instead, put an internalist spin on Mill's argument, and some things Mill says suggest that such a spin may be appropriate. "[Q]uestions of ultimate ends do

---

[31] Kant, *Groundwork*, p. 26 (4:415–416).
[32] Mill, *Utilitarianism*, p. 34.

not admit of proof,"[33] he says, echoing Hume's claim that "the ultimate ends of human actions can never, in any case, be accounted for by *reason*,"[34] and presaging the common internalist claim that the choice of ultimate ends, itself, lies beyond rationality. But if happiness is the ultimate end of every person, as Mill argues that it is, then it could serve as a source of reasons everyone can share.

The question this imperative immediately raises, however, and the question the Kantian may ask concerning the prudential imperative, is "*whose* happiness?" The utilitarian categorical imperative tells us to maximize happiness *in general*. But even if it is true that I necessarily value *my own* happiness above any other finite end, and that it is the only thing I value noninstrumentally, this says nothing about how I value *your* happiness or anyone else's. Sidgwick convincingly dismantles Mill's "proof" along these lines. That the general happiness ought to be desired, Sidgwick argues, "is not established by Mill's reasoning, even if we grant that what is actually desired may legitimately inferred to be in this sense desirable:"

> For an aggregate of actual desires, each directed towards a different part of the general happiness, does not constitute an actual desire for the general happiness, existing in any individual; and Mill would certainly not contend that a desire which does not exist in any individual can possibly exist in an aggregate of individuals. There being no actual desire—so far as this reasoning goes—for the general happiness, the proposition that the general happiness is desirable cannot be in this way established.[35]

Mill seems at times to recognize this problem. At the start of Chapter III of *Utilitarianism*, immediately preceding his "Proof" of the principle of utility, Mill asks what the source of the obligation of the moral law is, what the motives to obey it are, and how it derives its driving force. (Tellingly, he treats these questions as more or less equivalent.[36])

---

[33] Mill, *Utilitarianism*, p. 34.
[34] Hume, *Enquiry*, p. 293 (Second Enquiry, Appendix I).
[35] Sidgwick, *The Methods of Ethics*, p. 388.
[36] A slide between talk of obligating or justifying and motivating force is a common internalist "tell."

He does not say that the universally-shared end of happiness is the source of the motivation and the obligation to maximize happiness. Instead, he claims that the binding force of the principle of utility and our motivation to obey it depend on the presence of "external" sanctions (such as the threat of punishment or disapproval by others) and "internal" sanctions (such as an attack of guilty conscience).[37] But as we have seen, both these incentives to obey the moral principle are *external* in Kant's sense, and Kant has argued, in my view convincingly, that such ulterior motives cannot be the source of the normativity of the *moral* law, if it exists.

So Mill's view that we all value our own happiness noninstrumentally, which Kant shares, does not establish that *happiness* is the end on which the moral law is built, and cannot explain why we have reason to value and promote the happiness of others. Happiness, even if it is at some general level a universally shared end, cannot be the foundation for the moral law because what I in fact value when I set happiness as my end is not the same thing as what you value when you set happiness as your end. For I value *my* happiness and you value *your* happiness. Moreover (as Kant also suggests[38]), our concept of happiness is so nebulous that what I think constitutes happiness may be very different from what you think constitutes happiness, and whether it is or isn't is an entirely empirical question, which cannot be settled *a priori*. In any case, Kant says, we *do not* value happiness wherever we find it. Sadistic pleasures, for example, surely have no value. Kant writes:

> an impartial rational spectator can take no delight in seeing the uninterrupted prosperity of a being graced with no feature of a pure and good will, so that a good will seems to constitute the indispensable condition even of worthiness to be happy.[39]

So happiness is not really a case of an end that all rational beings share. It cannot provide every rational being with the same internal reason, and so it cannot form the basis of a categorical imperative.

---

[37] Mill, *Utilitarianism*, pp. 27–28.
[38] Kant, *Groundwork*, p. 28 (4:418).
[39] Kant, *Groundwork*, p. 7 (4:393).

Whether or not we agree with Kant's concession to the utilitarian that we always value our own happiness (and I'll return to this question in §5.3, below), or with his harsh assessment of the value (or lack thereof) of the happiness of wrongdoers, Kant's argument suggests a reason we have to value the happiness of others to which the utilitarian, who takes happiness to be fundamentally valuable and indeed the only unconditionally, noninstrumentally valuable thing, cannot appeal. We have reason to value the happiness of others because they value their own happiness, and we (for some reason) value *them*. As Parfit has pointed out, the classical utilitarian seems to have to prefer a world with many millions of inhabitants who are only slightly happy to a much less populated world in which all the inhabitants were extremely happy.[40] But this is very counterintuitive. As Jan Narveson has put it, what matters, morally, is *making people happy, not making happy people*.[41] These worries about utilitarianism already point strongly in the direction of Kant's conclusion that humanity, rather than happiness, should be the end on which moral laws are built.

But I am jumping ahead of myself.

4.4 Humanity As an End

At this point it is useful to take a much closer look at what Kant has in mind when he is speaking of *ends*. Kant's account of ends is somewhat ambiguous. At 4:427 he defines an end as that which "serves the will as the objective ground of its self-determination." This can perhaps be loosely translated like this: an end is the motive from which we perform a certain action. Kant adds that ends, "if given by reason alone, must hold equally for all rational beings."[42] In other words, if

---

[40] This is the so-called "Repugnant Conclusion." As Parfit expresses it, this version of utilitarianism commits its defender to the view that "for any possible population [of a reasonably large number of] people, there must be some much larger imaginable population whose existence, if other things are equal, would be better, even though its members have lives that are barely worth living." (See Parfit, *Reasons and Persons*, p. 388.)

[41] See Narveson, "Moral Problems of Population," p. 80.

[42] Kant, *Groundwork*, p. 36 (4:427).

the motive from which we perform an action is purely rational (i.e., is given to us by the requirements of rationality alone, and so is in no way based on individual inclination), then it is a valid reason for every rational being to perform the same action. The standard conception of ends is as effects of actions—the things at which our actions *aim*. But Kant has already hinted to us that the end that is to support the categorical imperative does not take the form of a desired effect of a possible action. So one question that our investigation of Kant's understanding of ends should answer is this: what does an end look like that is not the desired effect of an action?

Another confusing aspect of Kant's discussion of ends in 4:428 is that he seems to waver between searching for an end that is necessarily shared by all rational beings (that is, a universal end) and searching for something he calls an "end in itself." So another question our discussion of Kant's conception of ends should answer is how these two could amount to the same thing.

As I say, we are used to thinking of ends as the effects of our actions, or as things at which we aim. For example, in the case of the instrumental imperative I mentioned earlier—*if you want white teeth, brush them regularly*—having white teeth is the end at which we aim, and of which the action of regular brushing is to be the cause. Similarly, in the case of the prudential imperative, we see our happiness as our end because it is the thing at which we aim and which we hope our actions will bring into effect. Kant's conception of ends is somewhat different, and, though it can account for the kinds of things we generally see as ends, it allows for a larger variety of candidates. Allen Wood usefully explains Kant's broader conception of an end as "anything *for the sake of which* we act."[43]

This understanding of ends sits nicely with the version of internalism about reasons I have explored and defended. It is worth noting that it comes very close to Bernard Williams' own conception. Williams, remember, allows for the possibility that we have reason to perform actions that serve our ends in ways that are not straightforwardly

---

[43] Wood, *Kant's Ethical Thought*, p. 116.

instrumental (perhaps, for example, the action in question is constitutive of some end or commitment, or expresses that commitment),[44] and thus argues that the kinds of things that can occupy an agent's motivational set go beyond mere possible desired effects of actions. He thinks that principles, commitments, values, indeed (to borrow again from Wood), *anything for the sake of which we act* may belong in a motivational set.[45] The Wood interpretation gives a good general account of how Kant thinks of ends. But the function Kant's concept of ends plays in his argument is a more specific one. Kant thinks of ends as *worth-bestowers*—as things that bring value to our actions, or, as I will argue, to our other ends.[46]

The Kantian conception of ends as worth-bestowers will identify as ends all the things we usually think of as ends. Look, for example, at how this works in the case of the instrumental imperative just mentioned: if you want white teeth, brush them regularly. Now having white teeth is the end at work in the imperative because it is what gives value to my act of regular brushing. Without the end of having white teeth (or some other end), to which regular brushing is the means, such brushing would have no value for me at all. Again, the prudential imperative follows a similar course: if happiness were not valuable to me, my actions towards achieving happiness would have no value.[47]

But this conception will also allow for other kinds of things to be ends, and this suggests an answer to the first question about ends that I posed: how an end may be something other than the effect of an action. If an end is understood as a worth-bestower—as something that gives value to our actions or less fundamental ends, by being the

---

[44] Williams, "Internal and External Reasons," p. 104.

[45] Williams, "Internal and External Reasons," p. 105.

[46] Kant never defines an end in this way explicitly, but his discussion of ends in 4:428 repeatedly makes reference to their worth-bestowing quality, and this understanding is in no way incompatible with the definition he does give us of ends as reasons for acting.

[47] It might be argued that we don't always think of ends as *effects* of our actions. Sometimes, for example, we see our actions as intrinsically valuable, as when I paint for the sake of painting. Painting is not an *effect* of the activity of painting. If this is right, then Kant's understanding of ends is closer to our natural understanding than I suggest. This, if anything, makes the understanding of ends as worth-bestowers more persuasive: it can explain how an action can have worth independent of its effects, which is something utilitarians, for example, have trouble explaining.

thing for the sake of which we pursue those actions and ends—then there is no reason to think that only the effect of an action can be an end. Moreover, as my earlier worries about utilitarianism suggested, in the case of conditional ends-to-be-affected (such as white teeth or happiness) we will soon want (as I will argue) to go beyond seeing how they bestow worth on our actions and ask what it is that gives them (that is, the ends themselves) their worth. And this will not be the effect of an action; we often—perhaps usually—act for the sake of ourselves, and other people. We value happiness not as some kind of abstract good, for which people are a necessary carrier, but because *people value it*, and *we value them*. That is the sense in which humanity itself can be an end.

These thoughts in turn suggest an answer to the second question I posed: how the "universal end" and the "end in itself" can be one and the same. For they suggest that one thing that could be a universal end—that is, a worth-bestower for all rational beings—is something to which the worth of all actions and conditional ends may be traced back, but whose own worth is conditional on nothing. In other words: the thing that is of value in itself, and not just because it is desired, or, the *end in itself.*

The internalist structure Kant's argument for the formula of humanity will take is now clear. Its central idea is this: if there is one end whose value to us can be inferred from the value of all our contingently chosen ends—an end which is valuable to *each of us* to the extent that we are rational, because its value is a *condition* of the value of those other ends—then this end can perhaps serve as the basis of a moral law that each of us has *internal* reasons to uphold.

4.5 The "Unconditioned Condition" of Value

Kant's argument in 4:428 pulls his ideas about the nature of the end in itself together into a recognizable form: that of humanity. There are, I think, two kinds of argument running through Kant's discussion.

The first is a first-order normative argument based on Kant's intuitions about what is valuable; the second is a kind of structural argument about what our own ends and value-commitments, whatever they are, commit us to. As it stands, the first argument is more persuasive than the second. But they are, potentially, mutually reinforcing; and I think that the second, structural argument can be improved upon. When it is, it can provide an internalist defense of a first-order normative principle that the first kind of argument shows to be independently intuitively appealing. In what remains of this chapter, I will just set out Kant's two arguments, and flag some worries they raise and some gaps that they leave open. In the next two chapters, I'll try to fill in those gaps with a revised version of Kant's second, structural argument. In the final chapter, I'll begin to sketch the normative ethical view these Kantian internalist arguments entail.

I'll begin with the argument from normative-ethical intuitions about value. This argument is strongly suggested by a passage from 4:428, in which Kant draws a distinction between what he calls "subjective" and "objective" ends:

> Beings the existence of which rests not on our will but on nature, if they are beings without reason, still have only a relative worth, as means, and are therefore called *things*, whereas rational beings are called *persons* because their nature already marks them out as an end in itself, that is, something that may not be used merely as a means, and hence so far limits all choice (and is an object of respect). These therefore, are not merely subjective ends, the existence of which has a worth *for us*, but rather *objective ends*, that is, beings the existence of which is in itself an end, and indeed one such that no other end, to which they would serve *merely* as a means, can be put in its place, since without it nothing of *absolute worth* would be found anywhere; but if all worth were merely conditional and therefore contingent, then no supreme practical principle for reason could be found anywhere.[48]

Kant is pointing here to an intuitively very important distinction between two different ways in which something can have value. Something might have, as Kant says, "worth *for us*." Or it might,

---

[48] Kant, *Groundwork*, p. 37 (4:428) (emphasis in the original).

instead, be, like us, the sort of thing *to whom such other things have worth*. The former kind of thing has *subjective, conditional* value, because its value depends on our wanting or needing it. *We* are the condition of its value. Things like this matter only because *they matter to us*. But it seems like their *mattering to us* could make them matter only if *we matter*—if we have value. Otherwise, why would their mattering to us give them value? And on pain of regress or circularity, *our* having value cannot be, in the same way, conditional on our mattering *to someone*. In other words, the first, subjective kind of value turns out to depend on the second, objective kind. We must have a special, unconditional value.

John Taurek draws the same distinction very nicely. He points out that when we are deciding which *lives* to save or which *people* to rescue, we reason very differently from how we reason when we are deciding, say, which *objects* to rescue from a fire. In the case of objects, we consider how much they're each worth to us, and try to save as much value as we can. But people, he says, are different:

> when I am moved to rescue human beings from harm in situations of the kind described, I cannot bring myself to think of them in just this way. I empathize with them. My concern for what happens to them is grounded chiefly in the realization that each of them is, as I would be in his place, terribly concerned about what happens to him.... The loss of an arm of the Pietà means something to me not because the Pietà will miss it. But the loss of an arm of a creature like me means something to me only because I know he will miss it, just as I would miss mine....
>
> ...It is the loss to the individual that matters to me, not the loss of the individual.[49]

If we accept this distinction, we will recognize a need to treat *beings like us, to whom things matter* differently from how we treat *things that matter to us*. Every person may be an object of value to some other person. (In this regard, Taurek's "only" seems mistaken.) But she is always—as someone to whom things matter—at the same time an original source of value, and therefore an objective end-in-herself.

---

[49] Taurek, "Should the Numbers Count?," pp. 306–307.

Humanity, Kant concludes, should therefore be construed

> not as an end of human beings (subjectively), that is, not as an object
> that we of ourselves actually make our end, but as an objective end that,
> whatever ends we may have, ought as law to constitute the supreme lim-
> iting condition of all subjective ends....[50]

It's worth noting that the intuitive distinction to which Kant appeals in these passages does not seem to draw the line between types of ends where Kant wants it to be drawn. If the key distinction is between beings to whom things matter—objective ends—and the things that matter to them—subjective ends, then some "beings the existence of which rests...on nature" who are "without reason" should nonetheless fall on the objective side of the divide. For some such beings—non-rational animals, infants—surely are beings to whom things matter. The relevant question seems not to be whether a creature is rational, but whether it is conscious and sentient: a center of subjectivity. Humanity, on this line of reasoning, will prove to be only *one* kind of end in itself. There will be others.

This strikes me as a salutary, if significant, departure from Kant's view, which infamously has difficulties in accommodating our intuitions about our obligations to infants and lower animals. I will return to it in the last chapter of this book. But for now, let us take stock of how far this intuitive argument will take us. The answer, given the internalist goals of my project, is *not very far*. I've sketched an (I think) intuitively plausible picture of value. But nothing I've said thus far shows that this is a picture that cannot be rationally rejected. As Taurek notes, some utilitarians reject the picture. According to such utilitarians, happiness has unconditional value: its value does not depend on our valuing it. Rather, we have reason to value it because it is independently valuable. And such utilitarians may not recognize sentient beings as unconditionally valuable—their value—and our reason for protecting them—may depend on their ability to "produce" happiness.[51] Is there any way of rationally settling the disagreement,

---

[50] Kant, *Groundwork*, p. 39 (4:431).

[51] See Taurek, pp. 299–300. Some non-utilitarians will of course also reject this picture of value: they may think, for example, that some things, such as the natural world, have value independently of their having value *for* any sentient, valuing being.

despite the differences in what the disputants judge valuable at the outset? This, after all, was what I was after: a moral law that we're all required to uphold, regardless of our initial value commitments, on pain of *procedural irrationality*.

The second, structural argument Kant makes in defense of the formula of humanity seems designed to fill this need. He argues, as Christine Korsgaard puts it, by means of a "regress of conditions"— and takes himself to have shown that we're all committed to valuing humanity as an end in itself, regardless of what we contingently value, because of the relationship the end of humanity stands in to our other ends: its value is *the only possible condition* of the value of our contingent ends.

The frustrating thing about the argument for the formula of humanity as Kant lays it out in 4:428 is that he seems to make only half of it explicitly, and the less important half at that. Let's examine that argument piece by piece. After explaining his conception of ends, Kant begins:

> The ends that a rational being proposes at his discretion as *effects* of his actions (material ends) are all only relative, for only their mere relation to a specially constituted faculty of desire on the part of the subject gives them their worth, which can therefore furnish no universal principles, no principles valid and necessary for all rational beings and also for every volition, that is, no practical laws. Hence all these relative ends are only the ground of hypothetical imperatives.[52]

Kant is here reiterating the internalist thought that all of my discretionary ends—the things I happen to try to bring about—matter only because they matter to me, and they do that only because my faculty of desire happens to be constituted a certain way: I happen to want them. If I hadn't had the desires I have, I would have had no reason to pursue them; the mere fact that these are (as it happens) ends of mine can't give other people reason to pursue them. And indeed, even if we all happened to desire the same thing (as Hume, remember, thought

---

[52] Kant, *Groundwork*, p. 36 (4:428).

we did[53]), it would still be true that *had we not happened to share these values*, we would have had no reason to pursue their targets.

Because of this, no such discretionary end can ground categorical principles of practical reason—*moral laws*. At most (if Hume is right, and there is a universally valued end) they could ground imperatives to act that are *contingently* universal (so long as we're constituted the way we are). But the moral imperative, if there is one, *necessarily* binds all rational beings—we would not be tempted to withdraw a moral judgment if we were to learn that its object simply doesn't care.

Kant continues:

> But suppose there were something the *existence of which in itself* has an absolute worth, something which as *an end in itself* could be a ground of determinate laws; then in it, and in it alone, would lie the ground of a possible categorical imperative, that is, of a practical law.[54]

Here Kant says that if there is to be a categorically, unconditionally, necessarily binding moral law, it must be grounded in an end that we're all required to value, because it is valuable *in itself*, and not just because we happen to value it.

Kant then proposes what this end might be, and what the corresponding law would look like:

> Now I say that the human being and in general every rational being *exists* as an end in itself, *not merely as a means* to be used by this or that will at its discretion; instead he must in all his actions, whether directed to himself or also to other rational beings, always be regarded *at the same time as an end*.[55]

We are ourselves the end we were looking for—the things that have that special kind of value that is not conditional on *being valued*.

Why think this? Kant begins his defense of this thesis by means of a process of elimination. First, as we've already seen,

---

[53] Remember that Hume thought that all people, at least "while the human heart is compounded of the same elements as at present," valued social stability and the public good, at least to some extent (see §1.4 above).

[54] Kant, *Groundwork*, p. 36 (4:428).

[55] Kant, *Groundwork*, p. 37 (4:428).

> All objects of the inclinations have only a conditional worth; for, if there were not inclinations and the needs based on them, their object would be without worth.[56]

Kant continues:

> But the inclinations themselves, as sources of needs, are so far from having an absolute worth, so as to make one wish to have them, that it must instead be the universal wish of every rational being to be altogether free of them. Thus the worth of any object *to be acquired* by our action is always conditional.

Kant's claim here seems too strong: it's certainly not true that it's the wish of every rational being to be free of inclinations. But it is true that we don't see our inclination for something to be a sufficient condition for its worth. We have some inclinations—like cravings or addictions—we would rather be rid of. Our being inclined towards an end does not make it good. Even if it did, it would not follow that our inclinations have absolute worth: something may be valuable because of my need for it, but that doesn't make my *need* valuable. Even if my craving for a cigarette gives the cigarette some value, surely the craving itself has no value.[57]

The passage also suggests that the process Kant goes through to identify the end in itself is the one of tracing value-dependency indicated by my earlier discussion of his understanding of ends. The worth of our actions is based on the worth of the ends or objects at which they aim. The worth of those objects is in turn (in part) dependent on inclinations to them themselves, or, ultimately, on our tendency to have

---

[56] Kant, *Groundwork*, p. 37 (4:428). Allen Wood seems to interpret Kant differently here: he suggests that Kant is merely claiming that no object of inclination *considered simply as such* is an end in itself (though we may happen to have an inclination for something that *is* an end in itself). (See Wood, *Kant's Ethical Thought*, pp. 123–124.) But that would make Kant's claim tautologous, at least if we take an "end in itself" to be something that is *intrinsically* valuable: valuable by itself, in isolation, in virtue of its intrinsic properties. Because Kant would then be claiming that nothing can be intrinsically valuable (valuable in virtue of its intrinsic properties) in virtue of being an object of someone's inclination—a claim that seems fairly vacuous. What's more, as Wood acknowledges (p. 124), if this were Kant's meaning, it would do little to establish his apparent inference, at 4:428, that the worth of any object to be acquired by our action is always conditional.

[57] This passage shows that Kant does not think that *all* conditions of value are thereby made valuable. He explicitly says that inclinations are conditions (though perhaps not sufficient conditions) for the value of their objects. But he does not think it follows that the inclinations themselves are therefore valuable. This will be important later (see §5.4).

those inclinations, that is, on our neediness. And Kant points out (it seems to me rightly, although he puts the case too strongly) that neediness is not something to which we would attribute some sort of absolute worth, but is rather something we tend to regret.

The conclusion that therefore "the worth of any object to be acquired by our action is always conditional" is, however, somewhat premature. Because we are rational beings, some of the ends we set ourselves and the actions they demand are picked out not just by inclination but by our capacity for *rational choice*. Willing is, after all, an act of reason (although it is in some cases triggered by inclination). So the line of argument Kant follows in the case of inclinations should also be followed for the case of rational choice. This is the argument Kant fails to make explicit in this passage. But it would run roughly as follows:

> All objects of rational choice have only conditional worth; for if there were not our rational choices, or rather, our capacity for rational choice, their object would be without worth. That is, our actions gain their worth from the rationally chosen ends at which they aim, and these ends, in turn, gain their worth from the rational natures that set them. The worth of a rational nature is not based on any outside source, but rather such a nature is an end in itself, with absolute worth, and the source of worth of all of our ends and actions.

Therefore, Kant states, it is the rational nature of persons that marks them out as ends in themselves.

Why must we believe that our rational nature is an end in itself, on pain of irrationality? Kant says, towards the bottom of the paragraph I have been examining, that if we failed to attribute absolute worth to rational nature, "nothing of *absolute worth* would be found anywhere; but if all worth were conditional and therefore contingent, then no supreme practical principle for reason [i.e., no moral law] could be found anywhere."[58] But this formulation is surely somewhat question-begging. Kant cannot demonstrate the truth of the formula of humanity by maintaining that if his formulation is not true, then morality itself (or at least any kind of realist, objective conception of

---

[58] Kant, *Groundwork*, p. 37 (4:428).

morality) is a fiction. Kant's argument, as he himself admits, is not sufficient to show that the moral law is real, but, at best, what it would look like if it did exist—namely, that it would be a categorical imperative based on the (conjectural) universal end in itself: rational nature. Kant's argument aims to identify the conditions under which a moral law is possible—the existence of an end that can serve as the unconditioned condition of value—but he as yet provides no reason why we should suppose that the conditions for morality obtain. As yet, that is, he has not provided a response to the skeptical Humean view that rationality does not demand that we be moral.

Kant's argument, if it works, would, however, achieve something else that is of great importance to my project: it links the conditions for *morality* to the conditions for *practical reason* itself. It thereby ties the fate of the view that we all have reason to be moral to the fates of other less robust forms of faith in practical reason: indeed, to the very possibility of rational action. Kant argues that if we failed to attribute absolute worth to rational nature, then there would be nothing on which to support the worth of the contingent ends which we all value. If the ends that we set ourselves are valuable—if, that is, it is the case that we have *reasons* to act on them—then this can only be because the absolute worth of humanity can serve as a foundation for the worth of those ends. We must assume the worth of humanity if we are to defensibly claim that we value our own contingent ends with reason.

A question arises: let's grant for the time being that, since I value the ends I set myself, I must, if I am rational, also value *myself* as an absolute end. But I don't need to value the ends you set yourself, so why need I value *you* as an absolute end? In other words, how is the end picked out by this argument any more universal than the end of happiness we considered earlier?

Kant might respond: I have a distinctive kind of value not because my name is Julia Markovits, or because I'm my exact height, or because I was born on a Sunday, but because *my capacity for rational choice* gives me a worth-bestowing status. That this is so is clear from that fact that not just *any* end I set myself is valuable as a result, but only those ends I choose *rationally*. So Kant's argument implies that all rational beings must attribute value to their own persons *insofar as they exercise their capacity for rational choice.* But this capacity is, of course, not unique to me. It is also what makes every other rational being valuable in their own eyes. As Kant puts it:

> *rational nature exists as an end in itself.* The human being necessarily represents his own existence in this way; so far it is thus a *subjective* principle of human actions. But every other rational being also represents his existence in this way consequent on just the same rational ground that also holds for me; thus it is at the same time an *objective* principle, from which as a supreme practical ground, it must be possible to derive all laws of the will.[59]

So it is a characteristic inherent in rational nature *as such*, and not just my own rational nature, that it exists as an end in itself (or at least we must assume it to be an inherent quality of rational nature if we want to rationally act on the basis of our ends). This means, Kant says, that if I rationally value my own ends, then I must view rational nature as such, and therefore *any* rational nature, as an end in itself, including, for example, yours.

Kant concludes:

> The practical imperative will therefore be the following: *So act that you use humanity, whether in your own person or in the person of any other, always at the same time as an end, never merely as a means.*[60]

This, then, is how the Kantian argument is supposed to work. It begins from an optimism about what we have reason to do:

(1) I value the ends I rationally set myself, and take myself to have reason to pursue them.

It then appeals to an internalist-flavored premise:

(2) But I recognize that their value is only conditional: if I did not set them as my ends, I would have no reason to pursue them.

---

[59] Kant, *Groundwork*, pp. 37–38 (4:428–429).
[60] Kant, *Groundwork*, p. 38 (4:429).

But, Kant asks, why think that we can generate reasons to promote some end just by adopting it? We must, he says, think that we have the power to confer value on our ends by rationally choosing them:

(3) So I must see *myself* as having a worth-bestowing status.

From this Kant seems to infer that we must accord *ourselves* unconditional worth:

(4) So I must see myself as having an unconditional value—as being an end in myself and the condition of the value of my chosen ends—in virtue of my capacity to bestow worth on my ends by rationally choosing them.

But I recognize that the same argument holds from your perspective, and for your rational nature, and so consistency requires that I attribute the same worth-bestowing status, and so the same unconditional value, to *you*, and to any other *rational being*:

(5) I must similarly accord any other rational being the same unconditional value I accord myself.

Hence the formula of humanity:

(6) *So I should act in a manner that respects this unconditional value: I should use humanity, whether in my own person or in the person of any other, always at the same time as an end, never merely as means.*

What this imperative demands is that one never behave towards another person in a way that fails to respect the capacity for rational choice in which her humanity consists. For to neglect in one's actions to treat humanity (that is, the capacity for rational choice) as an end would be to disregard the very thing that gave those actions, and the personal ends at which they aim, their value.[61]

---

[61] This argument is an example of what Kant has called a "transcendental argument." It offers as a premise a description of the world as we take it to be, and works backwards from there to a conclusion about what must be the case for it to be like that. In this case, Kant argues that we take the world

4.6 Worries About Kant's Argument

Christine Korsgaard summarizes Kant's argument this way:

> If we regard our actions as rational, we must regard our ends as good;
> if so, we accord to ourselves a power of conferring goodness on the
> objects of our choice and we must accord the same power—and so the
> same intrinsic worth—to others.[62]

On its face, it exhibits some glaring vulnerabilities. Rae Langton observes that "an unsympathetic reader may be tempted to view it as a chain of non sequiturs." (She adds, "a sympathetic one will rightly ask to see more of the argument before coming to judgment.") But, she notes,

> It seems, on the face of it, that I could regard my actions as rational
> without regarding my ends as good. I could regard my ends as good
> without according to myself a power of conferring goodness on the
> objects of my choice. I could accord to myself a power of conferring
> goodness on the objects of my choice without according the same
> power to others. I could accord to others the power of conferring good-
> ness on the objects of their choice without according intrinsic value to
> them. I could accord intrinsic value to them without their having, or
> acquiring, intrinsic value.[63]

Langton has a point. The first step of the argument may be relatively unproblematic, if we understand the claim that an end is good, or valuable, as the claim that we have reason to adopt (pursue, protect, respect, or promote) it. And the last worry is one that Kant appears simply to concede: he does not take himself to have shown that the moral law is

to be full of valuable ends which we have reason to pursue, and that this can only be an accurate description of the world if a source for the value of those ends can be identified.

This is perhaps why Kant does not take himself to have conclusively proven the existence of a moral categorical imperative by the end of Section II of the *Groundwork*. It might yet turn out that our vision of the world as endowed with value, and of ourselves as acting for reasons, is simply a false one. (This might be the case, for example, if there was no freedom in the world, only the mechanical following of effect upon cause, as determined by physical laws.)

The transcendental nature of Kant's argument also suggests that Kant's moral imperative, although universally binding on all rational beings, is not *categorical* in the strictest sense of the word. It does apply to us *whatever we want or will*, but only provided that we want or will *something*. (This reflects Kant's internalism about reasons: we cannot be rationally bound by a law that is completely disconnected from any motivational facts about us.) I return to this issue in Chapter 6.

[62] Korsgaard, *Creating the Kingdom of Ends*, pp. 261–262.
[63] Langton, "Objective and Unconditioned Value," p. 169.

"real," but only that we're committed to it if we take any of our ends to be good. But what is supposed to be irrational (especially, *procedurally* irrational) about denying Kant's, second, internalist premise—about simply taking each of my ends to be valuable in itself, independently of my having chosen to pursue it? If I think this, then, it seems, I can see my ends as good without granting myself worth-bestowing status at all. And even if I concede that my end's value is somehow *conditional on me*, why conclude from this that I must have value, much less *unconditional, intrinsic* value? After all, hasn't Kant conceded (for the case of inclinations) that *some* conditions of value aren't, thereby, valuable themselves? This, at least, seems hard to question: infection makes penicillin valuable, but infection isn't therefore valuable, much less intrinsically valuable. And the cubic press, the machine which turns graphite into diamonds, makes carbon valuable, but is itself only instrumentally, not intrinsically valuable.

And it is far from clear, in any case, on the basis of what Kant has said, that *I* (rather than something else) must be the ultimate source of value of my ends, even if we allow that the source of their value, whatever it is, is intrinsically valuable. And even if *I am* the intrinsically valuable source of the value of my ends, what commits me to think *you* are an intrinsically valuable source of value, too? Why *can't* I think it's something special about *me* that gives me this status?

To these worries, Langton adds more troubling worries about the *conclusion* of Kant's argument. According to Korsgaard's Kant, she says,

> The ability of choosers to confer value on their choices—the ability of agents to be value-conferrers—is…the very source of the intrinsic value…of persons. We have intrinsic value because we value things as ends, conferring (extrinsic) value on them.[64]

As she puts it later: "I do value; therefore I have value."[65] But this, she worries, has decidedly troubling implications. In particular, and most worryingly for Langton, it seems to entail that persons who don't value things as ends—who cease to have desires—lose their value.

---

[64] Langton, "Objective and Unconditioned Value," p. 168.
[65] Langton, "Objective and Unconditioned Value," p. 169.

Langton considers Maria von Herbert, Kant's ill-fated young epistolary partner, struggling against an overwhelming depression: "I feel that a vast emptiness extends inside me, and all around me—," Maria writes, "so that I almost find myself to be superfluous, unnecessary. Nothing attracts me...." "Maria," Langton tells us, "does not value other things; and she does not value herself."[66] Must we, if we accept Kant's conclusion, agree with Maria that she has no value? Langton argues that this is the implication of the Kantian argument I have developed:

> [Maria von Herbert] does not value other things, and she does not value herself. We must assume that, in Korsgaard's terms, she does not confer value on other things and does not confer value on herself. But think: if we only have value because we *do value* ourselves, then our conclusion is a bleak one. Maria von Herbert *does not have value*. Maria von Herbert, acute philosopher, spurned lover, eloquent correspondent, is nothing. Sunk in apathy and self-loathing, she has lost what made her valuable. She thinks she does not matter—and *she is right*. Her conclusion that she should put an end to her life is, in these terms, justified. That is what we should say, and we should not shed tears when we learn that she put her conclusion into practice a few years later.[67]

Kant's conclusion may have other troubling implications. If it's our conferring value on other things through acts of rational choice that gives us our value, must we agree, with Kant, that animals and infants who have no rational capacities to exercise have no intrinsic value? This seems in tension with the "intuitive argument" I (loosely) ascribed to Kant—the one echoed by Taurek's point about the Pietà—according to which all beings to whom things matter have a special intrinsic value that things that *merely* matter *to us* lack.

The worries raised by Maria's predicament reach beyond cases of severe depression. If persons are valuable *because they make other things valuable*, doesn't that suggest that, even when they *do* confer value on some ends, they themselves have a kind of *instrumental,*

---

[66] Langton, "Objective and Unconditioned Value," p. 159.
[67] Langton, "Objective and Unconditioned Value," p. 181 (emphasis in the original).

extrinsic value—that their value somehow *derives from* the value they generate? On this picture, people would indeed seem to have the same sort of value as the cubic press. Such machines are valuable because they make other things valuable. Are we really to conclude that we're valuable only in the way the press is valuable—because we turn lumps of valueless world—like lumps of graphite—into the good stuff? Surely Kant was after the opposite conclusion—that the value of our ends *derives from our value*? Wasn't that, again, the point of the intuitive argument—the point about the special sort of value held by *beings to whom things matter*?

Kant's argument can, I think, be defended against some of these charges. And it can be supplemented and revised to avoid others. In its revised form, it may still have some counterintuitive implications. But it also, I believe, has significant intuitive appeal. It gains some of this appeal from its resonance with Taurek's point. It gains further appeal from its compatibility with the internalist conception of reasons, which, I've argued, we have independent reason to embrace. I will turn, in the next chapter, to spelling out this revised version of the Kantian view—one designed more explicitly to fit within an internalist conception of reasons.

5

Kantian Internalism

5.1 Skepticism About Procedural Practical Rationality

To recap: According to the version of internalism about practical reasons I am most interested in defending, for some agent A to have a reason to perform some action φ, that action must be related to A's "motivational set" in a particular way. More specifically, a reason for an agent to φ is a consideration that counts in favor of φ-ing—that throws its justificatory weight behind φ-ing—*in virtue of the relation it shows φ-ing to stand in to the agent's existing ends* (for example, by showing that φ-ing is a means to one of those ends, or constitutive of it, or valuable in consequence of the value of that end). Put in an oversimplified way, an internal interpretation of reasons is one that takes an agent A to have a reason to φ if and only if A has (or would, after procedurally rational deliberation, have) some end the attainment of which will be served by his φ-ing. It follows from the internalist picture that if we are rational *relative to our ends* (broadly understood), then we are rational, *all things considered*. On the externalist view, defended, for example, by Derek Parfit, what reasons we have need be in no way connected to the ends that we in fact hold.

I have argued (in Chapter 3) that we have good grounds for accepting this internalist account of reasons for action. I will not rehearse those arguments in favor of internalism here. I will instead try to defend the view against perhaps the most forceful objection leveled at it from the externalist camp: that it commits us to the undesirable conclusion that someone may have no reason to do what is in his own best interests, or to do as morality requires. I noted in Chapter 1 that the response of some prominent internalists to this objection, Williams, Harman, Foot, and Hume among them, has been to simply bite the bullet.[1] I believe, however, internalism about reasons places more restrictions on rational action than most externalists *and* internalists have allowed,[2] and in particular, that it is compatible with the view that we always have most reason to do as morality requires.

As I argued earlier,[3] the internalist/externalist distinction about reasons can be recharacterized as a distinction concerning the nature of practical reason. Parfit, following Williams, defines the difference between a *procedural* (internalist) and a *substantive* (externalist) notion of rationality as follows:

> To be procedurally rational we must deliberate in certain ways, but we are not required to have any particular desires or aims, such as concern about our own well-being.... To be substantively rational, we must care about certain things, such as our own well-being.[4]"

---

[1] As I discussed in Chapter 1, Williams has, for example, accepted the possibility of a cruel husband who in fact has no reason to be kinder to his wife. (See "Internal Reasons and the Obscurity of Blame," p. 39; on the possibility of people who have no reason to pursue what they need, see also, "Internal and External Reasons," p. 105). Harman, notoriously, has claimed that it would be false to say of Hitler that he had reason not to order the extermination of the Jews, or even that he *ought* not to have done so. (See "Moral Relativism Defended," especially pp. 3–11). Foot allows that some people may have no reason to do as morality requires. (See "Morality as a System of Hypothetical Imperatives", especially pp. 161–162.) And Hume infamously acknowledged such possibilities, writing of prudence,

'Tis [not] contrary to reason to prefer even my own acknowledg'd lesser good to my greater, and of morality,

'Tis not contrary to reason to prefer the destruction of the whole world to the scratching of my finger.

(See Hume's *A Treatise of Human Nature*, p. 416 (II, 3, iii).)

[2] Michael Smith is a notable exception (see *The Moral Problem* and "Internal Reasons," especially section 2).

[3] See §3.1.

[4] Parfit, "Reasons and Motivation," p. 101. Parfit introduces the labels "procedural" and "substantive," but he is drawing on a distinction Williams himself makes (see "Internal Reasons and the Obscurity of Blame," p. 36). Williams talks not about "procedural" versus "substantive" notions of rationality, but about the difference between setting normative standards for what counts as a "sound deliberative route," and setting such standards for what should belong in an agent's subjective motivational set "from the outside," as a result of "prudential and moral considerations."

Given the goals of my argument, this way of expressing the difference between procedural and substantive views of rationality is
question-begging. It assumes the truth of the conclusion I am arguing against: that on a procedural conception of rationality, we are not
rationally required to hold prudential or moral ends or commitments.[5]

It is not easy to restate the distinction without relying on this conclusion. I think that the two conceptions of rationality differ not in their
characterization of *whether* reason can demand that we hold certain ends,
but rather in their characterization of *how* and under what circumstances
reason can give us ends. According to a procedural notion of rationality,
the rational requirement to hold certain ends is generated indirectly by
the relation of those ends to other ends we do hold, as a result, in particular, of requirements of internal consistency and coherence.[6] One might
compare this to the case of theoretical reason, which may require us, by
means of standards of internal consistency and coherence, to hold certain beliefs in virtue of their relationship to other beliefs that we hold.
According to a substantive notion of rationality, reason may require us to
hold some (moral and prudential) ends directly, and regardless of what
else is true about us. I take this to be the distinction Williams and Parfit
have in mind, expressed now in a non-question-begging way. It is this
distinction with which I will work. I will draw on an expansion and revi-
sion of Kant's argument for the "formula of humanity" in the *Groundwork*
(spelled out in the last chapter) in support of the view that procedural
rationality can also demand of us that we hold particular ends.

I'll begin, however, by recalling why Hume thought that it could not.
In *A Treatise of Human Nature* Hume writes:

> A passion is an original existence, or, if you will, modification of exist-
> ence, and contains not any representative quality, which renders it a

---

[5] Another way of making this point is by pointing out that, drawn this way, the distinction
between procedural and substantive rationality makes internalism about reasons incompatible
with a rational requirement to be moral *by definition*.

[6] Of course, the standard of procedural rationality places many other requirements on us that
may not be requirements to hold certain ends; it dictates relations between our beliefs and intentions more generally. One prominent example of a requirement of procedural rationality which
need not be a requirement to hold a certain end is the *instrumental* requirement that we adjust our
means to our ends (discussed further below).

copy of any other existence or modification. When I am angry, I am actually possest with the passion, and in that emotion have no more a reference to any other object, than when I am thirsty, or sick, or more than five foot high. 'Tis impossible, therefore, that this passion can be oppos'd by, or be contradictory to truth and reason; since this contradiction consists in the disagreement of ideas, consider'd as copies, with those objects, which they represent.[7]

Beliefs—the "inputs" of theoretical reasoning—can themselves be rational or irrational, on Hume's view, because they can reproduce the world they represent well or poorly. But, because desires for particular ends are "original existences," Hume says, rather than interpretations of the world we see around us, they cannot be true or false in the same way. To say of a desire that it is contrary to reason would be like saying that it is contrary to reason to be thirsty, or sick, or five foot tall. Reason dictates relations between ideas, and hence determines the proper means of deliberation. But it cannot determine the desires that we deliberate about. Hume argues that it follows from this that it need not be irrational to be imprudent or immoral: again, if we are rational relative to our desires, then we are rational all things considered.

Hume sometimes writes as if he thinks we can never be truly *practically* irrational—that is, irrational in our actions and passions. He alleges that passions can be "unreasonable" only when they (i) are founded on the supposition of the existence of objects that don't really exist (as when, for example, we are afraid of ghosts), or (ii) rest on mistaken judgments of cause and effect (this is Hume's explanation of apparent cases of instrumental irrationality—when someone takes means insufficient to the satisfaction of her desires).[8] In both these cases, we seem to be guilty not of *practical* irrationality, but rather of holding false beliefs. Statements like these have led some interpreters (notably Elijah Millgram[9]) to class Hume as holding an *eliminativist* view of practical reason, according to which only beliefs, and not actions or desires, could ever be rational or irrational.

---

[7] Hume, *A Treatise of Human Nature*, p. 415 (II, 3, iii).

[8] Hume, *A Treatise of Human Nature*, p. 416 (II, 3, iii).

[9] See Millgram, "Was Hume a Humean?," especially §1.

As Christine Korsgaard has observed, this rather anemic analysis of practical irrationality seems to leave out some paradigm cases of irrationality, such as weakness of the will. She points out that practical and theoretical reason both have what she calls an "internalism requirement": we are not practically rational unless our recognition that some action is the means to an end we will is accompanied by a transmitting of *motive force* from the end to the means in question, any more than we are theoretically rational if we are able to perform logical and inductive operations without becoming *convinced* of the conclusions of those operations.[10] More generally, someone who fails to act as she knows she has most reason to act is practically irrational, just as someone who fails to believe what she knows she has most (epistemic) reason to believe is theoretically irrational. We are not rational if we merely pay the requirements of practical reason lip service.

Hume's leanings towards eliminativism are informative: his rejection of the possibility that desires can be irrational, especially when taken together with his caveat about the two sorts of cases in which we might say of a "passion" that it is "unreasonable," draws attention to a puzzle posed by his discussion. Hume writes that passions cannot "be oppos'd by, or be contradictory to truth and reason; since this contradiction consists in the disagreement of ideas, consider'd as copies, with those objects, which they represent." Unlike beliefs, desires, the suggestion is, cannot be true or false. The caveat suggests a similar focus: it notes that while passions cannot be true or false, they can result from or be explained by false beliefs. But how does this bear on the question of whether passions can be "contradictory to reason?" We know from the theoretical case that truth and rationality come apart. Truth is neither a necessary nor a sufficient condition for the rationality of beliefs: we might have a false but rational belief, and we might have a true belief that is irrational. So the mere fact that passions cannot be true does not obviously entail that they cannot be irrational.

---

[10]   Korsgaard, *Creating the Kingdom of Ends*, pp. 319–320.

There may be *a way* in which beliefs can be irrational that desires and ends can't be: beliefs can fail to accurately represent the world (or perhaps, the world as it appears to be), but desires, since they don't try to represent the world, can't be irrational *in that way*. But beliefs aren't just the *inputs* to reasoning but also its *outputs*; and the same, of course, is true of desires, intentions, and ends. Beliefs can be irrational in virtue of standing in the wrong relation to the world, but they can also be irrational in virtue of standing in the wrong relation *to each other*; they can conflict. And this latter kind of irrationality is also one that desires and ends can exhibit, even if they are "original existences."[11]

Our ends may conflict in a variety of ways, just as our beliefs may conflict in a variety of ways. My beliefs are irrationally inconsistent when I believe two propositions that straightforwardly contradict one another. This is the case when I believe that *p* and believe that *not p* at the same time. Similarly, I am practically irrational when I value an end—that is, take it to provide me with a valid reason for acting—when deliberating about one case, but overtly fail to value it—fail to recognize it as providing me with reasons for acting—when deliberating about another, relevantly similar case. For example, it would be irrational for me to take the value of a long and healthy life as a reason

---

[11] Hume's choice of analogies suggests another argument for the conclusion that passions cannot be irrational: remember his claim that they can no more be irrational than it could be irrational to be thirsty, or sick, or five feet tall. We are not guilty of irrationality if we find ourselves in these states not because as "original existences" they cannot be true or false, but rather because we generally have no control over such states. And it might be argued that our desires are at least often also beyond our control. But our actions and intentions generally are under our control. (Hume's word "passions," because it seems to be most naturally replaced by the more modern word "desires," conceals the fact that his theory, at least in the form adopted by Williams, is intended to describe the conditions not just for irrational desire, but for irrational action and intention as well.) It may well be irrational, if we are thirsty and desire not to be thirsty, to decline the offer of a drink. Similarly, it may well be irrational, if we are sick, to refuse the medicine we need to get better. And while it may not be irrational to have selfish desires (if we cannot help having them), it may be irrational to act on them. Whether such actions are irrational is the chief question we set out to answer at the start of this chapter, and Hume's argument fails, I think, to establish that it should be answered in the negative.

The Kantian point of view suggests that the Humean picture should be amended. As rational beings, we deliberate not about desires but about ends. That we may have conflicting desires is, unfortunately, simply a fact of human psychology. But, according to Kant, we cannot, if we are rational, will conflicting ends. Willing an end involves much more than desiring it or wishing for it: it involves a commitment to act towards it should the means be or become available.

not to smoke, but not to take it as a reason to stop drinking excessively. Of course, I may have overriding reasons to continue drinking which don't apply in the case of smoking—maybe drinking gives me significantly greater pleasure than smoking does. But this will not change the fact that the value of a long and healthy life should give me *some* reason—albeit a losing reason—to refrain from excessive drinking. The end of living a long, healthy life ought always to *motivate* me, even if it need not always *move* me.

But our beliefs may also be irrationally inconsistent or lacking in coherence in other ways. They are so, for example, if (i) I believe that *p* is true and know that *q* and *p* cannot both be true, but still believe that *q* is true. They are so, as well, if (ii) I believe that *p* is true, and know that the truth of *q* is a necessary consequence of the truth of *p*, but fail to believe that *q* is true (at least if it matters to me whether *q* is true).[12] To make a distinct point,[13] my beliefs are irrationally lacking in coherence if (iii) I believe that *p* is true, know that the truth of *q* is a necessary *condition* for the truth of *p*, but, again, fail to believe that *q* is true.[14] I believe that a similar set of restrictions binds the ends we may rationally hold, and that once these restrictions are identified, not just instrumental, but also prudential and moral requirements of procedural rationality emerge. I will try to show that this is the case, by examining the basis

---

[12] The parenthetical qualification is necessary here because I am probably not rationally required to believe all of the entailed consequences of my present beliefs when many of those consequences are irrelevant to me, especially when the entailment is not immediately obvious. (This point is due to John Broome. An alternative statement of the requirement, also suggested by Broome, is this: "Rationality requires of you that, if you believe p and you believe (if p then q), and if it matters to you whether q, then you believe q." (See Broome, "Does Rationality Give Us Reasons?," pp. 322–323.)) In what follows, I'll omit the qualification in the interests of simplicity.

[13] Is this point really distinct? Formally, it doesn't seem to be: there's no formal difference between *q*'s being a necessary condition for *p* and *q*'s being a necessary consequence of *p*. Both terms express, formally, simply the fact that *p* entails *q*. But I want to express the idea that if *q* is the condition for *p*, then *q* is the reason that *p*, and if *q* is the consequence of *p*, then *p* is the reason that *q*; consider "If it rains tonight (*p*), the park will be muddy tomorrow (*q*)"—*q* is a consequence of *p*; consider the different claim "if the park is muddy tomorrow (*p**), it will have rained tonight (*q**)"— *q** is a condition for *p**. We might say that in (ii), *q* is true *in virtue of p*, and in (iii), *p* is true *in virtue of q*. Alternatively, we might say that in (ii), *p explains q*, whereas in (iii), *q explains p*. Read in any of these ways, (ii) and (iii) do express distinct ideas.

[14] Again, the qualification "if it matters to me whether *q*" is probably needed; I leave it out for convenience.

for and implications of each of Kant's three imperatives of pure practical reason in turn. Here, for ease of reference, are Kant's imperatives of pure practical reason:

> The Instrumental Imperative: *if you fully will an effect or end you must also will the action or means requisite to it.*[15]
>
> The Prudential Imperative: *promote your own happiness*, or *take the means to your own greatest well-being.*[16]
>
> The Moral Imperative, or "Formula of Humanity": *so act that you use humanity, whether in your own person or in the person of any other, always at the same time as an end, never merely as means.*[17]

5.2 The Instrumental Imperative

Of all the species of skepticism about procedural practical rationality, skepticism about instrumental rationality is the least common. Most internalists, including Hume and Bernard Williams, allow that the scope of normativity of practical reason extends to cover corrections of instrumental rationality. So of Kant's three imperatives, the instrumental imperative, which tells us that we must will the necessary and available means to the ends that we will, has met with the least opposition. Most people would agree that if I will the end of having good dental health, and if I know that flossing my teeth regularly is the only available means to achieving that end, and I nonetheless do not intend to floss regularly, I am guilty of irrationality.[18] Note that Kant's imperative places a restriction on what we can rationally *will* or intend, rather than on what we can rationally *do*. Rationality is a property of my overall *mental* condition, and while actions can, I think, be irrational,

---

[15] Kant, *Groundwork*, p. 28 (4:417).

[16] Kant, *Groundwork*, p. 26–27 (4:415–416).

[17] Kant, *Groundwork*, p. 38 (4:429).

[18] Broome once again draws attention to a possibly needed qualification of this requirement of reason: he argues that we are only rationally required to *intend* the means to our *intended* ends if we think they will not come about unless we intend them. (See Broome, "Does Rationality Give Us Reasons?," pp. 322–323.)

they are irrational only when they result from mental failings, and not the interference of forces external to the mind. I cannot be rationally faulted for failing to floss if my hands are bound behind my back, though I may be faulted for continuing to intend to floss when I know I can't. Nor can I be *rationally* faulted if it *is* (in some central sense) possible for me to take the means to my ends, and I try to do so, but I fail out of incompetence (if, say, I'm so bad at flossing that, despite my best efforts, my trying to do so doesn't actually help promote my dental health).[19]

The failure of motivating force to carry through from ends to available known necessary means constitutes a procedural practical irrationality, just as the failure of conviction to carry through from a belief to the known necessary consequence of the belief constitutes a procedural theoretical irrationality: the former reveals a problem in the relationship between my ends, just as the latter reveals a problem in the relationship between my beliefs. The example runs parallel to the case of theoretical irrationality described at (ii) above. Just as my conviction that p, and my knowledge that q is a necessary consequence of p, require me to believe that q, my setting good dental health as my end, and my knowledge that regular flossing is a necessary and available means to that end, require me to also set regular flossing as my end. The point can also be expressed somewhat differently, in terms of valuing: it would be irrational to value good dental health, but not (derivatively) to value regular flossing. The (instrumental) value of regular flossing is simply a consequence of the value of good dental health, just as, in the theoretical case, the truth of q is a consequence of the truth of p.

---

[19] If the means to some end are not in my power, it is also not possible for me to will them—thus external restrictions on physical actions can place restrictions on mental actions as well. Just as I can't intend what I know I can't do, I also can't will what I know I can't do.

It might be suggested that I could act irrationally without being in an irrational mental state if I fail to be motivated to do what I will/intend to do, even though I will/intend to do as I have most reason to do. I'm not convinced that weakness of the will of this sort is even a conceptual possibility: being motivated to ϕ may be a constitutive part of an intention to ϕ.

There is a worry raised by this characterization of the instrumental imperative. We can imagine cases in which the only available means to ends that we will are prohibitively costly—perhaps even morally abhorrent. (Perhaps there's a life-threatening time-sensitive emergency I should respond to, and I'm contemplating flossing before I run out the door.) In such cases, is it still irrational for me not to take the only available means to my end? The question is a particularly worrying one from the Kantian perspective, because, if its answer is yes, then it would seem that Kant's instrumental and moral imperatives of reason, each of which he takes to apply universally and *a priori* to any of our actions, could conflict.

However, as Thomas Hill has pointed out, the Kantian imperatives need not conflict in cases like this. This is because the instrumental imperative is *disjunctive*: it states not that we must always will the means to our willed ends, but that we must *either* will the means *or* give up the end. Thus it is always possible to comply with both imperatives by simply giving up the end that requires immoral means, at least until less problematic means become available.[20] We might in such a case continue to will the end if we believe that less objectionable means will become available in the future (though they are not yet available). But in this case, we believe that the means we refuse to take are not *necessary* to the achievement of our willed end, so the instrumental imperative does not require us to take them.

The case of willing an end that can be achieved *only* by immoral means is similar to any nonmoral case in which we will conflicting ends. Here a comparison with the theoretical irrationality described at (i) above is useful: I cannot rationally believe that p is true, know that p and q cannot both be true, and still believe that q is true (if it matters to me whether q); I must, if I am rational, give up my faith in either p or q. Similarly, I cannot rationally will each of two incompatible ends.

---

[20] Hill, *Dignity and Practical Reason in Kant's Moral Theory*, p. 24. In giving up the end—that is, ceasing to *will* the end—one need not give up *wanting* or *wishing for* the end. It is, of course, perfectly rational to want or wish for an end to which no reasonable means are available—indeed, to which no means at all are available. As noted earlier, willing an end involves more than this: it involves something closer to a resolved intention to pursue the end.

I cannot will that I arrive at my lecture on time (if a punctual arrival would require me to ride my bicycle to class), and at the same time will to take a leisurely stroll to my department building. I must either give up on punctuality, or give up the stroll. In cases where the achievement of a contingently willed end requires immoral means—that is, means that violate Kant's moral imperative as expressed by the formula of humanity—the end with which my contingent end conflicts is the *rationally required* end of humanity itself. In such a case, I can rationally give up only one of the conflicting ends: my contingent end. (Of course, given the worries raised by Kant's argument, as I developed it in Chapter 4, it remains to be established that humanity *is* a rationally required end, on the internalist conception of rationality.)

The preceding discussion significantly oversimplifies the nature of the instrumental decisions we face. The circumstance in which there is only one means available to the achievement of a certain end is surely a rather special case. More commonly, there are a number of available means to take to an end, none of which is necessary to achieving it. Some means will stand out as better than the alternatives because pursuing them interferes less with our pursuit of the other ends we will. In this case, does the procedural conception of rationality I am defending require us to take means that seem to us at least as good as any of the available alternatives?

I think it does. (Forgive the rather reader-unfriendly use of schematic letters to represent ends and means, to which I'll resort for efficiency's sake.) Let's say I will three ends: X, Y, and Z. There are two possible means of achieving each of these ends, respectively: x_1 and x_2, y_1 and y_2, and z_1 and z_2. While it is possible for me to undertake all three of x_1, y_1, and z_1, allowing me to achieve all three of my ends, undertaking any two of x_2, y_2, or z_2 will preclude me from undertaking the third (or any alternative means to its associated end). What can be said of the scenario in which I choose to undertake x_2 and y_2, thereby ruling out the possibility of doing z_1 or z_2? Is such a choice procedurally irrational? If I make this choice, I achieve X and Y, but there are means that are necessary for the achievement of Z and that were available to me that I failed to take. True, z_1 and z_2 are not available to me *given* my decision to pursue x_2 and y_2; but the means to Z were available to me before I made that decision. Making that decision amounted to failing to will the available means to the achievement of Z, despite my commitment to achieving that end. And this violates the instrumental imperative of rationality.

Sometimes, of course, we find ourselves faced with choices that are not so straightforward: we are forced to make trade-offs. Perhaps we can either achieve X and Y, or achieve only Z. The account of instrumental rationality I am offering dictates that in cases of conflicting ends, where it is impossible to achieve all of the ends we set ourselves, we must give up some of the ends, until we are left with a compatible set. But there is in such a case more than one way to resolve the conflict. We can stop willing X and Y, or stop willing Z. Which end we give up will usually be a matter of preference—some of our ends are more important to us than others. But here the externalist worry once again rears its head: aren't there some ends which we simply oughtn't to give up when they come into conflict with others—ends which we have overriding prudential or moral reasons to pursue? And can a procedural account of rationality explain why this is the case?

5.3 The Prudential Imperative

Kant's prudential imperative is more problematic from an internalist perspective than his instrumental imperative for two reasons: first, as I noted in the last chapter,[21] it seems at least initially to fit more easily into a substantive conception of reason than a procedural one; for this reason, skepticism about prudential rationality is much more common among advocates of a procedural conception of practical reason than skepticism about instrumental rationality.[22] Secondly, the prudential imperative looks more likely to conflict with Kant's categorical moral imperative, in the sense that it may sometimes be impossible to

---

[21] See §4.2.
[22] As I have noted, both Hume and Williams are skeptics about prudential rationality.

comply with both. Both these difficulties result from the fact that the prudential imperative appears to posit a *necessary* end: Kant writes,

> [t]here is…*one* end that can be presupposed as actual in the case of all rational beings…, and therefore one purpose that they not merely *could* have but that we can safely presuppose they all actually *do have*, by a natural necessity, and that purpose is happiness.[23]

The imperative of prudence tells us to will the means to our own happiness.[24] The quoted passage raises several questions. Firstly, what does Kant mean when he writes that happiness is an end we hold by "natural necessity?" Are we also *rationally required* to hold it, as is suggested by the classification of the prudential imperative as an imperative of reason? How could this be, given a procedural conception of rationality? Secondly, what exactly does Kant understand under the concept of happiness, and why does he link it to that of prudence? Thirdly, given that the prudential imperative, unlike the instrumental imperative, seems to posit a necessary end, could the prudential and the moral imperatives conflict?[25]

I'll begin with the first of these questions. Kant's appeal in his discussion of happiness to the notion of an end we hold by "natural necessity" seems to contradict his idea of freedom. In *The Metaphysics of Morals* Kant writes:

> An end is an object of free choice;…and since no one can have an end without *himself* making the object of his choice into an end, to have any end of action whatsoever is an act of freedom on the part of the acting subject, not an effect of nature.[26]

---

[23] Kant, *Groundwork*, p. 26 (4:415).

[24] It is difficult to state precisely what Kant thinks the prudential imperative requires of us because he never actually states it in imperative form in the *Groundwork*.

[25] There are any number of competing possible interpretations of Kant's discussion of the prudential imperative in the *Groundwork*. While I think the interpretation that I offer in the pages that follow has some textual support, as well as the merit of allowing us to read Kant as employing a uniform conception of practical reason throughout his argument, I acknowledge that other interpretations may well be better supported by the text. My main interest is not in Kant interpretation, but in whether it is possible to build prudential and moral "oughts" on the foundation of a procedural conception of rationality. Kant's argument seems to me very suggestive in this regard.

[26] Kant, *The Metaphysics of Morals*, p. 516 (6:385).

Ends, Kant says, are—as a conceptual matter—freely chosen. (In the *Groundwork*, too, Kant defines an end as "that which serves the will as the objective ground of its *self-determination*."[27]) If our natural inclinations required us to adopt certain ends, then we would lack the free will that Kant takes to be a necessary condition of moral responsibility. But Kant seems in the *Groundwork* to suggest that all human beings by their nature necessarily will their own happiness, and set it as their end. Does it follow that the will does not freely choose its ends after all?

Moreover, if we understand happiness in an ordinary way—as an end that can compete with our other ends—then the claim that all human beings necessarily will their own happiness as an end (indeed, as the prudential imperative suggests, prioritize it above their other ends) seems both disconnected from prudential concerns, and, quite simply, empirically false. We would not describe, say, an artist, or a scientist, who places more importance on a successful career or on valuable contributions to her field than on her happiness as imprudent. We might well describe her as imprudent if she sacrificed her health or future well-being to the pursuit of success. Prudence seems much more strongly connected with concern for these things than for happiness. Moreover, as the example of the dedicated artist or scientist shows, people often *do* put other ends before happiness.[28]

More significantly, if we interpret "happiness" in this way, and take Kant's assertion that all rational beings have happiness as their end by "natural necessity" at face value, this does give rise to the possibility of conflict between the dictates of Kant's prudential and moral imperatives. As Thomas Hill notes,

> if we understand happiness in an ordinary way, there may be times when unless we do something immoral we shall lose all hope of happiness. Then if we cannot abandon the end of happiness, we cannot satisfy both the [moral] Categorical and the [prudential] Hypothetical Imperative.[29]

---

[27] Kant, *Groundwork*, p. 36 (4:427) (my emphasis).

[28] The claim that everyone *desires* his own happiness (though he may abandon it as an end) is more plausible, although there again seem to be counterexamples.

[29] Hill, *Dignity and Practical Reason in Kant's Moral Philosophy*, p. 25, footnote 3.

It was precisely the fact that any of our contingent ends *could be abandoned* that secured the compatibility of Kant's instrumental and moral imperatives. If the prudential imperative posits a particular end to be achieved that we *by our very nature cannot abandon*, then a possible incompatibility between the prudential and moral imperatives of reason poses a very real threat to Kant's picture of practical reason.

One response Kant might make to this worry is that we are required to abandon some natural end for the sake of a moral one only if it would be possible for us to do that. If we can't stop having happiness as one of our ends, we aren't then failing to do something we ought to do, since "ought" implies "can."[30] But as I noted earlier, this response doesn't seem to fit well with Kant's ideas about the freedom of the will. It also seems exceedingly unlikely that Kant would have excused us from doing what was morally best whenever it conflicted with our own self-interest. That seems to be resolving the potential conflict between the moral and prudential imperatives in the wrong direction, in favor of the latter.

The first task in addressing these difficulties will be to try to understand more fully just what, according to Kant, happiness is. The above objections give us good reason to doubt that Kant has an ordinary notion of happiness in mind. Kant tells us several things about happiness in the *Groundwork*. At 4:399 he writes of happiness that

> it is just in this idea that all inclinations unite into one sum.[31]

At 4:405 he reiterates:

> the entire satisfaction of [a human being's needs and inclinations] he sums up under the name of happiness.[32]

In the *Critique of Pure Reason*, Kant defines happiness in a similar way, again linking it to the idea of prudence:

> the doctrine of prudence [unifies] all ends that are given to us by our inclinations into the single end of *happiness*.[33]

---

[30] This response was suggested to me by Derek Parfit.
[31] Kant, *Groundwork*, p. 12 (4:399).
[32] Kant, *Groundwork*, p. 17 (4:405).
[33] Kant, *Critique of Pure Reason*, p. 674 (A800/B828).

And at 4:418 of the *Groundwork* he adds:

> For the idea of happiness there is required an absolute whole, a maximum of well-being in my present condition and in every future condition.[34]

These excerpts suggest that Kant understands happiness to be a kind of umbrella-end that gathers all of an agent's particular contingent (inclination-based) ends under one name.[35] If this way of understanding Kant's conception of happiness is the right one, then Kant's claim that all rational beings set happiness as their end seems not only more plausible than before, but indeed, almost trivially true. It merely amounts to the claim that if we value *each* of our contingent ends-to-be-effected, then we value *all* of our contingent ends-to-be-effected. And if, as the instrumental imperative requires, we must will the available means to each of our contingently willed ends, then, as the prudential imperative requires, we must will the means to all of our contingently willed ends.[36] We must do so not out of a natural necessity, but rather out of *rational* necessity: the inference seems to be one that is easily accommodated by a procedural conception of rationality.[37] The parallel with theoretical reasoning once again helps bring this out: if I believe p and I believe q and I believe r, then I am rationally required to believe p *and* q *and* r. The prudential imperative becomes simply a generalized form of the instrumental imperative.[38]

This understanding of happiness as a kind of umbrella-end helps to link Kant's prudential imperative to our more standard notion of

---

[34] Kant, *Groundwork*, p. 28 (4:418).

[35] This seems at least to be *one* of the central conceptions of happiness with which Kant works. In other passages he seems to appeal to a purely hedonistic conception. I adopt the conception above because it is, of course, far more congenial to my purposes.

[36] Remember that the instrumental imperative has already precluded the willing of incompatible ends (see §5.2 above).

[37] None of this helps explain why Kant claims we will our happiness out of a *natural* necessity. This raises further exegetical questions, but I'm more concerned here with piecing together a version of his view that can help underwrite my internalist argument than with interpreting Kant himself in a way that allows for consistency across his writings. This sticky task I leave to others.

[38] Although the conjunction principle of theoretical rationality to which I've just appealed seems intuitive enough, it raises a worry that a version of the familiar paradox about lotteries helps

prudence, and to more commonly recognized prudential ends, such as health and future well-being. The prudential imperative recommends the setting of health as an end because it is instrumentally valuable to many of our most important contingently willed ends: long life, a successful career, good spirits, and so on. It is true that the imperative does not give health the inviolable status of a necessary end. Nor do I think it should: there are certainly imaginable circumstances in which we should be willing to sacrifice concern for health for the sake of some more valuable end—perhaps a moral one.

But here a worry I raised at the end of my discussion of the instrumental imperative resurfaces. I pointed out there that when two or more of our contingently willed ends conflict, so that we cannot rationally will all of them, there are usually a number of ways in which we can revise our ends to make them coherent—it is, from the point of view of instrumental rationality, up to us which ends we abandon. The instrumental imperative leaves this indeterminate. Imagine a man who wants a long and happy life, in which he achieves success in his career and builds good relationships with family and friends. But he also wants a drink far more often than is compatible with his achieving or even pursuing his other goals. He cannot rationally *will* that he drink heavily as long as he rationally wills the achievement of his nobler ambitions. But can he rationally give up those other ends in favor of

---

to bring out. If I rationally ought to believe that *each* ticket in a million-ticket lottery won't win, does it follow that I rationally ought to believe that *all* of the tickets won't win?

The paradox doesn't present a problem for just the conjunction principle. That principle is merely a particular case of a more general and equally plausible principle of theoretical rationality that requires that I believe what is logically entailed by my other beliefs (at least if the entailment matters to me or is obvious).

How worrying need this be for my parallel account of practical rationality? I think it needn't be terribly worrying, because there seems to be no parallel problem raised by the conjunction principle when it is applied to the practical case. If I am committed to the value of p and committed to the value of q and committed to the value of r, it is plausible to claim that I am committed to the value of (p and q and r). The epistemic paradox seems essentially to concern the problem of how we should respond to extremely small possibilities, and there is no parallel to this problem in the case of the prudential imperative. Moreover, we feel the lottery paradox presents a paradox, and not merely a good reason to abandon the conjunction principle, precisely because each step in the story—certainly the appeal to the conjunction principle itself—is so plausible. In the absence of a good reason to abandon the conjunction principle in the practical case, I think we can retain it.

drinking himself into an early grave? Or, to borrow an example from Williams, can I rationally refuse the medicine I know I need? It seems, and the externalist would insist, that the imagined heavy drinker has *good reasons* to stop drinking—much better reasons than his reasons to abandon his other ends; similarly, it seems I have good reasons to take the medicine I know I need—prudential reasons that apply to me independently of any desire I have to take it. Does a Kantian internalist have to be skeptical about such reasons?

There are really two concerns raised by such examples. The first is that, faced with *conflicting* present inclination-based ends, a person could meet the requirements of procedural practical rationality by giving up the ends we intuitively feel he has good reasons not to give up. The second is that a person might simply lack *any* present inclinations to protect or promote his future well-being. Could such a person neglect his future needs and remain procedurally rational? I think both of these concerns can be addressed, but both will require an appeal to Kant's third imperative of practical reason—the moral imperative.

Let's begin with the case of the conflicted drinker. The first thing to note is that it is not so easy to give up, at will, a commitment to ends like a long, happy life, a successful career, and good relationships. So most people in the position of the heavy drinker will be in violation of Kant's instrumental and prudential imperatives. But what to say about someone who really does stop caring for these things, and prefers, instead, a drunken decline? Remember that the moral imperative required that we treat humanity as an end not only in others but also in our own persons. (A fuller examination and defense of that imperative, from within an internalist framework, will be developed in the next section, and what this entails for what we owe to ourselves (and others) will be explored in Chapter 7.) And it seems likely that respecting our own unconditional value, either as rational beings, or, more generally, as beings to whom things matter, will prohibit us from taking actions that will undermine our ability to achieve much of what matters to us, as well as very likely interfering with our ability to show the proper respect for others.

I will return to the task of fitting this imperative into a procedural conception of practical reason in a moment. For the time being, I want to emphasize that certain kinds of self-destructive behavior that are not irrational on instrumental or prudential grounds may turn out to be irrational, on the Kantian account I will develop, on moral grounds. It is likely that the behavior of the conflicted drinker will fall into this category. Undoubtedly, not all prudential ends that any externalist might think we have reason to adopt will be required by procedural rationality in the manner just sketched—there will likely be some differences between what the externalist and the Kantian internalist can claim we have reason to do. But I think the most important and most plausible of such ends will be required by the internalist conception of rationality I defend. I will say more in defense of this view in the next section, when I discuss Kant's moral imperative.

The problem of future ends is somewhat more complex. Most of us are presently concerned for our future well-being. Not all the inclinations we presently have are inclinations for the present. Philippa Foot points out:

[It is] useful to point to the heterogeneity within [the class of Kantian hypothetical imperatives]. Sometimes what a man should do depends on his passing inclination, as when he wants his coffee hot and should warm the jug. Sometimes it depends on some long-term project, when the feelings and inclinations of the moment are irrelevant. If one wants to be a respectable philosopher one should get up in the mornings and do some work, though just at that moment when one should do it the thought of being a respectable philosopher leaves one cold. It is true nevertheless to say of one, *at that moment*, that one wants to be a respectable philosopher....[39]

She adds in a footnote, "To say that at that moment one wants to be a respectable philosopher would be another matter. Such a statement requires a special connexion between the desire and the moment."[40] This is clearly true, and the distinction she relies on can clearly be

---

[39] Foot, "Morality as a System of Hypothetical Imperatives," p. 158 (my emphasis).
[40] Foot, "Morality as a System of Hypothetical Imperatives," p. 168.

drawn. I may now want to have children. But I don't want to have children now.

People who really live only in the present are very rare—indeed, I suspect there are no such people. But it nonetheless seems possible to imagine someone who has no concern at all for his future well-being, at least if that future is somewhat distant. And certainly, most of us at times discount the disvalue of future discomforts more than is merited on grounds of uncertainty. This seems like irrational behavior, but how can its irrationality be explained by the procedural conception? There need be no irrationality involved in believing that p is true now, while believing $not\ p$ will be true at some later time. A commitment to the value of now being pain-free doesn't obviously commit me to the value of being pain-free at some time in the future. But Kant implies, in the last of the passages from the *Groundwork* (4:418) quoted above, that happiness consists in *all* of our contingently willed ends: not only in the ends we will to achieve today, but also in our future willed ends. Thus he suggests that the prudential imperative requires us to take the means to these ends, as well as to our current ends.

I don't think this is correct. The prudential imperative alone does not explain the irrationality of failing to value the avoidance of future pains, in the absence of any present concern for that future. Here again, I think we must appeal to a version of Kant's moral imperative. When I value the avoidance of a present pain more than the avoidance of future pain I don't do so because I believe I will not then mind the pain as much as I do now. (If I did believe this, I would be guilty of holding irrational beliefs, and not of acting or willing irrationally.) Usually I recognize that *for my future self*, the future pain will be just as bad as the present pain would be for me, now. I know that that future self will want to avoid the pain, and will *will* its avoidance if possible. The requirement that I take that future end into account when I reason is therefore rather like my moral duties to other people. Just as I am rationally required, according to both the view set out in Chapter 4 and the expanded and revised version of it I will defend in a moment, to value the ends *other people* rationally set themselves, because I am required to value *them*, I am also required to value the ends I know

I will set myself at some future time. My imagined present-dweller owes his future self the same respect he owes to any other person.

I have now answered the first two of the three questions I posed at the beginning of my discussion of Kant's prudential imperative. I've tried to explain what Kant understands under the concept of happiness, and explored the relation of that end to other ends which we more commonly think of as prudential in nature: our health and future well-being. The third question asked whether the prudential imperative, which posits an end we are rationally required to will, could ever come into conflict with the moral imperative. The claim that the Kantian imperatives state requirements of rationality will be shaken if it is not possible to comply with all three imperatives at once, because they instruct us to do conflicting things.

This third question can now be answered: if happiness is understood simply as an "umbrella-end" that consists of all our individually willed contingent ends-to-be-effected, then the prudential imperative could not conceivably conflict with the moral imperative. The pursuit of the end of happiness would come in conflict with the moral imperative only if some component end of happiness came into conflict with that imperative. But as I argued in §5.2, if a contingently willed end comes into conflict with the moral (categorical) imperative, this simply means we are rationally required to give up the contingent end. Just as we can be released from the rational requirement to believe *p and q and r* by giving up belief in the relevant incongruent component belief, we can, in cases where the moral imperative conflicts with one of the component ends of our happiness, simply give up willing that component end. This does not mean that we need give up the end of happiness—understood as an umbrella end—since it still remains true that we will the attainment of all our (remaining) rationally willed contingent ends.

It is important to reemphasize the point that Kant (at least as I interpret him here) is using the notion of happiness in a very non-standard way in this argument.[41] It would be absurd to suggest that in doing our

---

[41] As I noted before (n. 35), Kant seems at times to be working with a much more standard, hedonistic, conception of happiness. It's not clear to me that a consistent conception of happiness

moral duty we will never sacrifice our own happiness (understood in the ordinary way), no matter how many important inclination-based ends doing so requires us to give up. And Kant, of course, allows that morality may require us to sacrifice many of our inclination-based ends—perhaps even most of them. The point is, rather, that if the argument of this section is sound, we can do this without violating the dictates of the prudential imperative, properly understood.

5.4 The Moral Imperative

The kind of skepticism about procedural practical rationality that I am most interested in contesting is, of course, skepticism about moral rational requirements. Both Williams and Hume argue that the adoption of a procedural conception of practical reason commits one to skepticism about moral rational requirements. A successful refutation of that skepticism has two components: firstly, it must show how there can be a particular moral end that is required by a procedural conception of practical reason. Secondly, it must show why such an end generates moral rational *requirements*, instead of functioning simply as one end among others. Why, in other words, does practical reason demand that we abandon our contingent and prudential ends in favor of our moral ends whenever the moral imperative and the instrumental or prudential imperatives threaten to conflict?

The previous chapter explored Kant's effort to achieve both these tasks: his argument for the formula of humanity. Kant's formula of humanity states:

> So act that you use humanity, whether in your own person or in the person of any other, always at the same time as an end, never merely as means.[42]

---

can be pulled out of Kant's work. As usual, my goal is not exegetical accuracy: I am borrowing from Kant only selectively, and interpreting his text with a somewhat loose hand, to suit the purposes of my own internalist argument.

[42] Kant, *Groundwork*, p. 38 (4:429).

I'll quickly summarize the argument. Kant develops the case for the formula of humanity through a process of tracing value-dependency. We pursue most of our ends because they are instrumental to the achievement of more fundamental ends. The ends that we pursue merely as means to other ends gain their value from the value of those more fundamental ends; that is, the value of the more fundamental ends is a condition for the value of our purely instrumental ends. But these more fundamental ends-to-be-effected are, according to Kant, also not valuable in themselves, but have as the source of their value the value of the rational natures that set them. Our ends are valuable only because we rationally choose to set them as our ends, and we are valuable. Thus the value of rational nature is, according to Kant, a condition of the value of the contingently chosen ends of our inclinations.

Here is Kant's argument again, broken into steps:

(1) I value the ends I rationally set myself, and take myself to have reason to pursue them.

(2) But I recognize that their value is only conditional: if I did not set them as my ends, I would have no reason to pursue them.

(3) So I must see myself as having a worth-bestowing status.

(4) So I must see myself as having an unconditional value—as being an end in myself and the condition of the value of my chosen ends—in virtue of my capacity to bestow worth on my ends by rationally choosing them.

(5) I must similarly accord any other rational being the same unconditional value I accord myself.

(6) *So I should act in a manner that respects this unconditional value: I should use humanity (that is, rational nature), whether in my own person or in the person of any other, always at the same time as an end, never merely as means.*

At the close of the last chapter, I raised some worries about this argument. What's irrational—more specifically, *procedurally* irrational—about simply taking each of my ends to be valuable in itself, unconditionally, and independently of my having chosen to pursue them? And even if I concede that their value is somehow *conditional on me*, why conclude from this that I must have unconditional, intrinsic value? We've seen that not all sources of value are themselves valuable, much less intrinsically so. Infection makes penicillin valuable, but isn't itself valuable; the cubic press makes carbon valuable, but is itself only instrumentally, not intrinsically valuable. And it is far from clear, in any case, on the basis of what Kant has said, that *I* must be the ultimate source of value of my ends, even if we concede that the source of their value *is* intrinsically valuable. And even if *I am* the intrinsically valuable source of value of my ends, what commits me to thinking *you* are an intrinsically valuable source of value, too?

My goal now is to fill in and revise the Kantian argument to provide answers to these questions. My hope is that once the argument is revised, it will also be less vulnerable to some of the worries raised by Kant's conclusion: in particular, Langton's worry about the value of the clinically depressed Maria von Herbert. I'll return to that worry below. First, let's see if the value-dependency-tracing argument can be made to work.

I noted when discussing the instrumental imperative that it would be irrational to value an end, but not value the necessary and available means to that end: thus it would be irrational to value the end of good dental health, but not value regular flossing. The value of the more fundamental end implies the value of the instrumental end. Kant's argument for his moral imperative suggests that the reverse implication may also hold: the value of an instrumentally valuable end implies the value of the more fundamental end to which it is instrumental. It would be irrational to value regular flossing without valuing good dental health (in the absence of other reasons for regularly flossing), or to value good dental health without valuing pain prevention or a longer life (or any of the other non-instrumentally valuable ends to which good dental health is the means). It would be equally irrational to value my contingent (non-instrumental) ends without valuing the source of *their* value—the value of the rational nature that set them. If I'm rational, I'll value flossing because I value good dental health because I value pain prevention because I value *me*.

The procedural nature of the conception of practical reason at work in this argument can again be brought out, as before, by means of a comparison to the case of theoretical reason. Just as I am *practically* irrational if I fail to value the only possible source of—and thus the condition for—the value of my contingent ends, I am *theoretically* irrational if (after informed deliberation) I fail to believe the proposition whose truth is the condition for the truth of my other beliefs. That is, I am theoretically irrational if I believe that *p* is true, know that the truth of *q* is a necessary *condition* for the truth of *p*, but fail to believe that *q* is true.

But why think that I am the only possible source of value of my contingent ends? Why can't I, rationally, just take them to be valuable in themselves, unconditionally? Let's start with the easier case: imagine a person who, when asked why he flosses regularly, responds that he does it for its own sake. And imagine that he gives a similar response when we ask him why he does all the other things he does. Such a person's value commitments would strike us as totally bizarre, in large part because of their total lack of internal coherence. There's just something arbitrary and dogmatic about valuing many such unrelated, unsystematic, contingently-chosen ends, without some more fundamental explanation for why they matter. Compare, again, the epistemic case: imagine a person who, when asked why she believes each of the things she believes, responds, "I just *do.*" Rational people's sets of beliefs are not so piecemeal and disconnected; their beliefs cohere and support each other. Justification may have to bottom out somewhere; but it had better not bottom out in *too* many unrelated articles of faith—especially not articles of faith about which there is irresolvable disagreement between otherwise rational agents.

So one advantage of valuing humanity as an end in itself, and recognizing it as the source of the value of my other ends, is that it can lend a kind of unity to my set of ends. A set of contingent ends that includes the end of humanity is rationally preferable to one that does not because it is, to borrow a term from Michael Smith, more *systematically justifiable*. Smith writes (of *desires*, as opposed to ends),

> we may properly regard the unity of a set of desires as a virtue; a virtue that in turn makes for the rationality of the set as a whole. For exhibiting

> unity is partially constitutive of having a systematically justified, and so
> rationally preferable, set of desires, just as exhibiting unity is partially
> constitutive of having a systematically justified, and so rationally pref-
> erable, set of beliefs.[43]

The virtue of willing a mutually supportive, systematically justified
set of ends is a virtue of procedural practical rationality, as the analogy to the epistemic case once again helps bring out: it's a matter (at
least in the first instance) of my ends' standing in the right *relations to
each other*, not *simply* of my holding or failing to hold a particular end.
Smith argues that one of the most important ways in which procedurally rational deliberation can bring it about that we acquire new ends is
through such a process of systematic justification—an attempt to bring
unity to our ends.

If this is right, then there is rational pressure on us, as Kant thought,
to search for "an unconditioned condition" of value—an answer to the
string of why-questions we might ask about the value of the things we
happen to care about. And Kant's argument gives shape to the plausible thought that things matter only because they matter to us, and
we matter. A world with no sentient beings in it would have no value.
But the argument so far cannot explain on its own why it's procedurally irrational to trace the chain of value-dependency among our ends
back to a different starting point. Many ends, it seems, could increase
the coherence and systematic justifiability of our set of ends if we came
to see them as the source of value of those ends.

However, to count as rational, it's not enough simply to restructure
my ends in a way that makes them systematically unified. Derek Parfit
observes:

> Consider…Smith's claim that we can be rationally required to have a
> more unified set of desires. Mere unity is not a merit. Our desires would
> be more unified if we were monomaniacs, who cared about only one
> thing. But if you cared about truth, beauty, and the future of mankind,
> and I cared only about my stamp collection, your less unified set of

---

[43] Smith, *The Moral Problem*, p. 159. Smith compares his account of this process of acquiring unifying desires through deliberation to Rawls' account of *reflective equilibrium* as a method for acquiring beliefs in a general principle given a particular set of specific beliefs.

desires would not be, as Smith's claim seems to imply, less rational than mine.[44]

Parfit's point shows that not any kind of unity of ends is, intuitively, equally rational. But he is skeptical that the *internalist*, committed as she is to a *procedural* conception of rationality, has the resources to explain why.[45] Nonetheless, I think the claim that any contingent set of ends will be more *procedurally* rational for including a commitment to the value of persons (rather than some other "source of value") can be defended.

Recall Hume's recognition, discussed in the very first chapter of this book, that *moral* judgments lay claim to a validity that is *non-parochial*—that can be recognized from any perspective. Hume says:

> When a man...bestows on any man the epithets of *vicious* or *odious* or *depraved*, he then...expresses sentiments, in which he expects all his audience are to concur with him. He must here, therefore, depart from his private and particular situation, and must choose a point of view, common to him with others; he must move some universal principle of the human frame, and touch a string to which all mankind have an accord and sympathy.[46]

I think Hume's observation applies to value-judgments—indeed, to *reasons*-judgments—more generally. If I begin, as Kant says we do, from an optimism that that some of the things that matter to me *really matter*—that I have genuine reason to pursue and protect and respect and promote them—then I am claiming more for my ends than just that they're *what I'm after*. In this way, my ends resemble my beliefs: if I take my beliefs to be rational, then I take them to be justifiable in a way that *others* should be able to recognize; I'm not merely saying they're what I happen to think.

Here's how Onora O'Neill makes the same point:

> If thoughts and knowledge claims are to be seen as reasoned, they must at least be followable in thought by others who hold differing

---

[44] Parfit, *On What Matters*, Volume One, p. 80.

[45] Parfit speaks of "subjectivism," not internalism, but the views are in the relevant respects the same.

[46] Hume, *Enquiry*, p. 272 (Second Enquiry, IX, i).

views...If principles of action are to be offered as reasons for action to others...they must at least be principles that could be adopted by those others and used to organise their action.[47]

Reasons claims, as she puts it, must appeal to "outsiders." And

'Outsiders' would legitimately view any claim that principles of reason are to be identified with the specific beliefs or norms of groups from which they are excluded as fetishising some arbitrary claim....In a world of differing beings, reasoning is not complete, or we may say (and Kant said) not completely public when it rests on appeals to properties and beliefs, attitudes and desires, norms and commitments which are simply arbitrary from some points of view.[48]

This doesn't mean that others must be able to take that very end I see as providing me with a reason to do something as a reason for *them* to do the same thing. That something will benefit *my child* may be a reason for me but not a reason (at least, not a reason of the same strength) for a stranger. But the stranger must be able to, at least in principle, see how that consideration functions as a reason in *my* circumstances—he must see that if it were *his* child, the fact would provide him with a reason. There can be agent-relative reasons, on this view, but there cannot be reasons that are recognizable as such only from a fully parochial perspective. I suspect, however, that I can recognize an agent-relative reason of this sort for someone to do something only if I recognize a related agent-neutral value: that is, for example, I can recognize your agent-relative reason to do what benefits your child only if I also think there is some kind of agent-neutral value in people's benefitting their own children. Your action's share in this value is what makes your reason non-parochial.[49,50]

---

[47] O'Neill, "Constructivism in Rawls and Kant," p. 358.

[48] O'Neill, "Constructivism in Rawls and Kant," p. 359.

[49] It doesn't follow in any obvious way from this that there can't be *deontological* obligations: obligations to benefit one's own children that don't amount to obligations to ensure that parents in general benefit their children. I won't address this question further here.

[50] Compare also Michael Smith's claim, in "Internal Reasons," that

[p]art of the task of coming up with a maximally coherent and unified set of desires is coming up with a set that would be converged upon by rational creatures who too are trying to come up with a maximally coherent and unified set of desires; each rational creature is to keep an eye out to her fellows, and to treat as an

So much, then, for stamp collecting. It doesn't even provide systematic justification to *my* ends, much less make sense from the perspective of anyone else's. One of the main arguments I offered in favor of
the internalist conception of reasons in Chapter 3 was that it seems less
dogmatic than externalism—more epistemically humble, as I put it
there. But to insist that stamp collecting is an ultimate worth-bestower
is *very* dogmatic. Even if stamp collecting became *all* I cared about,
so that my own value-commitments looked quite systematically justifiable, I would fail terribly at demonstrating epistemically healthy
humility. I would totally dismiss most other people's perceptions of
value from the start, with no way of defending the dismissal.[51] So it's
important that the end I recognize as the source of value, and so of
systematic justification, for my ends make sense as a potential source
of value for the ends of others.

But stamp collecting is, of course, not the only, or most plausible,
alternative source of systematic justifiability. *Happiness* (understood
now in its ordinary, non-Kantian sense) seems like a plausible (and
philosophically popular!) candidate. Perhaps we should think our
ends are valuable not because we choose them, and we're valuable, but
because they make us happy, and happiness is valuable. (If this is right,
then there is still a sense in which persons are the condition of the value
of their ends, but only because persons are the *vehicle*, so to speak, for

aberration to be explained, any divergence between the sets of desires they come
up with through the process of systematic justification. (p. 118)

Smith thinks that this aim of convergence is part of our ordinary concept of a reason—which he
argues is *nonrelative*. He doesn't claim to have shown that such convergence is possible, and so
doesn't take himself to have established that there *are* any reasons in the nonrelative sense (though
he seems optimistic). See section 2 of "Internal Reasons." My aim here is to defend this more
ambitious claim.

   Kenneth Walden makes a related point in his "Laws of Nature, Laws of Freedom, and the Social
Construction of Normativity." He argues that to act for reasons is to act in a manner that is susceptible to a certain kind of *explanation*—a rationalizing explanation. But explanations, by their nature,
he argues, are general: if my action is to be rationally explainable then the same explanation must in
principle hold for other, similarly situated agents.

   [51] In this way, I would be like a chicken sexer who thinks she's always right, even when she disagrees with other chicken sexers and cannot point to any independent criterion to show that she's
better at chicken sexing or to prove her approach gets it right. See §3.2.

the happiness their ends produce. Maybe the most appealing way to think of this is by analogy with musical instruments: on the utilitarian picture, our value is a bit like the value of a musical instrument. We're valueless hunks of matter until we're "strummed" or "played" by the world, by life, and then we "sing"—we produce experiences that, like the music produced by a strummed instrument, are where the real value lies.) Perhaps Kantian internalism mistakes the value of happiness for the value of getting what we want, when in fact, getting what we want is valuable only when and because it makes us happy.

Parfit, in fact, suggests that internalists who claim that our desires or choices give us reasons are succumbing to just this confusion. He writes:

> When people claim that our desires give us reasons, it is very often…facts about what we would enjoy, or find painful or unpleasant, that they really have in mind. Such facts give us reasons that are *hedonic* rather than *desire-based*.
> …[S]ome people mistakenly believe that hedonic reasons are desire-based.[52]

In this way, the Kantian argument I've laid out may seem to lead us back in the direction of the utilitarian conclusion I dismissed in the last chapter.

Taking happiness to be the "unconditioned condition" of value makes pretty good sense of most of my commitments, and of many of the commitments of others. Sidgwick, for one, thought that it did better, in that regard, than the assumption that human life was what was ultimately valuable. He argued that it would be a mistake to value human life in the absence of—even at the expense of—happiness. There would be nothing good, he says, about preserving a life that is full of misery.[53]

Sidgwick seems, here, to be assuming that the only reasons for action provided by values are reasons to preserve or make more of what's valuable. But, as T. M. Scanlon has pointed out, many of our values give

---

[52] Parfit, *On What Matters*, Volume One, p. 67.
[53] Sidgwick, *The Methods of Ethics*, p. 397.

us reasons that are not reasons to create more of that value. The value of friendship, for example, does not primarily give us reasons to bring about and prolong states of affairs that involve friendship, but rather gives us reasons to structure our interactions with our friends in ways that express loyalty, attention, concern, and so on.[54] We might even, for the sake of the value of friendship, perform an action that we know will bring a friendship to an end. If my friend is in an abusive relationship, the value of our friendship may give me conclusive reason to report the abuse to the police, because I know that my friend's life depends on my doing so. I may be required to do so even if the inevitable result of my doing so is that she feels betrayed, and no longer wants to be my friend.

Kant's broader conception of ends, which I explored in §4.3, and in particular, his claim that *humanity* is an end, provides us, of course, with another example of a value that is not a source of reasons to *make more of* what is valuable. The value of humanity as an end in itself does not provide a reason to have as many children as we can, or to encourage population growth. It may not even (despite Kant's own expressed views on suicide) provide us with reasons to extend an existing human life as long as possible. On the Kantian picture, the value of humanity is not an end to be produced or effected but rather an "*independently existing* end,"[55] whose existence as a value must inform our actions if we are to act fully rationally. Thus it gives us reason not to act in ways that conflict with the recognition of and respect for that value. How exactly that constrains our actions is not at all clear. I will set this difficult question aside for now. I will take some initial steps towards investigating it in the final chapter of this book.

And despite the importance almost everyone attaches to happiness, it cannot, it seems, explain the value we attribute to all our ends. Many people value ends quite independently of whether they generate happiness. This may be true of some of the ends they value the most. Think of the theoretical physicist, or indeed the philosopher, in dogged and

---

[54] Scanlon, *What We Owe to Each Other*, pp. 88–90.
[55] Kant, *Groundwork*, p. 44 (4:437).

laborious pursuit of some fundamental truth. The value of these ends does not seem to be derivable from the value of happiness. So the assumption that happiness is "the source of value" will still force us to dismiss many value-commitments out of hand.[56] The commitment to persons, or humanity, as the source of value, with the ability to confer value on their chosen ends, fares better: it allows us to begin with the default assumption that everyone's ends matter, and correct that assumption only when it actively conflicts with the commitment to the value of humanity.

A clarification is in order. The goal isn't, of course, to find an ultimate end that will accommodate *everything* individual people happen to value. The point of a moral principle, after all, is partly to *correct* our value commitments. But it shouldn't dogmatically rule out some people's values as mistaken from the start. We should grant anyone's ends, not just our own, the benefit of the doubt, as a kind of working assumption, and correct that assumption only when we need to. This at least is the goal and appeal of the internalist project, as I have interpreted it. If we assume that people are the source of value, then their value can, at a first pass, explain the value of *any* chosen end, though that end could *later* turn out to be irrationally adopted if it (or its pursuit) necessarily conflicted with respect for the special value of persons.

These considerations may lead you to think, however, that I have been focusing on the wrong version of utilitarianism. Perhaps the assumption that happiness is the fundamentally valuable thing dogmatically rules out some people's value-commitments as mistaken from the start, because some people have ends whose value cannot be explained by the value of happiness. This fact may undermine hedonistic forms of utilitarianism, but it suggests that a *desire-satisfaction* version of utilitarianism might fare better. There seems to be nothing problematically dogmatic about the assumption that it's the satisfaction of people's desires (broadly understood), whatever they are, that's

---

[56] I have also argued that the assumption that happiness, as opposed to the persons and creatures who can be happy, is the end in itself has implausible normative implications. See §4.2.

the ultimate source of value; and doesn't a commitment to this value serve just as well as a commitment to the value of humanity as a source of systematic justification for our motley collection of ends?

But there is, on reflection, something very odd about the idea that desire-satisfaction could be the ultimate end—the intrinsically valuable source of value of all our other ends.[57] We might think that it's valuable to satisfy our desires because we think what we desire is itself valuable. But this won't do, of course, for the present purpose. If satisfying our desires is valuable because our desires point us towards ends that are valuable independently of our desiring them, then our ends aren't valuable *in virtue of* satisfying our desires, and the value of desire satisfaction isn't the source of or explanation for their value after all. Coming to value desire satisfaction can't then provide greater systematic unity to our set of ends.[58]

If desire satisfaction is to serve as a source of systematic justifiability for our individual, disunified ends, those ends must be valuable in virtue of their satisfying our desires. Why should we think the value of our ends depends on our desires in this way? A natural thought may be that the satisfaction of desire is valuable, not because of the independent value of the ends we desire, but because of the positive experiential state it involves—because of *what it's like* to have our desires satisfied. But to answer that way is, of course, to revert to hedonistic utilitarianism and the problems it brings with it.

According to the view under consideration, the satisfaction of desires is, instead, intrinsically valuable. And it is all that's intrinsically valuable. We ourselves, on such a view, would again be valuable only as *vehicles* or *mediums* for desire—no more intrinsically valuable than the cold stone from which the Pietà was carved. But if the *objects* of our desires have no value in themselves, and the *experience* of having our

---

[57] Roger Crisp also notes the oddness in the idea that desire-satisfaction itself is the ultimate good-making property (see "Well-being," §4.2).

[58] Similar obstacles face the view that preference satisfaction is desirable because certain experiences or ends can be *made* valuable by the fact that they satisfy desires of the agent, just as, say, taking an interest in a game or a sport can make the experience of watching it or playing it valuable. This gives preference satisfaction the same kind of instrumental value as the cubic press.

desires satisfied has no value in itself, and *we*, the *subjects* of the desire, have no value in ourselves, then why should the satisfaction of *our* desires have any value at all? This seems mysterious, unmotivated. The question brings us back around to the Kantian line of thought I have been pushing, which provides an answer: it matters that *we* get what we desire, when it matters, because *we matter*.

The argument from systematic justifiability explains why there is rational pressure on all of us to value humanity as an end, regardless of our contingent ends and commitments, and so provides the first necessary component of a successful internalist defense of the thesis that rationality requires us to be moral. But the argument also provides the second necessary component of such a defense: it explains why the rationally required end of humanity is not just one end among others, but trumps those others in cases of conflict, and so can be a source of moral *requirements*. Because the value of humanity is, on the view I've defended, a condition of the value of any other end whatsoever, it is always procedurally irrational to fail to treat it as an end for the sake of promoting some particular (even prudential) end-to-be-effected. This is because such an end could have no value (and thus could generate no reasons for acting) independent of the value of humanity itself.

Consider a miser, who values money because of the good things it can get him, but then sacrifices those good things for the sake of accumulating more money. The person who violates the moral imperative for the sake of promoting some conditionally valuable end—who, say, uses and manipulates others for personal gain, without regard to their interests—is guilty of precisely the same sort of *procedural* irrationality. Thus Kant's moral imperative can never be overridden by instrumental or prudential concerns. Even on an internalist view of practical reason, we always have most reason to do as morality requires.

In brief, if I'm procedurally rational, I will try to restructure what I care about in such a way as to make my ends more systematically justifiable without ruling out the value of your ends from the start. Assuming that we matter—that is, adopting humanity as an end and recognizing it as the source of value for the ends we set—is ideally suited to the purpose. We might well be more procedurally rational if we came to treat humanity as an end in itself, and as a source of value for our other ends, as well as the ends of other people; if we learned to give up our contingent ends when their pursuit is incompatible with respecting the value of others as ends in themselves; if we learned to recognize that what matters to us isn't all that matters; and if we learned to recognize that some of what matters to us doesn't really matter, after all.

I have been trying to fill in the gaps in Kant's argument, to make clear why there is rational pressure on us—even on an internalist, procedural conception of rationality—to comply with Kant's formula of humanity. Along the way, I hope it has also become clear why Kant is not, in fact, guilty of the mistaken inference that he is sometimes accused of making: from the claim that X is the source of, or condition for, the value of Y to the claim that X must therefore be valuable, perhaps even intrinsically valuable. Kant recognizes, as I've noted, that not all conditions of value are themselves valuable—he thinks inclinations, though conditions of value of our chosen ends, are not valuable in themselves. Kant's idea is not that, *because* we're the source of value of our chosen ends, we must *therefore* be valuable in ourselves. Rather, it's the *way* we bestow value on our ends that matters: we do this by being *the more fundamental ends for whose sake we pursue our contingent ends.* By contrast, we don't value or pursue or create penicillin *for the sake of* the infection that is a condition of its value. We do these things for the sake of *health*, not illness—health is the more fundamental end that makes the development of antibiotics a valuable end. And ultimately, Kant might add, *our health* is valuable because *we* are valuable.

This point goes a considerable way towards defusing Langton's other worry, about the value of Maria von Herbert.[59] Langton, remember, restates the view of value she attributes to "Korsgaard's Kant" this way:

> The ability of choosers to confer value on their choices—the ability of agents to be value-conferrers—is…the very source of the intrinsic

---

[59] I say only "a considerable way" because I don't think it goes all the way to defusing the worry. A related worry survives, which I discuss below (see §6.1).

value...of persons. We have intrinsic value because we value things as ends, conferring (extrinsic) value on them.[60]

This comes close, I believe, to characterizing the Kantian position. But it's not *quite* right, and the mischaracterization is what leads to the most pressing version of the problem of Maria von Herbert.

In one sense, I believe, it *is* in virtue of our ability to confer value on our choices that we have a special value. But we don't have this special value because we make things valuable. Our value is not like the (instrumental) value of the cubic press, which turns ordinary carbon into diamond. We have the special value we have, I have suggested, because we aren't just beings *that matter to someone*, but rather we're *beings to whom things matter*. We are centers of subjectivity. This was Taurek's point about the crucial difference between a person and the Pietà. For all its priceless beauty, if the Pietà survived the nuclear holocaust but no sentient beings did, it would lose its value. But my value does not depend on my being *of* value to anyone—I am, as Kant says, valuable *in myself*.

What if (unfortunate soul!) I not only matter to no one, but nothing matters to me? Now we are arriving at Maria's predicament. But it doesn't seem to follow from Taurek's point, which, I argued, is the driving normative-ethical intuition behind the Kantian argument, that Maria has no value. Maria is, after all, still a center of subjectivity, not a mere thing, even if, at the moment, nothing matters to her. Things, after all, don't suffer depression; and though they may self-destruct, they don't commit suicide.

But what of the Kantian internalist argument itself? Does *it* entail, as Langton suspects, that Maria has no value? The answer, again, is no. As Langton says, the Kantian (as I've portrayed her) reasons like this: "I *do* value; therefore I *have* value."[61] But the "therefore" in this argument represents an *inference* from the first proposition to the second; it does *not* indicate that the first proposition *explains*, or *makes*

---

[60] Langton, "Objective and Unconditioned Value," p. 168.
[61] Langton, "Objective and Unconditioned Value," p. 169.

true, the second. That is, my drawing the inference shows I'm committed to the second proposition, about my value, because I'm committed to the first, about my valuing; it does not show that I'm committed to the further view that I have value *because* I do value—that this is what *makes* me valuable.

In fact, as we've seen, Kant would reject this claim. Consider a less fundamental step in his process of tracing value-dependency. Say that if I value flossing, I must value good dental health, because it's the only (plausible) source of the value of flossing. It certainly doesn't follow from this that good dental health is valuable *because* or *in virtue of* its conferring value on flossing. *That's* not what *makes* health valuable. This would, absurdly, suggest that the value of good health derived from the value of flossing, in much the same way as the value of the cubic press comes from the value it confers on carbon (to return to my earlier analogy). If humanity were valuable in this way, its value would be purely instrumental. But our value, on Kant's view, is not instrumental, and it does not derive from the value of our ends. It is because *their* value derives from *ours* that our *commitment* to their value puts rational pressure on us to recognize our own.

So we should not conclude, as Langton worries we must, that Maria has no value because she does not value. We have learned, by reasoning from our *own* values, that *she has value*—indeed, intrinsic, unconditioned value—just like we do. And we should indeed mourn her suicide as a great loss.

This makes the Kantian argument much more acceptable. But, unfortunately, it does not entirely defuse the worry Maria's case poses. There's a lingering question about what Maria *herself* should think. *She*, after all, rejects the very first step of the Kantian argument: that there are valuable ends she has reason to pursue.[62] I turn to this worry, and related worries, below.

---

[62] Though Maria seems to embrace the conclusion of the Kantian argument directly. There's nothing in the correspondence Langton presents to suggest that she thinks persons, in general, valueless, and indeed she long refrains from suicide for fear that it would violate the moral law.

6

Is the Moral Imperative Categorical?

6.1 A First Response: the Problem of Maria Revisited

I want to begin with a final analogy between the picture of procedural practical rationality that I have sketched and the case of theoretical rationality. It may seem surprising that, as I have argued, the mere exercise of our faculties of practical reason in willing, regardless of which ends we contingently will, can commit us, if we are rational, to willing a particular, substantive end. But there is again a familiar analog in the case of belief, provided by Descartes' *Cogito*. Descartes argues that there is one substantive belief that we must all hold, on pain of irrationality, if we believe anything at all: that we exist. I have argued, following Kant, that there is one substantive end that we must all will, on pain of irrationality, if we will anything at all: that of humanity.

I say: *if we will anything at all*. On one prominent and natural understanding of the claim that moral requirements are *categorical*, such requirements bind us regardless of *any* facts about what we desire or will. In my view, Kant's internalism does commit him to rejecting the claim that the moral law is categorical *in this sense*. At least, the version of Kant's argument that I've presented and defended commits *me* to rejecting this claim, whether or not Kant himself would have wished to retain it. After all, I've argued that our reasons to be moral can be derived from facts about what we will, combined with facts about what procedural rationality requires of us: our commitment to the value of our contingently willed ends rationally commits us to the value of another end—humanity—that forms the foundation for the moral law. The claim that moral reasons are internal reasons is precisely the claim that they can be derived in some way from the contents of our motivational sets—that facts about those sets *are* relevant to establishing that we are subject to moral requirements, as well as to discovering what those requirements are.

However, according to the argument I have developed, all of us are subject to the *same* moral requirements regardless of differences in our contingently willed ends. It is our commitment to the value of those ends, *whatever they may be*, that gives rise to the rational requirement to treat humanity as an end. The Kantian moral law might therefore be called categorical in a somewhat weaker sense: it is a law of reason that binds us regardless of what we desire or will, *provided that we will something*.

As I've said, however, such moral judgments are justified only if and because we can back them up with claims about what we are rationally required to value *given that we value something*, regardless of what that something is, and regardless of whether we in fact comply with this rational requirement. Thus a true nihilist, someone who values nothing—whose motivational set is simply empty—and who thus fails to meet the conditions necessary for the moral rational requirement to get a hold on her, may escape the "categorical" imperative I have described. On my view, it seems, I must retract the claim that, say, Jones ought not to torture cats, if I discover that Jones is a true nihilist. And, to return to the troubling case of Maria von Herbert, we must, it seems, retract the claim that Maria ought not to commit suicide, if we find, as Langton suggests, that she *really values nothing*. (We need not conclude, I argued in the previous chapter, that Maria in fact has no value, or that her suicide is nothing to be mourned, or that we should do nothing to save others like her. Nor need we think that Jones' violent acts are nothing we should abhor, or try to prevent.)

Do Jones and Maria really have *no reason* to avoid such acts? This is, admittedly, counterintuitive. But the force of the counterintuition can, I think, be softened somewhat. Firstly, a true nihilist in the sense I have in mind—someone who really sees no value in anything, and no reason to do anything—is not likely to go around torturing cats.[1] Nor is she likely to commit suicide. As Kant noticed, suicide is not really the action of a true nihilist; the suicidal person has an end, if it is only to put an end to her own suffering.[2] (And it is worth noting that Maria, indeed, seems to have felt the force of the categorical imperative: she long refrains from suicide for fear that it will violate the moral law.) It seems to me that it is not easy to act (voluntarily) in a way one believes one has no reason at all to act. This is what makes wagers like that described in Gregory Kavka's "The Toxin Puzzle" so hard to win. Of course, performing a random action, such as jumping in the air three times, in order to disprove this assertion is a hopeless way of disproving it—your reason for jumping in the air will have been provided by your goal of disproving the assertion.

A profession to nihilism is, of course, not a way out of moral condemnation. It is not so easy, I have maintained, to imagine a case of true nihilism. In fact, I am not at all convinced that true nihilism is even a psychological possibility for recognizably human agents. But it may be. If we did encounter a true nihilist, how prepared would we be to say of her that she ought to act in certain ways? I'm really not sure. I could, of course, make many other normative claims about her case; I could say that it would be good for the rest of us (and for her) if she did this or refrained from doing that. I think I would balk at making any claims about what she ought or has reason to do.

When Bernard Williams introduced the amoralist's challenge— the challenge to which this book aims to provide a response—he drew attention to precisely the difference between nihilism and more

---

[1] While a fair amount of destruction has certainly been wrought in the world by persons describing themselves as nihilists, this self-description is unlikely to have been an accurate one.

[2] Kant, *Groundwork*, p. 38 (4:429). This is why Kant characterizes suicide as using humanity in your own person as a mere means to your end (of "maintain[ing] a tolerable condition up to the end of life"). It does not seem clear to me that Kant's argument entails the hard line on suicide that he takes, however.

motivated wrongdoing that concerns us here. "'Why should I do anything?'," he writes:

> Two of the many ways of taking that question are these: as an expression of despair or hopelessness, when it means something like 'Give me a reason for doing anything; everything is meaningless'; and as sounding a more defiant note, against morality, when it means something like 'Why is there anything that I should, ought to, do?'
>
> Even though we can paraphrase the question in the first spirit as 'Give me a reason...', it is very unclear that we can in fact give the man who asks it a reason—that, starting from so far down, we could *argue* him into caring about something.... What he needs is help, or hope, not reasonings....
>
> I do not see how it could be regarded as a defeat for reason or rationality that it had no power against this man's state; his state is rather a defeat for humanity. But the man who asks the question in the second spirit has been regarded by many moralists as providing a real challenge to moral reasoning. He, after all, acknowledges some reasons for doing things; he is, moreover, like most of us some of the time. If morality can be got off the ground rationally, then we ought to be able to get it off the ground in an argument against him; while in his pure form—in which we can call him the *amoralist*—he may not be actually persuaded, it might seem a comfort to morality if there were reasons which, if he were rational, would persuade him.[3]

I have been hoping, of course, to provide an argument of just this sort: an answer to this second kind of question. I'm inclined to agree with Williams that a question of the first sort (if, again, there can be anyone to ask it) is not one we can or should aim to resolve through moral reasoning.

This conclusion would be a kind of corollary to the thought Williams expresses in "Persons, Character, and Morality," about the limits to the demands morality can make of us. There he writes:

> There can come a point at which it is quite unreasonable for a man to give up, in the name of the impartial good ordering of the world of moral agents, something which is a condition of his having any interest in being around in the world at all.[4]

---

[3] Williams, *Morality: An Introduction to Ethics*, pp. 3–4.
[4] Williams, "Persons, Character, and Morality," in *Moral Luck*, p. 14.

Morality, Williams thinks, cannot require us to do something that takes away the condition for our having any interest in the world. And if we have no interest in the world to begin with? Then, perhaps, morality cannot require us to do *anything*.

This may also be the seed of truth in Williams' discussion of blame, which I considered in §1.4. *Pace* Williams, we don't (I argued there) withhold blame from a person who lacks certain elements in his motivational set: who simply doesn't care about the well-being of (some) others, or their good opinion. But we might withhold blame from a person, if indeed there can be such a person, whose motivational set is completely empty: who cares about nothing at all.⁵

---

⁵ The case of Maria von Herbert—and the shadow of the possibility of true nihilism she casts—raises a perhaps more fundamental question about the view I've been defending. I argued in the last chapter that Maria *has value*, even if she truly values nothing, though *she* may have no *reason* to protect or promote or respect that value. *We* have reason to promote and protect and respect her value. But what if we *all*, like Maria, fall into a motivating-sapping depression? What if we all cease, entirely, to care? What if nothing matters anymore to any of us?

If we follow the line of argument sketched above, it seems we must conclude that none of us have any moral reasons at all—that morality simply ceases to have application in the world like the one I am imagining. Does it also follow that the world is drained of value? That none of us, after all, have value, at least until we start to care again?

This even grimmer conclusion *need* not follow. It follows only if we accept buck-passing about value: the view that *what it is* for something to have value is for there to be reason to respect or protect or promote it. But it is open to the Kantian internalist to reject buck-passing about value. She could then embrace internalism about reasons, but leave the door open to *externalism* about *value*. That is, she could think what we have *reason* to do depends, in the complicated way described in Chapter 2, on our antecedent ends, and the constraints of procedural rationality. But there could be *value* in the world that is not constrained, in this way, by what we care about, and what we could reason our way to caring about.

This view is not as disjointed as it may at first appear to be. Most of the arguments I advanced in Chapter 3 in favor of the internalist picture of reasons were epistemologically, as opposed to metaphysically, motivated. And it is *reasons*, in particular, that I take to be epistemically constrained: what we have *reason* to do, and correspondingly, what we *ought* to do, depends to some extent on our evidence, and on what desires, broadly understood, we can hold on to if we exhibit certain epistemic virtues, like coherence and humility. It's not at all clear to me that what is valuable must be epistemically constrained in the same way.

In this way, the distinction between *value* and *reasons* may resemble the distinction between *truth* and *justification*: what is true is in no way constrained by our evidence and our antecedent beliefs; but what we are justified in believing may well be.

If we were to accept this mixed position, then the arguments of the preceding chapters would concern what we have *reason* to do, and what we *will value*, if we're rational, as opposed to what *has value*; on the view I'm tentatively floating here, these might, at times, come apart.

Thanks to Ruth Chang, Jamie Dreier, Alex King, and Alex Mechanick for pressing me on this point.

6.2   A Second Response: the Categorical "Use" of "Ought"

Philippa Foot points out that the thesis that moral oughts are categorical is in part a thesis about how we *use* such oughts: we don't think, when we say of someone that he ought morally to do such-and-such, that we must first examine his desires. And we don't feel we have to retract our moral ought claims when we discover that the agent we are describing lacks particular relevant desires, such as the desire to be moral, or certain concerns, such as concern for the well-being of others. Moral ought claims differ in this way from merely instrumental ought claims, which we do retract when we find the relevant desire is absent. Foot writes:

> Is Kant right to say that moral judgments are categorical, not hypothetical, imperatives? It may seem that he is, for we find in our language two different uses of words such as 'should' and 'ought', apparently corresponding to Kant's hypothetical and categorical imperatives, and we find moral judgements on the categorical side. Suppose, for instance, we have advised a traveler that he should take a certain train, believing him to be journeying to his home. If we find that he has decided to go elsewhere, we will most likely have to take back what we said: the 'should' will now be unsupported and in need of support. Similarly, we must be prepared to withdraw our statement about what he should do if we find that the right relation does not hold between the action and the end—that it is either no way of getting what he wants (or doing what he wants to do) or not the most eligible among possible means. The use of 'should' or 'ought' in moral contexts is, however, quite different. When we say that a man should do something and intend a moral judgement we do not have to back up what we say by considerations about his interests or his desires; if no such connexion can be found the 'should' need not be withdrawn. It follows that the agent cannot rebut an assertion about what, morally speaking, he should do by showing that the action is not ancillary to his interests or desires.[6]

The internalist moral imperative I defend is categorical in this sense, given a natural interpretation of Foot's phrase "considerations about

---

[6]   Foot, "Morality as a System of Hypothetical Imperatives," p. 159.

his interests or his desires." We are not, I have argued at length, required to back up moral judgments by pointing to any *particular actual* desires or interests of the agent we are judging. So, for example, we are not required to retract our assertion that the cruel husband of Williams' example ought to be kinder to his wife when we discover that he has no desire to be so. He, like the rest of us, is subject to a rational pressure to treat persons as ends in themselves, including his wife.

Foot acknowledges that there is truth to the claim that moral requirements are categorical, at least to the extent that this is an assertion about linguistic usage. But, she claims, Kantians mean more than this when they insist moral imperatives are categorical: they intend to attribute an "inescapability," a "special dignity," a "necessity" to such requirements that they take hypothetical imperatives to lack.[7] This stronger claim, however it is interpreted, cannot, she argues, be established by appeal to the observation about linguistic usage alone. (She marks the difference between the weaker and the stronger theses by distinguishing between the "non-hypothetical *use* of 'should' [or 'ought']," of which she takes moral judgments to be examples, and a "non-hypothetical imperative," of which, she argues, we cannot show moral requirements to be examples.[8]) The linguistic observation, she points out, can be made of types of judgments and types of rules that clearly lack the inescapability, dignity, and necessity we want to attribute to moral imperatives. "For instance," she notes,

> we find this non-hypothetical use of 'should' in sentences enunciating rules of etiquette, as, for example, that an invitation in the third person should be answered in the third person, where the rule does not *fail to apply* to someone who has his own good reasons for ignoring this piece of nonsense, or who simply does not care about what, from the point of view of etiquette, he should do. Similarly, there is a non-hypothetical use of 'should' in contexts where something like a club rule is in question. The club secretary who has told a member that he should not bring ladies into the smoking-room does not say 'Sorry, I was mistaken' when

---

[7] See Foot, "Morality as a System of Hypothetical Imperatives," p. 160.

[8] Foot, "Morality as a System of Hypothetical Imperatives," pp. 160–161 (my italics). See also Foot, "A Reply to Professor Frankena," in *Virtues and Vices*, p. 176.

informed that this member is resigning tomorrow and cares nothing about his reputation in the club. Lacking a connexion with the agent's desires or interests, this 'should' does not stand 'unsupported and in need of support'; it requires only the backing of the rule. The use of 'should' is therefore 'non-hypothetical' in the sense defined.[9]

As Foot remarks, if a non-hypothetical *use* of "ought" or "should" were sufficient to make the resulting imperative categorical in the (somewhat nebulous) strong sense described above, then even rules of etiquette would qualify as categorical imperatives. Since the defenders of Kantian ethics whom she is addressing would doubtless deny rules of etiquette this status, they must offer some alternative account of the sense in which the moral imperative is categorical to that provided by these observations about use.

Foot has a suggestion to make about what this other account might be that is very relevant to the project I have undertaken. She writes:

> Very roughly the idea seems to be that one may reasonably ask why anyone should bother about what should (from the point of view of etiquette) be done, and that such considerations deserve no notice unless reason is shown. So although people give as their reason for doing something the fact that it is required by etiquette, we do not take this consideration as *in itself giving us a reason to act*. Considerations of etiquette do not have any automatic reason-giving force, and a man might be right if he denied that he had reason to do 'what's done.'
>   This seems to take us to the heart of the matter, for, by contrast, it is supposed that moral considerations necessarily give reasons for acting to any man.[10]

Foot goes on to adopt an internalist conception of what it is to have a reason. She writes, in a manner reminiscent of Williams,[11] that "the man who rejects morality because he sees no reason to obey its rules can be convicted of villainy but not of inconsistency."[12] She declares that "[i]rrational actions are those in which a man in some way defeats

---

[9] Foot, "Morality as a System of Hypothetical Imperatives," p. 160.

[10] Foot, "Morality as a System of Hypothetical Imperatives," p. 161.

[11] Foot's article was originally published in 1972, *before* Williams' "Internal and External Reasons" (which was first published in 1980). As noted earlier, Foot later revised or withdrew some of her internalist views.

[12] Foot, "Morality as a System of Hypothetical Imperatives," p. 161.

his own purposes, doing what is calculated to be disadvantageous or to frustrate his ends. Immorality," she concludes, "does not *necessarily* involve any such thing."[13]

I have argued, in the preceding chapter, that violating the moral imperative expressed by the formula of humanity does involve us in inconsistencies—in procedural irrationalities—in a way that simply violating rules of etiquette would not. The moral imperative is categorical in the stronger sense, while rules of etiquette are not, because the end on which it is built—the end it asks us to respect—is one that all rational beings must hold to the extent that they are procedurally rational. This is not true of the end of propriety, on which rules of etiquette are built—this end is certainly optional from the perspective of rationality.

6.3 A Third Response: Categorical Imperatives and Practice Rules

The important similarities and differences between moral rules and rules of etiquette can also be brought out another way, by appealing to a distinction of John Rawls', between two types of rules. Rawls distinguishes between what he calls the "summary conception" and the "practice conception" of rules.[14] *Summary rules*, also called "rules of thumb," are guidelines for acting that we form on the basis of an assessment of what was generally the best way of acting in similar circumstances in the past (hence the name). They allow us to decide how to act without reassessing the relevant reasons anew each time we find ourselves in such circumstances. They are rules of convenience—allowing us to reach decisions more quickly and easily, and perhaps also more appropriately, reaping the benefit of past experience. Summary rules are instrumental to achieving certain ends. An act-utilitarian might, for example, advocate making use of the rule "Don't lie" because lying

---

[13] Foot, "Morality as a System of Hypothetical Imperatives," p. 162.
[14] Rawls, "Two Concepts of Rules." See especially pp. 18ff.

usually results in unhappiness, and following a rule against lying makes us better at avoiding unhappiness than evaluating the potential effects of each possible lie on a case-by-case basis. When the particular end at which the rule aims is *known* not to be served by following the rule in a particular case (when, for example, it is known that telling a lie in particular circumstances will increase happiness) then the rule loses its binding force.

Hypothetical imperatives of the sort Foot considers above, such as "Take the 7.15 train," (and hypothetical uses of "ought," such as "You ought to take the 7.15 train,") while they do not exactly express *rules* for action, share some features of summary rules. Like such rules, they are justified on *instrumental* grounds—taking the train is supposed to be required because it is deemed instrumental to the achievement of some other end, such as arriving at home in time for dinner. Like summary rules, they lose their binding force when it becomes evident either that they don't promote the end in question (perhaps the 7.15 train arrives too late for dinner) or that the end in question is not in fact valued (perhaps the addressee has made other dinner plans).[15]

Practice rules have a more complex structure. Such rules serve to *define* practices—they establish offices, and specify actions allowed under the practice, and offenses against it. Practice rules have a different sort of authority from that of summary rules. They do not depend on their own instrumental value on some occasion of action for their binding force. We might ask whether the *practice* that each subsidiary practice rule contributes toward defining is justified, and the justification we offer or seek may, for some practices at least, be instrumental in nature. The practice of baseball, for example, might be thought to aim at the ends of providing entertainment, and developing, showcasing, and rewarding skills of certain kinds. These ends might be described as ends *external* to the practice. Some practice rules may

---

[15] The analogy is only partial, not perfect. Summary rules can also act as stand-ins for Kantian categorical imperatives, without standing in instrumental relations to some end-to-be-effected. "Always do what your wise Auntie Maud advises you to do," is one example. "Don't lie" may be another. We sometimes have good reasons to make use of such rules. But fundamental moral rules will never be summary rules. Thanks to Adrian Moore for this point.

even be preferable to others on external grounds. That is, there may be argument among fans of a sport about whether the external ends of the sport would be better served by some possible rules (perhaps a rule allowing for the use of a "designated hitter," or a rule allowing batters a fourth strike) than by others. But such a disagreement is accurately described as a disagreement about what the rule *should be*, and not about what the rule is, and a rule does not cease to apply to a practice participant on some occasion just because it fails, on that occasion, to best promote the ends external to the practice. As Rawls says:

> In a game of baseball if a batter were to ask 'Can I have four strikes?' it would be assumed that he was asking what the rule was; and if, when told what the rule was, he were to say the he meant that on this occasion he thought it would be best on the whole for him to have four strikes rather than three, this would be most kindly taken as a joke.[16]

Categorical uses of words like "ought" and "should" are often appropriate in discussions of practice rules, as Foot's observations help to bring out. The rules of etiquette define a practice in Rawls' sense. As she notes, we are not tempted to withdraw claims such as "You ought to keep your elbows off the table when you eat" when we find out that the person we are addressing would rather keep his elbows on the table, any more than we would be tempted to revise the rules of baseball for a batter who wants a fourth strike. But it is equally clear that the "ought" we employ in this case—the "ought" of etiquette—is not the same as the all-things-considered "ought" of moral judgment—the "ought" I have equated with "has conclusive reason to." We might, in such cases, perfectly consistently, though admittedly somewhat confusingly, maintain that we ought not to do as we ought.

When do categorical uses of "ought" expressing practice rules signify the presence of genuine reasons? Answering this question might help to distinguish such mere categorical *uses* of "ought" of from true categorical imperatives—*oughts* that are categorical in the strong sense of giving everyone (barring the hypothetical nihilist) reasons for

---

[16] Rawls, "Two Concepts of Rules," p. 26.

acting. I have said that the usual way to justify a practice is to appeal to ends external to that practice that are valuable, and to indicate how the practice is instrumental to achieving those ends.[17] In the case of baseball, those external ends are, let's say, providing entertainment and developing certain skills. In the case of etiquette the external end justifying the practice might (to take a generous view of the matter) be the avoidance of giving offense, the easing of social interaction, or perhaps (to take a less generous view) the establishment of a readily recognizable social stratification. Practice rules are designed to advance such ends.

Practice rules serve another purpose as well—they define ends *internal* to the practice—ends the pursuit of which *requires* adherence to the rules. These ends can only be achieved by means of obedience to the rules of the practice, and they contribute to the instrumental value of practices—practices would not serve to promote the ends external to them nearly so well if the internal ends were not established. One cannot win a game of baseball by taking advantage of the allowance of a fourth "strike." One cannot avoid defeat in a game of chess by moving one's king two spaces instead of one. Nor can one achieve propriety while eating with one's elbows on the table. Winning is an end internal to the practice of most games, and propriety is the end internal to the practice of etiquette. In each case, the presence of the internal end contributes to the instrumental value of the practice: baseball and chess would be much less fun, and would build fewer skills, if it was not possible to win at them in a fair contest; and it could at least be argued that if everyone simply tried to avoid giving offense, and tried to put others socially at ease, they would be less successful at doing so than if they aimed instead at propriety.

When we take the internal perspective to a practice, we come to value the ends internal to it, and so come to have reasons to comply

---

[17] Here, as is generally the case throughout this book, I intend "instrumental" to be broadly understood—practices may serve ends by being somehow expressive or constitutive of them, as the practice of playing a game may be constitutive of the end of expressing enthusiasm for life.

with its rules—there is no other way for us to obtain the internal end. But in most cases, we *need* not take the internal perspective to a practice. Some practices purport to be justified by external ends we don't think are valuable—this may be true of etiquette, on the less sympathetic picture presented above. In such cases, we will have no reason at all to obey its rules, despite their categorical form.

Some practices promote external ends that are valuable, but these ends can be achieved by means of participation in any one of several practices, as is the case with most games and sports. Taking up baseball or taking up basketball may be equally good means of having fun. Alternatively, some practices aim at ends which are valuable, but which give us only sufficient and not most reason to pursue them. The development of the logical reasoning skills that can be achieved by means of taking up chess is a valuable goal, but the development of musical skills that would result from taking violin lessons may be just as valuable, and it would not be irrational for me to spend my limited time and energy in pursuit of this goal instead. In both of these cases, while we have sufficient reason to adopt the internal perspective to such practices, we are not rationally required to do so. We can choose, rationally, not to participate in them. Thus their rules *need* not provide us with reasons, again, despite their categorical form.

I may have sufficient reason to violate the rules of a practice even if I (generally) take the internal perspective towards that practice— even if, that is, I'm a participant in the practice in question. This will be the case, at least sometimes, when the goals external to the practice are better served by my violating its rules (and ceasing, temporarily, to participate in it) than by my adhering to them, or when new, more important goals interfere.[18] Rawls is right that we would not usually withdraw our claim that a player ought to be ruled out after taking a third strike when we discover that a relevant desire is lacking. The

---

[18] Thanks again to Adrian Moore for drawing my attention to this last possibility, and for illustrating it with a real-life example from football: when West Ham played Everton in December of 2001, Paulo di Canio intentionally caught the ball in the middle of play, in obvious violation of the rules, when an opposing player went down with what looked to be a very serious head injury.

rules of baseball don't make exceptions for or cease to apply to such cases. But we might decide that, *all things considered*, we ought not to declare the player "out" in special circumstances (though we *ought, as far as the rules go*, to rule him out)—when, for instance, the player is a five-year-old kid in a backyard game who hasn't hit the ball all day. In such a case, we have most reason not to do as the rules demand, once again, in spite of their categorical form.[19]

It seems that many practice rules—rules connected with what Foot would call categorical uses of "ought"—do not constitute categorical imperatives: we may not have most reason to comply with them. What's different about the moral categorical imperative? I have argued that it is a rule of reason. It is one of many rules that define the practice of procedural rationality. These rules are rules of practice, not rules of thumb: they serve to define types of actions—willing, acting for reasons—that are not available to people who do not adhere to them, at least to an extent. Like the other examples of practice rules I have discussed, they take the categorical form. But the moral imperative, as a law of reason, also differs in important respects from the other examples of practice rules. Firstly, moral rules, and other rules of reason, are not binding on us in virtue of being instrumentally valuable. Our participation in the practice of morality, and more broadly, that of rationality, is not justified on instrumental grounds. One sometimes finds

---

[19] Rawls sometimes seems to argue that though "one can be as radical as one likes" about practices, "in the case of actions specified by practices the objects of one's radicalism must be the social practices and people's acceptance of them" and not the particular actions themselves. (See Rawls, "Two Concepts of Rules, p. 32.) This suggests that when a practice is justified, all actions required by its rules are also justified. The above example is intended to show that this may not always be the case. Here the practice of baseball is surely justified, but one ought, in this instance, to break its rules.

Rawls might respond that the justified action provided by the example is not one of "allowing a fourth strike," as there is no such action ("strikes" exist only within the practice of baseball, and its rules allow only three of them). The justified action of the example might be described instead as "an additional throwing of the ball after three strikes have been pitched, for the purpose of persuading the player he has not yet struck out." This answer strikes me as unsatisfactory: the principle suggested above—that all actions required by the rules of justified practices are themselves justified—still fails under the redescription of the example: we still have an example of a case where an action required by the rules of a justified practice—calling the player out—is not justified, all things considered.

morality or a particular moral principle defended on instrumental grounds, for example, by appeal to self-interest, or even evolutionary theory. Even if having certain moral dispositions were in the agent's best interests, or were fitness-promoting, nothing *normative* would follow from this alone. It cannot be the case that fundamental moral laws derive their normative force from their tendency to promote such goals. The value of such goals must itself first be established by means of moral argument. (Recall also Kant's argument, discussed in §4.1 above, against the possibility of grounding the bindingness of moral requirements in some external end or ulterior motive.)

It might be objected here that our reasons to be rational must sometimes be based on the value of ends to which rational behavior is a means. This is clear from the fact that we can sometimes have powerful instrumental, prudential, or even moral reasons to be at least locally *irrational*, as Derek Parfit has shown. He imagines cases in which what we have most reason to do is to cause ourselves to be for brief periods deeply irrational (perhaps by taking a pill).[20] However, in these cases we are still being rational, broadly speaking, even if we are temporarily and in some respects irrational—we are, after all, doing what we have most reason to do. If, in such a case, we decided against being locally irrational—if, that is, we behaved in a way that was locally rational, we would be guilty of broad irrationality—of failing to do what we had most reason to do. Let's imagine a case where my only reason to be rational is clearly instrumental in nature—I'm taking a mathematics prize examination, and my only reason to do well in it is to obtain the prize. Even here, it is, I think, a mistake to conclude that the laws of rationality, which guide me as I tackle the questions on the exam, get a grip on me only because I value the prize. After all, the *instrumental* reason I have to do well on the exam—the reason provided by the prize—*itself* gets a grip on me only because I take the internal perspective to the practice of rationality. It is not because of my desire for the prize that I occupy that perspective.

---

[20] Parfit, *Reasons and Persons*, pp. 12–13.

This brings us to a second, closely-related way in which the moral categorical imperative differs from the practice rules that I discussed earlier, in which we find categorical *uses* of "ought," but, it seems, no genuine categorical imperatives. The practice of rationality, of which the moral imperative is one rule, cannot be questioned from the outside. When we ask "is the practice of rationality justified?," as we did of those other practices, we appeal to the very standards whose reason-giving force we are trying to question. Justification is a matter of providing sufficient reason—it is itself part of the practice of rationality. This does not mean that we can never question proposed principles of rationality—some philosophers spend a good deal of their time doing just that. But such questions must necessarily be asked from within the practice of rationality, and must appeal to principles of rationality that we do not doubt. As Thomas Nagel has put it in *The Last Word*, his defense of the objectivity of reason, the "validity [of reason] is unconditional because it is necessarily employed in every purported challenge to itself."[21]

Nagel goes on to address an obvious worry this line of argument raises. He grants:

> This response to subjectivism may appear to be simply question-begging. After all, if someone responded to every challenge to tea-leaf reading as a method of deciding factual or practical questions by appealing to further consultation of tea leaves, it would be thought absurd. Why is reasoning about challenges to reason different?
>
> The answer is that the appeal to reason is implicitly authorized by the challenge itself, so this is really a way of showing that the challenge is unintelligible. The charge of begging the question implies that there is an alternative—namely, to examine the reasons for and against the claim while suspending judgment about it. For the case of reasoning itself, however, no such alternative is available, since any considerations against the objective validity of a type of reasoning are inevitably attempts to offer reasons against it, and these must be rationally assessed....In contrast, a challenge to the authority of tea leaves does not itself lead us back to tea leaves.[22]

[21] Nagel, *The Last Word*, p. 7.
[22] Nagel, *The Last Word*, p. 24.

Nagel argues that it is not possible for us to look at reasoning as simply something we do—something without normative force. If we are fully committed to the validity of, say, the principle of *modus ponens*, then we cannot at the same time think of this commitment as simply a psychological fact about us, a fact that has nothing to do with the normative force of the principle. "This," Nagel writes, "is merely an instance of the impossibility of thinking 'It is true that I believe that p; but that is just a psychological fact about me; about the truth of p itself, I remain uncommitted.' "[23]

The strangeness of the question "Is the practice of rationality justified?" is clear if we take rationality to consist in responsiveness to reasons. If being rational is a matter of doing what one has sufficient reason to do, and if a practice is justified if we have sufficient reason to participate in it, the question appears to read, "Do we have sufficient reason to do what we have sufficient reason to do?" The question seems tautological. John Broome has recently questioned whether the above interpretations are the right ones to make.[24] He argues that being rational is a matter of complying, in our reasoning processes, with certain requirements (of which the law of non-contradiction and the principle of *modus ponens* are prominent examples). Doing what we have sufficient reason to do, he maintains, is an entirely different matter. Conflating the two is simply a matter of mixing up *reason*, the mass noun (we might call this "*Reason* with a capital 'R' "), with *reason*, the count noun. The requirements of rationality describe Reason, and need not tell us anything about what reasons (small "r") we have.

Broome's doubts are worth raising. But I have tried, in the last four chapters of this book, to argue that the assumption of a close relation between what reasons we have and what rationality requires of us is well founded, and furthermore, that the fact of this close relation does not significantly limit the scope of normativity of practical reason.

---

[23] Nagel, *The Last Word*, p. 32
[24] Broome, "Does Rationality Give Us Reasons?," especially §5.

I have argued that what we have reason (small "r") to do depends on the (purely procedural) requirements of Reason (capital "R"), as they apply to our existing ends and commitments. I have also argued that this account of when we have a reason is compatible with the existence of universal moral reasons—of a moral imperative that is categorical in the strong sense.

7

What Do We Have Moral Reason To Do?

7.1 Persons and Things

If the internalist argument for categorical moral reasons I've developed in the preceding chapters succeeds, *what is it we have reason to do*? I've argued that we all have internal reasons to comply with a version of Kant's categorical imperative. Kant's formula of humanity tells us:

> so act that you use humanity, whether in your own person or in the person of any other, always at the same time as an end, never merely as means.[1]

But taken on its own, this instruction is somewhat cryptic. What exactly do Kant's formula and the Kantian internalist argument I've developed entail about which actions are morally permissible or required?

What I will have to say about this important question will be provisional and exploratory in nature. For this reason, it may, I am afraid, disappoint. But the exploratoriness is, I think, inevitable. As Allen Wood has argued, Kant's formula is not designed to provide, on its own, clear answers to specific questions about what to do. Despite Kant's efforts to explain his various formulations of the moral law by applying them to particular examples in the *Groundwork*, Kant's categorical imperative doesn't provide a straightforward, "plug and chug"

---

[1] Kant, *Groundwork*, p. 38 (4:429).

test for the permissibility of maxims. This, Wood says, simply reflects Kant's conception of the system of moral philosophy, which consists both of a fundamental, *a priori* principle and of a body of empirical information about humans and the circumstances in which they act (which Kant called "practical anthropology"). We can get a specific set of moral rules or duties or verdicts out of the former only by carefully and nondeductively *interpreting* it in the light of the latter.[2]

So, Wood argues, we should not mistake Kant's proposed fundamental principle for the kind of "scientific" principle from which we could simply *deduce* a conclusion about what to do in any given circumstance (of the sort that Sidgwick and some modern-day utilitarians, and perhaps some Kantians, too, are arguably after). Instead, Wood says,

> The first principle is . . . fundamentally an articulation of a basic value. The rules and duties represent an interpretation of the normative principles applying that basic value under the conditions of human life. In their application, moreover, the rules or duties themselves require interpretation, and admit of exceptions, by reference to the first principle.[3]

This seems to me exactly right: the best way to characterize the formula of humanity—certainly in the role it plays in my defense of it—is as "an articulation of a basic value." And what I hope to do now is to take some initial interpretive steps towards exploring what recognition of that basic value requires of us given the circumstances of our lives.[4]

Kant's argument, as I have developed it, tells us that all people are ends in themselves, intrinsically valuable, the source of the value of all the other things we pursue, and the ends for the sake of which we ultimately act. They have their special value in virtue of being the kinds

---

[2] Wood, "Humanity As End In Itself," p. 61.

[3] Wood, "Humanity As End In Itself," pp. 59–60.

[4] In doing so, I will draw significantly from the work of others, including Christine Korsgaard ("Creating the Kingdom of Ends: Reciprocity and responsibility in personal relations," in *Creating the Kingdom of Ends*), Rae Langton ("Duty and Desolation"), Peter Strawson ("Freedom and Resentment"), Onora O'Neill ("Between Consenting Adults"), Thomas Hill (*Dignity and Practical Reason in Kant's Moral Theory*), and Derek Parfit (*On What Matters*).

of beings *to whom things matter*—who have ends of their own that matter to them—as opposed to merely mattering *to* us, having value *for* us. This distinguishes persons from things, and establishes persons as "ends in themselves." Kant's principle as I read it is, at heart, an *anti-objectification* principle. Kant tells us that we must, in all our actions, respect the status of persons as ends in themselves, by never using them merely as a means, as we might a mere thing, but always, at the same time as an end—as something whose special value as a person we recognize and respect.

It seems clear enough what is involved in using someone as a means—we do this whenever we make use of their body or attributes or capacities to help serve our own ends. There are, surely, plenty of harmless ways of doing this. When I hug you on a cold night, I may be using you to keep me warm. When I ask you how to spell a word, I am using you as a means to avoid an embarrassing error. When I ask you for an introduction to your friend, I am using you as a means to get to know someone new. When I pay you to drive me to the station in your taxi, I am using you as a means of getting there. Indeed, I use others as means in all of the myriad ways in which I rely, every day, on their help. When I act in these ways, I may, in one respect, be treating others as I would a thing—using you as a dictionary, or a hot water bottle. But my attitude to you, more generally, is quite different from my attitude towards things, and this would be reflected in this and other interactions I have with you. Kant's formula, accordingly, does not forbid treating someone as a means, but rather treating someone *merely* as a means, and not at the same time as an *end*.

It is important to notice that the requirement that we treat others as ends goes well beyond the prohibition on treating them as mere means. After all, I can, it seems, avoid using people as mere means by simply ignoring them altogether. But if I do that, I am not treating these people as ends, and so am not complying with the formula of humanity. As this brings out, Kant's formula is in fact quite demanding. It tells us that we shouldn't *just use* people, and so issues a negative prohibition on certain forms of exploitation and objectification, which I'll consider more carefully below. But the formula calls for considerably more than this: it adds, to its prohibition on treating others as mere means, a positive exhortation to also treat them *as ends*.

What is it to treat another person as an end? This question has, I think, many answers. First and perhaps most straightforwardly, treating someone as an end, rather than a means, may be a matter of valuing that person non-instrumentally. If I keep you as a friend *only* because you're useful to me as a source of introductions to a social circle to which I would not otherwise have access, I am *merely using* you in a way that is condemned by the formula of humanity.[5] The phrase "trophy wife," used to describe a young, attractive woman who is valued merely as a status symbol by her older husband, picks out another example of this sort of objectionable objectification of persons. I should, instead want you for my friend (or wife) and value you in your own right, not (or not primarily) as a means to some further good, like your social connections or my social status. If I value you in your own right, non-instrumentally, I am not treating you merely as a means.

But this can't be all that's involved in recognizing the special value you have as a person, since we often value *things* as ends in this way, not just people. I may value a painting non-instrumentally—in its own right, and not, say, as an investment, or status symbol, or because of some other further good it can bring me. So it is possible for me to treat a person as my end in this way while still, in an important sense, *objectifying* her—that is, without respecting the special status she has, as an end *in herself*, that objects, like paintings, lack. It is easy enough to objectify people in this sense in the context of personal relationships. We do this when we focus exclusively on what someone means *to us*,

---

[5] Does this formulation condemn too much? My interest in my cab driver, for example, does not seem to stretch much beyond my interest in getting to the station. Do I then use her merely as a means? I would hope not. If I did, then I would, for example, not pay my fare, if I could get away with it. But I do pay my fare, and not just as a matter of convenience. If, in fact, I pay it only because it's the easiest option, then I may well be treating her as a mere means, and my behavior may well be objectionable under the formula of humanity.

rather than on *their* interests (except to the extent that their interests affect their value to us). This, too, is a familiar enough failing in personal relationships.[6]

Christine Korsgaard points out that it is *this* sort of objectification, rather than *merely using* people, that Kant sees as the chief danger posed by sexual relationships. She writes:

> what bothers him is not the idea that one is using another person as a means to one's own pleasure. That would be an incorrect view of sexual relations, and in any case any difficulty about it, would, by Kant's own theory, be alleviated by the other's simple act of free consent. What bothers Kant is rather that sexual desire takes a *person* for its object. He says: "They themselves, and not their work and services, are its Objects of enjoyment."[7]

The quote is from Kant's *Lectures on Ethics*, and she includes a longer passage, too, that makes the point quite clear:

> Man can, of course, use another human being as an instrument for his service; he can use his hands, his feet, and even all his powers; he can use him for his own purposes with the other's consent. But there is no way in which a human being can be made an Object of indulgence for another except through sexual impulse... it is an appetite for another human being.[8]

The potential problem with sexual love is that it sees its object not as a mere means, but as an end to be possessed, rather than as an end in itself. Recall Kant's distinction between "objective" and "subjective" ends, which John Taurek picked up on and which played such a crucial role in the arguments of Chapters 4 and 5:

---

[6] This book's cover image, David Hockney's painting "American Collectors (Fred and Marcia Weisman), explores this slide between the way we value people and the way we value objects—even those objects we value non-instrumentally. Look once at the painting, and you see two art collectors, standing amongst objects from their valuable collection. Look again, and the collectors themselves can seem to belong to the collection, echoing the form of other statues, colorful and static and carefully, precisely placed. Perhaps the husband is surveying his collection, his wife now its prized member. Or perhaps it is she who standing amidst her possessions, husband included, looking out at the viewer.

[7] Korsgaard, *Creating the Kingdom of Ends*, p. 194. The quote from Kant in this passage is from his *Lectures on Ethics*, p. 162.

[8] Kant, *Lectures on Ethics*, p. 163, quoted by Korsgaard, *Creating the Kingdom of Ends*, p. 194.

> [Persons]…are not merely subjective ends [like things], the existence of which as an effect of our action has a worth *for us*, but rather *objective ends*, that is, beings the existence of which is in itself an end, and indeed one such that no other end, to which they would serve *merely* as means, can be put in its place…[9]

He draws the same distinction between kinds of value again in somewhat different terms, in a later passage from the *Groundwork*, this time distinguishing between two different kinds of "subjective" ends:

> What is related to general human inclinations and needs has a *market price*; that which, even without presupposing a need, conforms with a certain taste, that is with a delight in the mere purposeless play of our mental powers, has a *fancy price*; but that which constitutes the condition under which alone something can be an end in itself has not merely relative worth, that is, a price, but an inner worth, that is, *dignity*.[10]

As Korsgaard explains, regarding someone as a sexual object is less like regarding him or her as a *tool*, valuable to us because it serves our needs—as having what Kant called a "market price"—and more like regarding him or her as an *aesthetic object*, something whose value to us does not depend on its serving some purpose—as having what Kant called "fancy price." This is more problematic than being seen as a tool, because it's not clear how someone could consent to being regarded as an end to be achieved or possessed without giving up her respect for her own status as an end in herself. As Korsgaard puts it in a footnote: "Being useful is no threat to your dignity, but being delectable is."[11]

So treating someone as an *end in herself*, as having *dignity*, rather than *price*, in the manner required by the formula, goes beyond not merely using her as a *means*, and also beyond treating her as an end in the sense of valuing her non-instrumentally. What more does it involve? Remember that on Kant's broader conception of ends, as those things for the sake of which we act, I may pursue something as an end, non-instrumentally, but still *for the sake of* some more fundamental

---

[9] Kant, *Groundwork*, p. 37 (4:428) (emphasis in the original).
[10] Kant, *Groundwork*, p. 42 (4:434–435) (emphasis in the original).
[11] Korsgaard, *Creating the Kingdom of Ends*, p. 214 (note 11).

end. When I pursue a painting that I value as an end, I do so for *my* sake—*I* am, in Kant's sense, the ultimate end for the sake of which I act. In this second, non-instrumental, kind of objectifying relationship I've been discussing, we pursue people in the same way: for *our own sakes*, ultimately, and not *theirs*. This, then, is one way in which we can treat others as ends in themselves: we can act *for their sakes*, rather than (just) for ours. We can recognize them not only as beings that *matter to us*, and have value because of that, but also, at the same time, as beings *to whom things matter*, who therefore confer value on their own ends.

An element of that, as Kant emphasizes, is acknowledging the value of others' ends by making them our own. Kant's formula is, in this way, notably demanding. Kant writes:

> Now, humanity might indeed subsist if no one contributed to the happiness of others but yet did not intentionally withdraw anything from it; but there is still only a negative and not a positive agreement with *humanity as an end in itself* unless everyone also tries, as far as he can, to further the ends of others. For, the ends of a subject who is an end in itself must as far as possible be also *my* ends, if that representation is to have its *full* effect in me.[12]

This is one way in which I can act out of recognition of other's value-conferring status.

There are of course incredibly difficult and important questions to be asked and answered here about the extent of our obligations to help others achieve their ends. These are precisely the sorts of questions to which Kant's categorical imperative, on its own, provides no clear answer. I will not try to tackle them here. But as Kant argues, and Onora O'Neill has emphasized, there is another tricky line to be walked here, a thin line between (to use Kant's labels) too much *love* for others and too much *respect*. In *The Doctrine of Virtue*, Kant writes:

> The principle of *mutual love* admonishes [rational beings] to constantly *come closer* to each other; that of the *respect* they owe one another, to keep themselves at a *distance* from one another.[13]

---

[12] Kant, *Groundwork*, p. 39 (4:430).
[13] Kant, *The Metaphysics of Morals*, pp. 568–569.

Both love and respect are ways of recognizing the status of others as ends in themselves; but each on its own also threatens to lead us into violations of the formula of humanity. Love, says O'Neill, "requires us to make the other's ends, whose achievement would constitute his or her happiness, in part [our] own." Respect, on the other hand, requires that we "recognize that others' maxims and projects are *their* maxims and projects. [We] must avoid merely taking over or achieving the aims of these maxims and projects, and allow others the 'space' in which to pursue them for themselves."[14]

So one aspect of treating others as ends *in themselves*—as opposed to merely ends *of ours*—is doing things *for their sake*, while leaving them room to exercise their capacities for free choice. But the anti-objectification principle that underlies Kant's formula—that *persons* have a special value, as *beings to whom things matter*, that mere objects, which may matter *to us*, lack—is more generally suggestive. To think about what it might entail, it helps to think about what is distinctive about persons, and our interactions with them, and what it might mean to treat a person as we'd treat a mere thing.

When Kant draws the distinction between persons and things, he emphasizes one difference in particular: a person, he says, is a "being the existence of which is in itself an end, and indeed *one such that no other end...can be put in its place*."[15] Persons, unlike things, in other words, are *nonfungible*. This, in fact, is the main point of the related distinction between *price* and *dignity* that he later draws: "[w]hat has a price," he says, "can be replaced by something else as its *equivalent*; what on the other hand is raised above all price and therefore admits of no equivalent has a dignity." Persons, Kant tells us, are essentially irreplaceable; but things are replaceable—another with the same properties would do just as well.

This seems clearly true of things we value purely as *means*—as instruments. It's less clear that this is true of those things we value as *ends*—not in themselves, but for *our* sakes. Rae Langton points out:

---

14   O'Neill, "Between Consenting Adults," p. 265.
15   Kant, *Groundwork*, p. 37 (4:428) (*my emphasis*).

> We often value particular items in such a way that they aren't replaceable by a duplicate: it is this very teacup that I value, this very house, this very painting.[16]

This is true. But usually, when it is true, it's true because of the relation of the object to a *person*—it's that relation that makes the object irreplaceable. I value *that very painting*, and not a copy, because that one is a genuine Leonardo. I value *this very house*, because it's the one I grew up in. I value *this very teacup*, because we brought it back from that holiday we took together. Objects whose value to us depends on their relation to a person inherit some of the nonfungibility of that person. They become nonfungible because they are, in a sense, nonduplicatable. We may find an identical cup, with all the same properties; the house for sale next door may look just like mine; an unusually skilled forger may paint a faithful copy of the *Mona Lisa*; but the objects themselves will have different relational properties—they will be related to different people. *This* teacup didn't make it back with us from Cornwall. Someone else imported it. *This* house was not the scene of my childhood memories, but of someone else's. And even if our forged painting is produced, it turns out, by Leonardo's identical twin brother, the copy will differ from the original in a crucial respect—its author will be a distinct center of subjectivity, with a distinct, unique, perspective on the world.

Persons have value that is nonfungible not only because each person is unique, but also, perhaps more importantly, because of the value they have as ends in themselves. They not only matter *to us*, in their own special way, but things matter *to them*. In addition to the unique value they may have for others, the fate of each person is of course of special and terrible significance to himself. It is this insight that led John Taurek to conclude that respecting the special value had by persons, as opposed to objects, has dramatic implications for how we may make trade-offs between the competing interests of different people. When fungible goods are threatened, he says, a certain aggregative, maximizing attitude seems like the right one to adopt: these things

---

[16] Langton, "Duty and Desolation," p. 486 (note 9).

have value to us, and our goal is to preserve as much of what is valuable as we can. But to make the same sort of calculation when it's *people's* interests at stake is to fail to respect them as not just having value for us, but being, themselves, valuers.

Taurek writes:

> It seems to me that those who, in situations of the kind in question, would have me count the relative numbers of people involved as something in itself of significance, would have me attach importance to human beings and what happens to them in merely the [aggregative, maximizing] way I would to objects which I valued....
>
> But when I am moved to rescue human beings from harm in situations of the kind described, I cannot bring myself to think of them in just this way. I empathize with them. My concern for what happens to them is grounded chiefly in the realization that each of them is, as I would be in his place, terribly concerned about what happens to him.[17]

Taurek thinks it follows from this difference that the *number* of people whose good is at stake should not be taken into consideration when making decisions that involve trade-offs between the interests of different people. It's far from clear to me that this does follow. Scanlon, for example, draws a very different conclusion from a very similar premise. He writes:

> respecting the value of human life is in [a] way very different from respecting the value of objects and other creatures. Human beings are capable of assessing reasons and justifications, and proper respect for their distinctive value involves treating them only in ways that they could, by proper exercise of this capacity, recognize as justifiable.[18]

Scanlon makes it clear that "the justifiability of a moral principle depends only on various *individuals'* reasons for objecting to that principle and alternatives to it."[19] In discussing trade-offs between the interests of different people, he writes:

> Utilitarianism, and most other forms of consequentialism, have highly implausible implications, which flow directly from the fact that their

---

[17] Taurek, "Should the Numbers Count?," pp. 306–307.
[18] Scanlon, *What We Owe to Each Other*, p. 169.
[19] Scanlon, *What We Owe to Each Other*, p. 229.

mode of justification is, at base, an aggregative one: the *sum* of a certain sort of value is to be maximized.... A contractualist theory, in which all objections to a principle must be raised by individuals, blocks such justifications in an intuitively appealing way. It allows the intuitively compelling complaints of those who are severely burdened to be heard, while, on the other side, the sum of the smaller benefits to others has no justificatory weight, since there is no individual who enjoys these benefits [summed together] and would have to forgo them if the policy were disallowed.[20]

But Scanlon goes on to argue that we *can* justify to each individual a decision to save a greater number of lives rather than a lesser.[21] I won't try to weigh in on whether Taurek or Scanlon has better understood what's involved in respecting the unique value of persons.[22] Allen Wood is right that Kant's formula is unlikely to settle questions like this one its own, without a lot of additional normative-ethical legwork. He is also right that the formula of humanity "provides us with the right value-basis for settling difficult issues, and that on many difficult issues, it is an advantage of [the formula] that different sides can use it to articulate their strongest arguments."[23]

So far, we have seen that the requirement to value persons as ends in themselves involves not *merely* using them as instruments in our plans; it involves not merely treating them as valuable *to us*—to be pursued and protected for *our own sakes*—but also as valuable in themselves, independently of our interest in them, with ends of their own, and the moral status to confer value on those ends. We have seen that recognition of this status requires us to adopt others' ends as our own, but without taking over those ends. Our recognition of other people as ends in themselves, with the capacity to choose their own projects and plans, requires us to give them space to carry out those plans without too much interference from us. And we have seen that respecting the special value had by persons, as opposed to things, requires

---

[20] Scanlon, *What We Owe to Each Other*, p. 230.
[21] See Scanlon, *What We Owe to Each Other*, Chapter 5.
[22] My sympathies are with Scanlon (though not with all the details of his argument).
[23] Wood, "Humanity as End in Itself," p. 65.

recognizing them as *nonfungible*, though the implications of this for how we may treat them are far from clear.

There is still more we can say. In discussing what it is involved in treating persons as ends in themselves (rather than as mere means, or as merely having value *to us*), both Christine Korsgaard[24] and Rae Langton draw on Peter Strawson's classic essay "Freedom and Resentment," in which Strawson perceptively describes two different attitudes we can adopt in our interactions with other human beings. Here's Strawson:

> What I want to contrast is the attitude (or range of attitudes) of involve-ment or participation in a human relationship, on the one hand, and what might be called the objective attitude (or range of attitudes) to another human being, on the other. Even in the same situation, I must add, they are not altogether exclusive of each other; but they are, profoundly, opposed to each other. To adopt the objective attitude to another human being is to see him, perhaps, as an object of social policy; as a subject for what, in a wide range of sense, might be called treatment; as something certainly to be taken account, perhaps pre-cautionary account, of; to be managed or handled or cured or trained; perhaps simply to be avoided, though this gerundive is not peculiar to cases of objectivity of attitude. The objective attitude may be emotion-ally toned in many ways, but not in all ways: it may include repulsion or fear, it may include pity or even love, though not all kinds of love. But it cannot include the range of reactive feelings and attitudes which belong to involvement or participation with others in inter-personal human relationships; it cannot include resentment, gratitude, forgive-ness, anger, or the sort of love which two adults can sometimes be said to feel reciprocally, for each other. If your attitude towards someone is wholly objective, then though you may light him, you cannot quarrel with him, and though you may talk to him, even negotiate with him, you cannot reason with him. You can at most pretend to quarrel, or to reason, with him.[25]

Strawson's "objective" attitude has much in common with our attitudes towards things, or inanimate forces of nature. We may fear the falling rock, or the flooding waters, we may seek to avoid them,

---

[24] Korsgaard, *Creating the Kingdom of Ends*, p. 196; Langton, "Duty and Desolation," p. 486.
[25] Strawson, "Freedom and Resentment," p. 9.

or "manage" them, guarding as best we can against the damage they threaten to do, but we don't, ordinarily, *resent them*, or *blame them*, for that damage. (Sometimes, we do: we kick the door that slams on our finger; we shout at the computer that, crashing, loses our work; we kiss the goalpost the blocks our opponent's shot. But when we do these things, we are making the inverse mistake to the one Kant's formula warns us against: instead of objectifying persons, we are anthropomorphizing objects.)

Sometimes though, as Strawson notes, we take the objective attitude towards another human being: we see his behavior as something to be feared, perhaps, or managed, or just waited out, but not to be blamed or resented. In some cases, this may be the appropriate attitude to take, as when we're dealing with very young children, or with the clinically deranged—with people who lack the ordinary rational capacities of persons. As Williams noted (and I discussed in Chapter 1), *blame* assumes the presence of a *reason* to which its target is capable of responding. The same is true of resentment, and of the other reactive attitudes that are characteristic of the "participant" attitude Strawson describes. When we take the objective attitude towards people who lack normal rational capacities, we do objectify them in a way—we treat them, in one respect, as we would an object; but in this respect—in that we cannot *reason with* them—they *are* like objects. (In many other respects, including those I have discussed, they are still like people, and not like objects. In those respects, Kant's formula tells us we must still treat them as ends in themselves: we may not treat them as mere means, nor as mere ends to be possessed; we must recognize them as ends in themselves, and so as sources of value for *their* ends; and to that extent, we must make their ends our own.[26])

But sometimes we adopt the objective attitude towards people with whom we *could* instead reason—towards people with whom taking the participant attitude is open to us. We do this, for example, when we judge others (or ourselves) to have been overcome by their emotions. It is common to think of the emotions as a kind of *internal weather*—as

---

[26] For more on how we must treat such people, see §7.3, below.

forces of nature that move us against our will. I recall an irate teacher once railing at a student for having failed to follow the argument of a lesson. When the student, bewildered, asked, "Professor, what is it you want me to *do*?" he responded, with some self-awareness, "Just wait until the storm blows over." This teacher was taking the objective attitude towards *himself*, and advising his student to do the same. But it is hard not to see such behavior in a psychologically healthy human being as involving a voluntary ducking of responsibility, a willing abdication of the capacity to respond to reasons—and as such, a kind of objectification of himself, a failure to treat himself as an end.

A more insidious form of this species of objectification, discussed by Langton, to great effect,[27] is the characterization of women as governed by their emotions, rather than by their rational wills, and so as beyond the reach of reasoning. The widespread diagnosis of *female hysteria* in the eighteenth, nineteenth, and early twentieth centuries illustrates this phenomenon. Any number of "symptoms" of "nervousness" or dissatisfaction were attributed to this "malady." In 1908, the *London Times* published an editorial claiming that suffragettes protesting for the right to vote were "suffering from hysteria;" such questioning of the mental health of feminist activists was not unusual. And a notorious article written by the renowned professor of pathology Almwroth

---

[27]   See her description of the case of Maria von Herbert in "Duty and Desolation." Herbert writes to Kant for moral advice, both about the permissibility of deceiving a friend, and about the moral status of suicide (which she contemplates in the desolation that results in part from the damage done to her friendship). Kant at first responds to her with seriousness, but later dismisses her letters as the communications of a woman suffering from female hysteria. Langton writes:

> It is hard to imagine a more dramatic shift from the interactive stance to the objective. In Kant's first letter, Herbert is 'my dear friend', she is the subject for moral instruction, and reprimand. She is responsible for some immoral actions, but she has a 'heart created for the sake of virtue', capable of seeing the good and doing it. Kant is doing his best to communicate, instruct, and console.... He treats her as a human being, as an end, as a person. This is the standpoint of interaction.
>
> But now? Herbert is *die kleine Schwirmerin, the little dreamer, the ecstatical girl, suffering a 'curious mental derangement', lost in the 'wanderings of a sublimated fantasy', who doesn't think.* ... Herbert, now deranged, is no longer guilty. She is merely unfortunate. She is not responsible for what she does. She is the pitiful product of a poor upbringing. She is an item in the natural order, a ship wrecked on a reef. She is a thing. ("Duty and Desolation," p. 500)

Wright attributed feminist demands to the "physiological emergencies" that constantly threatened women.[28] Not only did such treatment objectify women by failing to recognize their status as rational beings, capable of responding to reasons, filling roles of responsibility, and making plans and setting ends of their own. It also, consequently, resulted in another kind of objectification: a failure to treat women as sources of value, and thus a failure to recognize *their ends* as valuable, to recognize those ends' frustration as the more likely source of women's dissatisfaction, to share those ends, and to help further them.

As Strawson emphasizes, adopting the objective perspective towards someone dramatically changes the nature of the interactions that we can have with her. Sometimes, this is exactly the point. As Strawson says, we sometimes adopt the objective perspective towards someone "as a refuge...from the strains of involvement."[29] Resentment, certainly, can be draining, and absolving someone of responsibility is sometimes easier than forgiving. But adopting this attitude comes at a cost, both to its object and to ourselves. Over time, it makes genuine friendship impossible. This is because friendship necessarily involves some sharing of ends.

Langton writes:

> When you hold someone responsible, you are prepared to work with them, view them as someone who has goals of their own that you might come to share, or as someone who might come to share your goals. You are prepared to *do something with them*, in a sense very different from the sense in which you might do something with a tool. When my friend and I make a cake, I'm *doing something with* my friend, and I'm *doing something with* flour, chocolate, cherries, brandy—but there is a difference. My friend, but not the flour, is doing something with me. My friend, and not the flour, is doing what I am doing, sharing the activity. As a human being, she can choose ends of her own, and can choose to make them coincide with mine. The standpoint we take towards human beings is interactive, and it is different from the standpoint we take with things.[30]

---

[28] See Elaine Showalter's "Hysteria, Feminism, and Gender," in *Hysteria Beyond Freud*, p. 320.

[29] Strawson, "Freedom and Resentment," p. 9.

[30] Langton, "Duty and Desolation," p. 487.

We cannot *do things with* people, in the sense that entails their also *doing things with us*, if we adopt the objective perspective towards them. Doing things *together*, in that sense, is another way of showing respect for the special value had by persons—another way of treating them as ends in themselves.

Indeed, it represents a kind of *apotheosis* of treating others as ends in themselves, which is why Korsgaard tells us that "[t]o become friends is to create a neighborhood where the Kingdom of Ends"—Kant's moral ideal—"is real."[31] If you are genuinely my friend, I will value you as an end, not just a means. And I will value you not just for *my* sake, but also for yours. I will see you as an end in yourself, and the things that matter to you will matter to me too, for your sake. I will make your ends my own, and will try to secure them. But I will not *take them over*, leaving you no space to pursue them yourself. Because as your friend, I will want us to do things *together*—that is, after all, what friends do. And if we're to do things together, then I cannot, as we have seen, take Strawson's objective attitude to you—see you a thing buffeted by the forces of nature. For I cannot act *together* with a thing that has no will of its own.

7.2 Consent

I also can't act together with a thing that *has* a will of its own but that does not *share my ends*. So even if I adopt a participant attitude in our relationship—even if I treat you as responsive to reasons and having a will and ends of your own—I will still fall short of the ideal of cooperation if I *coerce* you into acting as I wish or *deceive* you about what it is we are doing. If I coerce or deceive you into helping me pursue my end, then it cannot be one of your ends, too. As Kant writes of one kind of deception:

> he whom I want to use for my own purposes by [a false] promise cannot possibly agree to my way of behaving towards him, and so himself contain the end of this action.[32]

---

[31] Korsgaard, *Creating the Kingdom of Ends*, p. 194; Langton concurs; see "Duty and Desolation," p. 492.
[32] Kant, *Groundwork*, p. 38 (4:430).

Rae Langton says: "To deceive is thus to make a person thing-like: something that cannot choose what it does."[33] What if, she imagines, she enlists her friend's help to bake a cake, but without revealing that her intent is to use that cake to seduce her friend's notoriously sweet-toothed boyfriend? "Now," she says, "I am *doing something with* my friend in the very same sense that I am *doing something with* cherries and chocolate, flour and brandy."[34]

Langton is partly right: when we deceive or coerce people, we *make use* of their capacities to serve our own ends, just as we might make use of a tool with certain handy functions. Langton's imagined friend is a good baker, just as her oven might be. But in another respect, when we deceive or coerce people we are not treating them as we would a thing, or as something that cannot choose what it does. We can't, after all, coerce or deceive a *thing*. And it is precisely because people *can* choose what they do, and have ends of their own, that we can coerce them, and would choose to deceive them.

Coercion, unlike force, uses a person's ends against her; it *persuades* her to act, by upping the stakes, for her, of non-compliance. Far from overriding a person's rational capacities, coercion asks her to employ them—a person generally has *good reason* to do as she is coerced to do, though she would not have such reason, of course, were it not for the coercive threat. Deception is, in this respect, a little different: the person who is deceived may act as she has no (objective) reason to act. But she, like the victim of coercion, acts rationally—she responds correctly to her *subjective* reasons. And again, the deceiver is *making use of* her victim's rational faculties—*convincing* her to act a certain way, by controlling her evidence about how she should act.

As this brings out, there are ways of *using* people that are very different from the ways we can *use* objects. Consider the two senses of the word "manipulation." In one sense of the word, we can manipulate an object: the surgeon manipulates her scalpel when she performs an operation; in the same sense, the physical therapist may manipulate her

---

[33] Langton, "Duty and Desolation," p. 489.
[34] Langton, "Duty and Desolation," p. 490.

patient to loosen a joint. But the kind of manipulation we usually have in mind when we speak of manipulating people—the kind involving coercion, deception, seduction—is not something we can do to things.

Coercion and deception nonetheless undermine Kant's ideal of cooperation, in which respect for the humanity of another is most fully realized. Coercers and deceivers make it impossible for their victims to *act together* with them, by preventing the sharing of important ends. They also, usually, fail to treat their victims as sources of value, by failing to properly take into account how what they do matters to their victims. And they use their victims, and especially, their victims' rational capacities—a central manifestation of their personhood—as a mere means to their ends.

We may be able to avoid these pitfalls if we give others an informed say in how we treat them. This thought, coupled with the examples to which Kant himself appeals to illustrate the formula of humanity, have led many Kantians to interpret the formula as entailing a kind of *consent requirement*.

Kant says, in explanation of his formula:

> rational beings … are always to be valued at the same time as ends, that is, only as beings who must be able to contain in themselves the end of the very same action.[35]

And (again) to account for the wrongness of making false promises:

> he whom I want to use for my own purposes by [a false] promise cannot possibly agree to my way of behaving towards him, and so himself contain the end of this action.[36]

And finally, in the *Critique of Practical Reason*:

> [a] rational being … is not to be subjected to any purpose that is not possible in accordance with a law that could arise from the will of the affected subject himself; hence this subject is to be used never merely as a means but as the same time an end.[37]

---

[35] Kant, *Groundwork*, p. 38 (4:430).
[36] Kant, *Groundwork*, p. 38 (4:430).
[37] Kant, *Critique of Practical Reason*, p. 210 (5:87).

In all three of these passages, Kant can be read as claiming that treating others as ends is in part a matter of treating them only in ways to which they can consent.[38] But formulating a plausible, meaningful consent requirement can be surprisingly tricky. Is a person able to share the ends of my action only if he actually *has* consented to it, or at least *would actually* consent to my performing it if I asked him?

This may be an ideal to aim for, but it cannot be a *requirement* for morally permissible actions. The fact that a very self-interested person would refuse to consent to an act that would greatly benefit someone else at minor cost to himself does not entail that we ought not to perform it. As Derek Parfit points out, even in those cases where the withholding of consent to an action is not something for which we would blame a person, we often feel that we are morally required (or at least morally permitted) to perform the action anyway. Rescue cases, in which the rescuer must choose between saving one person or a group of five people, might take this form. The one may perfectly justifiably withhold consent to our leaving her to die, but we are still morally required, or at the very least morally permitted, to save the five. As this last case brings out, there will also be many occasions for action in which we cannot possibly secure *everyone's* consent, because the only actions to which some parties would be willing to consent will be rejected by others.[39]

---

[38] One difference between Kant's various appeals to consent, which I will not address in what follows, concerns the question of what it is that the persons affected by our actions must be able to consent *to*. The two passages from the *Groundwork* suggest that the targets for moral evaluation under the consent principle are particular actions. The passage from the Second Critique, by contrast, suggests that the target of evaluation might be broader—it might be the "law" in accordance with which we act. The first, narrower, interpretation is reflected in Korsgaard's and Parfit's versions of the principle. The second, broader, interpretation is reflected in the work of contractualists such as Rawls and Scanlon. Rawls argues that the basic structure of society should be organized according to the principles that would be agreed upon by rational, mutually disinterested agents who are ignorant of specific facts concerning their social status or contingent aims and desires. Scanlon's consent principle states that an act is wrong if it would be disallowed by any principle that no one could reasonably reject. (See Rawls, *A Theory of Justice*, and Scanlon, *What We Owe to Each Other*.) Parfit also considers an interpretation of Kant's argument that applies the test of the consent principle to principles for acting rather than to specific actions. He calls this the "Kantian Contractualist Formula." According to this formula, "Everyone ought to follow the principles whose universal acceptance everyone could rationally will." See Parfit, *On What Matters*, Volume One, p. 342.

[39] See Parfit, *On What Matters*, Volume One, p. 180.

Moreover, as Onora O'Neill has argued,[40] actual consent often does little to secure the permissibility of actions. She points out that even in the case of explicit contracts, where the actions consented-to are supposed to be explicitly spelled out, ignorance and duress can lead people to consent to things they would never have agreed to under conditions of full information and free choice. Indeed, the legalese of explicit contracts often makes informed consent particularly hard to obtain in these cases. Sometimes, one suspects, intentionally so: too much information can deceive as assuredly as too little. O'Neill mentions the "widespread European use of 'treaties' to 'legitimize' acquisition of land or sovereignty by seeking the signatures of barely literate native peoples with no understanding of European moral and legal traditions."[41] The baffling complexity of modern-day mortgage and credit card contracts with variable interest rates provides a more recent example.

Even where the best efforts to obtain genuine informed consent are made, serious obstacles to meaningful consent remain. It can be impossible to strike a working balance between too much information and too little: "Patients," O'Neill points out, "cannot easily understand complex medical procedures; yet if they consent only to a simplified account, they may not consent to the treatment proposed."[42] And often, even when parties *are* making a genuinely informed choice, they are choosing from a dramatically limited set of options. (O'Neill gives, as examples, a choice of husbands in a society where there is a firm expectation that women will marry, and a choice of jobs in an economic system where non-employment is not an option for most people.) Sometimes, just how limited our set of options is can be difficult to discern from within the walls the limits build, throwing up yet another obstacle to meaningful, informed consent. Adaptive preferences present a related worry. And some people will, even with clear eyes, repeatedly allow themselves to be taken advantage of.

---

[40] O'Neill, "Between Consenting Adults," pp. 254–256.
[41] O'Neill, "Between Consenting Adults," pp. 254–255 (note 1).
[42] O'Neill, "Between Consenting Adults," p. 256.

Of course, treating people in ways to which they do not consent isn't the only way of violating the dictates of the formula of humanity. Taking advantage of someone may well fail to respect his status as an end in himself in other ways, some of which I discussed in the previous section. But we may nonetheless think that poorly informed consent, or consent among severely limited options, or the consent of a self-denier or "pushover" do *no* work justifying an action—that whatever moral work consent *can* do, it is *not* doing it here. If so, we will want to look beyond the appeal to *actual consent* to understand the role consent and its absence play in determining the permissibility of action.

Some philosophers have pushed a weaker interpretation of Kant's formula: perhaps it requires us merely to make it *possible* for others to consent to our treatment of them. The second passage from the *Groundwork* lends some support to this interpretation. Kant, remember, writes that I violate someone's status as an end in himself when I make a lying promise to him because he "*cannot possibly agree* to my way of behaving toward him, and so himself contain the end of this action." Korsgaard's reading of Kant's principle puts emphasis on the "possibly." Thus she writes:

> Kant's criterion most obviously rules out actions which depend on force, coercion, or deception for their nature, for it is the essence of such actions that they make it impossible for their victims to consent. If I am forced, I have no chance to consent. If I am deceived, I don't know what I am consenting to. If I am coerced, my consent itself is forced by a means I would reject. So if an action depends on force or deception or coercion, it is impossible for me to consent to *it*. To treat someone as an end, by contrast, is to respect his right to use his own reason to determine whether and how he will contribute to what happens.[43]

On Korsgaard's interpretation of Kant's formula, we may not treat people in ways to which their giving consent is *impossible*. This principle has the advantage that it seems to fit Kant's discussion of examples well, particularly in the case of the lying promise. It also has the

---

[43] Korsgaard, *Creating the Kingdom of Ends*, pp. 295–296.

more significant advantage that it reinforces some of the intuitions that made the formula of humanity appealing in the first place. If what is most valuable and inviolable in human nature is a person's capacity to rationally choose ends for himself, then force, deception, and coercion do seem to be particularly grave offenses.[44]

A possible consent requirement seems, however, both too permissive and too restrictive. It is too permissive because it does not condemn any actions that *were* consented to, and thus, *a fortiori*, it was *possible* to consent to, even if their victims should *not* have consented to them. Appeals to possible consent thus seem to inherit all the difficulties of actual consent.

Such a requirement looks too restrictive because it condemns actions to which the affected person could not possibly consent, but to which he or she should have or would have consented had consent *been* possible. Parfit points out that Korsgaard's test, as it stands, would condemn lifesaving surgery on people who are unconscious.[45] The same may be true of acts that protect the interests of people whose whereabouts we don't know.

Korsgaard might respond to this objection that it is not "the essence of such actions that they make it impossible for their victims to consent," as it is in the case of "actions which depend on force, coercion, or deception for their nature." In the first example, it is the patient's unconscious state, rather than the act of performing lifesaving surgery, that makes consent impossible. Similarly, in the second example, it is our ignorance of the whereabouts of the beneficiaries, not our beneficial act itself, which makes consent impossible. Crucially, in both these cases, *we* are not responsible for the impossibility of consent. What we may not do, according to Korsgaard's Kant, is *make* it impossible for others to consent to our actions. Coercion and deception do just that. What's more, this shift in emphasis to what *we* make possible or impossible may help alleviate some of the worries

---

[44] O'Neill also interprets Kant's formula in terms of a Possible Consent Principle (see "Between Consenting Adults," pp. 105–125).

[45] Parfit, *On What Matters*, Volume One, p. 178.

the possible consent requirement seemed to inherit from the actual consent requirement. *We* may not withhold crucial information from people with whom we interact; *we* may not dramatically limit their options, and thereby coerce them into giving consent; *we* may not bully them into self-denial. We must do *our* best to give them genuine power of choice over their situation. But if their information is lacking, their options are limited, and they are self-denying independently of us, we cannot be faulted for that.

It's not clear, however, that this response can do the work that Korsgaard needs it to do. It seems we are sometimes morally required to deceive a person, even though our act of deception is what makes their consent impossible. Parfit offers an example that helps bring out this intuition:

[C]onsider

> *Fatal Belief:* I know that, unless I tell you some lie, you will believe truly that *Brown* committed some murder. Since you could not conceal that belief from Brown, he would then murder you as well.
>
> If I say nothing, you could reasonably complain with your dying breath that I ought to have saved your life by deceiving you. I could not defensibly reply that, since I could not have deceived you with your consent, this way of saving your life would have been wrong. My life-saving lie *would* be like life-saving surgery on some unconscious person. Just as this person would consent to this surgery if she could, you would consent to my deceiving you. It is a merely technical problem that, if I asked you for your consent, that would make my deceiving you impossible.... Since you would consent to my deceiving you if you could, my lie would be morally as innocent as some lie that was needed to give someone a surprise party.[46]

---

[46] Parfit, *On What Matters*, Volume One, pp. 178–179. Korsgaard suggests that Kant's formula, and her interpretation of it via the consent principle, run into the greatest difficulties when dealing with evil (see Korsgaard, *Creating the Kingdom of Ends*, p. 100; also, Ch. 5: "The Right to Lie"). But Parfit's *Fatal Belief* example could be restructured so that it doesn't rely on the presence of evil. We can imagine, instead, the following case of *Vertigo*: You must cross a deep ravine by means of a narrow bridge, but suffer from severe fear of heights. Half way across the bridge and afraid to look down, you ask me how deep the ravine is. I know that if I answer you truthfully, you will be paralyzed with fear and dizziness, and may well lose your balance. If I tell you instead that the ravine is quite shallow, and you safely cross to the other side, have I done a moral wrong?

Korsgaard's consent requirement might be reformulated to avoid some of these worries. In some cases, she could argue, a general, tacit, *advance* consent to harmlessly deceptive actions of a certain type may be inferred. In this way, for example, celebrating a surprise party may after all be something that we do together—an end that we can share. Whether this response generalizes is unclear—it seems much more far-fetched, for example, to suggest that you had a genuine opportunity to tacitly accede, in advance, to my plan of deception in *Fatal Belief*.

In any case, the fact that you would have good reason to condone my deception in *Fatal Belief after* I acted[47] makes the fact that you could not have consented to it before I acted seem morally irrelevant.[48] Moreover, as with actual consent, securing the possibility of genuine consent or dissent, in what Parfit calls the "act-effecting sense"—where the person's consent or dissent will effectively determine my course of action—may be impossible in cases where different parties' interests conflict. *A* may dissent from my performing the only action to which *B* would give her consent. If that's the case, then I cannot give both *A* and *B* the power to determine how I act. What's more, often I *should* not give others such veto power over what I do: if I can prevent grave harm to *A* at a small cost to *B*, then I should do so, whether or not *B*, selfishly, dissents from my plan of action. And if I can save *A* only by deceiving or coercing *B*, then I should do so.[49]

A reexamination of the objections raised against the first two inter-pretations of Kant's formula as a consent principle points in the direc-tion of a formulation that avoids the problems of both. I objected to an actual consent requirement on the grounds that a person might fail to consent to some act to which she *should* consent. I objected to both an *actual* consent requirement and a *possible* consent requirement that a

---

[47] Parfit points out that if you had the ability to make yourself lose particular memories, you could have and would have consented to my lying to you without making that lie impossible.

[48] Although consent after the fact raises its own problems: in particular, when, as in some cases of adaptive preference or cognitive dissonance, the act itself secures the later consent.

[49] For example, we should (*contra* Kant) surely deceive the murderer at the door, who has come to ask the whereabouts of our friend. Korsgaard agrees, and explains this departure from Kant as a move from ideal to non-ideal theory. See "The Right to Lie," in *Creating the Kingdom of Ends*.

person may in fact consent to an act to which she *should not* consent. And finally, I objected (following Parfit) to a possible consent requirement that a person might have good reason to approve of an act to which she could not possibly consent, and good reason to consent to an act to which she would not *actually* consent, so that I ought not make it possible for her to exercise power over what I do. All these objections suggest that there is a standard for consent, and that what matters for the moral permissibility of an action is whether the person affected by it has sufficient reason to consent to it, not whether she would consent to it, or subjectively could consent to it.

Parfit offers a third interpretation of Kant's formula that takes this conclusion into account. According to his principle, which I will call the *Rational Consent Principle*, "It is wrong to treat anyone in any way to which this person could not rationally consent."[50] The emphasis here is on "rationally." The question is whether our actions are rationally justifiable from the perspective of the people whom they affect. Parfit elaborates: "[w]e ought to act with some aim that other people could *rationally* share, so that they could rationally consent to our way of treating them."[51] (If he is to avoid the objections he raises to the *possible* consent requirement, Parfit must mean here to appeal to what we could rationally choose, if we were in a position to choose, as if from outside our lives, what happens to us.[52]) He argues that, in many cases, we have sufficient reasons to do either what is best from our own point of view, or what would be best from an impartial point of view. We could rationally consent to acts that would be best from an impartial point of view, as well as to acts that, though not impartially best, would be significantly better for us or for those we love.[53]

His test therefore produces the right answer in the case of the person who allows himself to be taken advantage of by consenting where he did not have sufficient reason to consent—consent in this case, though

[50] Parfit, *On What Matters*, Volume One, p. 181.

[51] Parfit, *On What Matters*, Volume One, p. 182.

[52] We might compare this to Michael Smith's appeal to the well-placed advisor who shares our values, which I discuss in §2.2 above. Thanks to a reader for OUP for this point.

[53] Parfit, *On What Matters*, Volume One, p. 186.

possible, and indeed *actual*, was not *rational*. His test also produces the right answer to cases where the affected person either should have consented, but did not consent, or would have consented, but could not consent. If the act under evaluation is best by far from the point of view of the person affected (as is the case in the lifesaving surgery example, and in *Fatal Belief*), then that person could rationally have consented to it, and the act is permissible under the Rational Consent Principle. If the act under evaluation is best from an impartial point of view (as, for example, in rescue cases like the one described above), then again, according to Parfit, any person affected by it could rationally consent to it, even at great cost to himself.

Parfit's Rational Consent Principle provides a more satisfying interpretation of Kant's formula than appeals to actual or possible consent, largely because it does a better job of matching our intuitions about particular cases. Moreover, it seems to capture much of what was appealing about Kant's formula of humanity. It resonates with Scanlon's observation, which I quoted earlier:

> respecting the value of human life is in [a] way very different from respecting the value of objects and other creatures. Human beings are capable of assessing reasons and justifications, and proper respect for their distinctive value involves treating them only in ways that they could, by proper exercise of this capacity, recognize as justifiable.[54]

But it might be objected to Parfit's principle that it is no longer, strictly speaking, really about consent. That is, Parfit's test is a test for the *sufficiency of reasons*, and could in fact be rephrased without making reference to consent at all. We might, for example, restate it as the *Rational Justification Principle*: an act is permissible only if there is sufficient reason for it to be performed from the perspective of the persons whom it affects.

Of the versions of the consent requirement I have discussed, only the first, the actual consent requirement, really allows the concept of consent, as we usually understand it, to do work in establishing the

---

[54] Scanlon, *What We Owe to Each Other*, p. 169.

permissibility of actions. That principle, we have seen, is problematic. But in some cases, the fact of consent does seem to make a difference to the moral permissibility of an action. Thus in most cases, a doctor may operate on a man to remove one of his kidneys for donation only if he *actually* consented to the operation. And a rapist cannot defend his act by claiming that his victim *could* have rationally consented to having sexual intercourse with him. Hypothetical consent is no kind of consent at all.[55]

This does not strike me as a devastating objection to the Rational Consent Principle. For one thing, some acts are *by their nature* consensual, in that nonconsensual versions of them are not plausibly described as the same act-type. Rape is not the same act-type as consensual sex, and a fistfight counts as a boxing match only if consent was given first. Moreover, as Parfit notes, we can sensibly ask if someone could have rationally consented, in advance, to our treating them a certain way *without their consent*, and while the answer will often be "no" (as in the case of rape, and in most cases of organ donation), it may sometimes be "yes." So the Rational Consent Principle will not collapse into an actual consent requirement. We may sometimes have sufficient reason to consent to limiting our future freedom in this way.[56] "Before the discovery of anaesthetics," Parfit points out, "many people freely consented to being later coerced during painful surgery."[57] We might similarly argue that we could rationally consent, in advance, to a policy of saving the greater number of people, even over the objections of the members of the smaller group, so long as we didn't know, in advance, which group we'd be likely to belong to should the need for a rescue arise.

It seems to me plausible to interpret Kant's formula of humanity as implying, in part, a test for the sufficiency of reasons. It would not be the first of Kant's formulations of the categorical imperative that was intended to play just this role. Christine Korsgaard, for one, has

---

[55] This is not to say that tacit or implicit consent—the fact that I *would* have consented had I been asked, and that this is known about me—cannot in some cases do the work of consent in justifying actions.

[56] Parfit, *On What Matters*, Volume One, p. 193.

[57] Parfit, *On What Matters*, Volume One, p. 179.

interpreted Kant's formula of universal law as "a test of the sufficiency of the reasons for action and choice which are embodied in our maxims."[58] That formula, remember, states: "*act only in accordance with that maxim through which you can at the same time will that it become a universal law*."[59] Kant's arguments begin from the premise that we are all equally bound by the requirements of morality. His worry, when arguing for the formula of universal law, is that we may make exceptions for ourselves as moral agents. It is this tendency to make exceptions of ourselves that the test proposed by the formula is supposed to check. But the test seems to have stated its requirement the wrong way around. According to it, we are to ask ourselves before we act, "Could I rationally will that everyone act this way?" But the more natural question to ask, when seeking to determine whether our reasons for acting are sufficient, is "Could everyone (affected by my actions) rationally will that I act this way?" And this, as we have seen, is the requirement established by the formula of humanity, if we take it to entail Parfit's Rational Consent Principle.

As an interpretation of Kant, however, the Rational Consent Principle runs up against a significant concern, which can be brought out by responding to an objection to hypothetical consent principles raised by Onora O'Neill. O'Neill objects to a version of the Rational Consent Principle on the following grounds:

> Many conceptions of rationality presuppose a given set of desires. If these are the actual desires of the consenter, appeal to hypothetical consent will not overcome the worry that a consensus may be iniquitous or reflect local ideology. Yet if there is no appeal to the consenter's actual desires, then the theory may be too weak to determine what would rationally be consented to. Given that there are many rationally structured sets of hypothetical desires, rational structure alone cannot determine what would rationally be consented to.[60]

This concern appears to be a recreation of the worry about internalism that is brought out by Williams' example of the cruel husband. If what we could rationally do is relative to our desires (or, more broadly, our

---

[58] Korsgaard, *Creating the Kingdom of Ends*, p. 79.
[59] Kant, *Groundwork*, p. 31 (4:421).
[60] O'Neill, "Between Consenting Adults," p. 109.

motivational sets), then might it not turn out that what we can rationally consent to reflects iniquities in our character or local ideologies? Just as the Kantian argument can, I think, provide a solution to the worry raised by Williams' example, it can also respond to O'Neill's worry. According to Kantian internalism, the motivational sets of *fully procedurally rational* persons contain only those contingent ends that are compatible with the laws of procedural rationality, of which Kant's moral categorical imperative is one. Thus the possibility that the consent of (hypothetical) fully rational beings reflect iniquities or local ideologies is ruled out by Kant's internalist argument.

But viewed in this light—that is, taken as a piece in Kant's larger moral-rationalist project—the Rational Consent Principle gives rise to a different problem: it seems to be circular over at least a subset of the cases it is supposed to evaluate. Here is one way the principle could be problematically circular: it could tell us that an act is wrong if and only if it treats someone in a way to which she could not rationally consent; and then it could tell us that we could rationally consent to be treated a certain way if and only if the act in question is not wrong. The circularity worry raised by the Kantian principle is similar. The Rational Consent Principle is, on Kant's view, not only a *moral law*, whose content depends on what it is rational to do, but also itself a *law of reason*, which at least in part *determines* what it is rational to do. The formula of humanity, from which the Rational Consent Principle was derived, is, after all, one expression of Kant's categorical imperative of practical reason. Kant's argument has this structure:

(i) *The Formula of Humanity*: It is a law of reason that we must in our actions always take humanity to be an end in itself. We are behaving rationally only to the extent that our actions respect the status of humanity as an end in itself.

(ii) *The Rational Consent Principle*: Treating humanity as an end in itself means treating human beings only in ways to which they could rationally consent.

(iii) The giving of consent is one of our actions which, if we are fully rational, must be governed by the Formula of

Humanity. Our consent is rational only to the extent that it is compatible with respect for humanity as an end in itself.

(iv) Therefore, we can only rationally consent to actions that treat humanity as an end in itself.[61]

But, according to (ii), treating humanity as an end in itself involves treating human beings only in ways to which they could rationally consent. Hence the circularity arises. It arises despite the fact that this way of spelling out the Rational Consent Principle determines which acts one could rationally consent to without appealing an act's "rightness" or moral permissibility as grounds for rational consent. The grounds for rational consent to an act are, according to Kant, the same as the conditions for the moral permissibility of that act. But this is a different claim from the claim that the grounds for rational consent to the act are *that* it is morally permissible.

None of the versions of a consent requirement on action that I've explored offer completely satisfactory rules for action. But we'd do well to remember Allen Wood's admonishment that we should not be searching for such rules in Kant's formula of humanity in the first place. We ought to try, as far as possible, to interact with others through cooperation, rather than manipulation:

- We should try, where possible, to influence them by appealing to their rational faculties, rather than through means that undermine or circumvent those faculties.
- When only one person's interests are at stake, we should aim, when possible, to give that person power over how our acts affect him—to offer him the genuine possibility of meaningful consent or dissent.
- When many people's interests are at stake, we can try to give each person as much power over the proceedings as is compatible with the same power for others.

---

[61] This condition for rational consent (provided by the categorical imperative) includes the limitations on rational consent provided by the instrumental and prudential imperatives. That is, we could not rationally consent to any action that undermines our subjective ends when their promotion would not conflict with the necessary end of humanity.

- We should leave others as much freedom to pursue their chosen ends as is compatible with these and other requirements of the formula of humanity, and where possible, aid them in their pursuit of those ends.

7.3 Infants and Animals

Before closing, I'd like to briefly consider what the Kantian formula I have defended tells us about our treatment of nonrational beings: of infants and young children, of those who are severely mentally incapacitated, and of animals. In *Kant's* argument for his formula of humanity, only *rational* nature is a source of value. And in case we missed the point, he reiterates it when he draws his crucial distinction:

> Those beings whose existence rests not on our will but on nature, if they are *non-rational beings*, have still only a relative worth, as means, and are therefore called *things*, while *rational* beings, on the contrary, are called *persons*, because their nature already distinguishes them as ends in themselves....[62]

But, I have maintained, Kant was wrong to draw the line between *persons* and *things*—between *ends in themselves* and everything else—where he does. Kant's argument, at least as I have revised and redeveloped it, relies on drawing it in a different place: between *beings to whom things matter* and the *things that matter to them*. We are all committed, I've argued, to the nonfungible, noninstrumental, intrinsic, and value-conferring value of beings that value. And that class surely includes not just *rational* beings, but any creatures with a mental life sophisticated enough to count as centers of subjectivity.

I believe that the Kantian internalist argument commits us, on pain of procedural irrationality, to recognizing the moral status of all such creatures as ends in themselves. But it certainly doesn't follow that animals, say, or infants, or the severely cognitively impaired or mentally ill

---

[62] Kant, *Groundwork*, p. 37 (4:428) (my emphasis).

should be treated as "persons" in *all* of the respects I have been exploring. Scanlon's injunction, that we treat human beings only in ways that
they could recognize, through the proper exercise of their rational
capacities, as justifiable, does not apply to animals. Nor, of course,
does any requirement to obtain their consent. And we cannot aim to
do things together with animals, infants, and the insane, as we can with
each other. Nor should we adopt towards them the fully participant
perspective. It is understandable but not reasonable to resent an infant
for waking you up six times a night. Or to resent the dog for destroying
yet another pair of shoes. So friendship is not the moral ideal at which
our relationships with nonrational beings should aim.

But we can recognize such beings as ends in themselves in many
other respects: we may not treat them as mere means, nor as mere
ends to be possessed; we must recognize them as having a value that
is independent of the value they have *for us*, and so as sources of value
for *their ends*; and to that extent, we must make their ends our own.[63]
(There is no danger, however, in this case, of allowing love to inappro-
priately swamp respect.)

Our duties towards animals differ, therefore, in important respects,
from our duties towards people. They differ also from our duties
towards infants, young children, and the mentally ill. This is because,
in the case of children, we must respect not just the ends that they are,
but also the ends they are starting to become. Peter Strawson, after
distinguishing between the objective and participant attitudes we can
adopt towards others, perceptively writes:

> parents and others concerned with the care and upbringing of young
> children cannot have to their charges either kind of attitude in a pure or
> unqualified form. They are dealing with creatures who are potentially
> and increasingly capable both of holding, and being objects of, the full
> range of human and moral attitudes, but are not yet truly capable of
> either. The treatment of such creatures must therefore represent a kind

---

[63] Nonrational beings can't, of course, bestow value on their ends by rationally choosing
them. And their desires are no surer an indicator of what has value for them than ours are (as any
dog owner will know). But they, like us, have *interests*. We can ask of such beings: what do their
actual motivations, coupled with standards of procedural rationality, entail for what we have reason to do for them?

of compromise, constantly shifting in one direction, between objectivity of attitude and developed human attitudes. Rehearsals insensibly modulate towards true performances. The punishment of a child is both like and unlike the punishment of an adult.[64]

And he adds, considering the case of the mentally ill:

> Again, consider—a very different matter—the strain in the attitude of a psychoanalyst to his patient. *His* objectivity of attitude, *his* suspension of ordinary moral reactive attitudes, is profoundly modified by the fact that the aim of the enterprise is to make such suspension unnecessary or less necessary.[65]

I cannot put it better.

7.4 Immorality As Irrationality?

At the outset of this book, I raised a worry: my goal would be to identify universal moral *internal* reasons—to show that everyone has reason to be guided by the same moral principle, regardless of their contingent antecedent ends and motivations, on pain of *procedural irrationality*. But, the worry was, wasn't it unsatisfying to suggest that someone who has failed to act as she has a *moral* reason to act is guilty merely of a *procedural* irrationality? Could we possibly be persuaded by the conclusion of an argument that reduces a moral wrongdoing to an error in reasoning?

Scanlon discusses this objection to what he calls "formal" accounts of the importance of moral reasons (he labels Kant's a formal account). A formal account is one that "appeal[s] to considerations that are as far as possible independent of the appeal of any particular ends."[66] Such accounts, he writes,

> might provide the secure basis that some have sought for the demand that everyone must care about morality, [but do] not give a very satisfactory description of what is wrong with a person who fails to do so.[67]

---

[64] Strawson, "Freedom and Resentment," p. 19.
[65] Strawson, "Freedom and Resentment," pp. 19–20 (emphasis in the original).
[66] Scanlon, *What We Owe to Each Other*, p. 150.
[67] Scanlon, *What We Owe to Each Other*, p. 151.

This fault, the thought is, is not just an irrationality (as is the fault of someone who fails to adhere to the principles of logic); there is something more deeply wrong with the person. Someone who acts very wrongly is doing something more—something worse—than behaving very irrationally.

When I flagged this concern in §1.2, I suggested that the worry should be postponed until the end of the book, after we'd seen what failing to live up to the demands of procedural rationality could look like. I hope the intervening arguments will have convinced the reader that there is nothing dryly mechanical about the exercise of procedural rationality. Not all errors in reasoning are, in that respect, on a par. And there are some kinds of procedural concerns that are intuitively moral. Fairness is one of these. I believe that Kant's moral theory takes rightness to be a kind of fairness. Kantian internalism's central claim is that we behave irrationally when we fail to recognize others like us as our equals, in the sense that their goals and needs matter as much, objectively, as ours do. The exercise of our procedural rationality involves us in the task of examining our own ends in a manner that does not dismiss those of others. If we accept this task, we can indeed become better people through the exercise of *moral* reason.

Bibliography

Arpaly, Nomy. 2003. *Unprincipled Virtue: An Inquiry into Moral Agency.* New York: Oxford University Press.

Brink, David O. 1986. "Externalist Moral Realism," in *The Southern Journal of Philosophy,* Vol. 24, No. S1, pp. 23–41.

Broome, John. 2005. "Does Rationality Give Us Reasons?," in *Philosophical Issues,* Vol. 15, No. 1, pp. 321–337.

Chang, Ruth. 2013. "Grounding Practical Normativity: Going Hybrid," in *Philosophical Studies,* Vol. 164, No. 1, pp. 163–187.

Crisp, Roger. 2013. "Well-Being," *The Stanford Encyclopedia of Philosophy* (Summer 2013 Edition), Edward N. Zalta (ed.), forthcoming URL = <http://plato.stanford.edu/archives/sum2013/entries/well-being/>.

Cummiskey, David. 1996. *Kantian Consequentialism.* Oxford: Oxford University Press.

Dancy, Jonathan. 1986. "Two Conceptions of Moral Realism," in *Proceedings of the Aristotelian Society,* Supp. Vol. LX, pp. 167–187.

Darwall, Stephen. 1992. "Internalism and Agency," in *Philosophical Perspectives,* Vol. 6, Ethics, pp. 155–174.

Falk, W.D. 1947. "'Ought' and Motivation," in *Proceedings of the Aristotelian Society,* New Series, Vol. 48, pp. 111–138.

Falk, W.D. 1986. *Ought, Reasons, and Morality: The Collected Papers of W.D. Falk.* Ithaca: Cornell University Press.

Finlay, Stephen and Mark Schroeder. 2008. "Reasons for Action: Internal vs. External," in *The Stanford Encyclopedia of Philosophy* (Fall 2008 Edition), edited by Edward N. Zalta, URL = <http://plato.stanford.edu/archives/fall2008/entries/reasons-internal-external/>.

Foot, Philippa. 1978. *Virtues and Vices.* Berkeley: University of California Press.

Goldman, Alvin. 1979. "What is Justified Belief?," in *Justification and Knowledge,* edited by George Pappas. Dordrecht: Reidel, pp. 1–23.

Harman, Gilbert. 1975. "Moral Relativism Defended," in *The Philosophical Review,* Vol. 84, No. 1, pp. 3–22.

Harman, Gilbert. 1975. "Reasons," in *Critica,* Vol. 7, No. 21, pp. 3–13.

Harman, Gilbert. 1978. "What Is Moral Relativism?," in *Values and Morals,* edited by Alvin Goldman and Jaegwon Kim. Dortrecht: Reidel, pp. 143–61.

Harman, Gilbert. 2000. "Is There a Single True Morality?," in *Explaining Value and Other Essays in Moral Philosophy*. Oxford: Clarendon Press, pp. 77–99.

Herman, Barbara. 1993. *The Practice of Moral Judgment*. Cambridge, MA: Harvard University Press.

Hill, Jr., Thomas E. 1992. *Dignity and Practical Reason in Kant's Moral Theory*. Ithaca: Cornell University Press.

Hobbes, Thomas. 1994/1651. *Leviathan*, edited by Edwin Curley. Indianapolis: Hackett Publishing Company.

Holmes, Richard. 1985. *Acts of War: The Behaviour of Men in Battle*, New York, NY: Simon & Schuster, Inc. (The Free Press).

Hume, David. 1975/1777. *Enquiries Concerning Human Understanding and Concerning the Principles of Morals*, edited by L.A. Selby-Bigge and P.H. Nidditch. Oxford: Oxford University Press (Clarendon Press).

Hume, David. 1978/1740. *A Treatise of Human Nature*, edited by L.A. Selby-Bigge and P.H. Nidditch. Oxford: Oxford University Press (Clarendon Press).

Johnson, Robert N. 1999. "Internal Reasons and the Conditional Fallacy," in *The Philosophical Quarterly*, Vol. 49, No. 194, pp. 53–71.

Johnson, Robert N. 2003. "Internal Reasons: Reply to Brady, Van Roojen and Gert," in *The Philosophical Quarterly*, Vol. 53, No. 213, pp. 573–580.

Kant, Immanuel. 1981/1775–1780. *Lectures on Ethics*, translated by Louis Infeld. Indianapolis: Hackett Publishing.

Kant, Immanuel. 1992/1764. *An Inquiry Concerning the Distinctness of the Principles of Natural Theology and Ethics* (the "Prize Essay"), in *Theoretical Philosophy, 1755-1770*, translated and edited by David Walford. Cambridge: Cambridge University Press, pp. 243–275.

Kant, Immanuel. 1996/1788. *Critique of Practical Reason*, in *Practical Philosophy*, edited and translated by Mary J. Gregor. Cambridge: Cambridge University Press, pp. 133–271.

Kant, Immanuel. 1996/1797. *The Metaphysics of Morals*, in *Practical Philosophy*, edited and translated by Mary J. Gregor. Cambridge: Cambridge University Press, pp. 353–603.

Kant, Immanuel. 1997/1781/1787. *Critique of Pure Reason*, translated by Paul Guyer and Allen Wood. Cambridge: Cambridge University Press.

Kant, Immanuel. 1997/1785. *Groundwork of the Metaphysics of Morals*, translated by Mary J. Gregor. Cambridge: Cambridge University Press.

Kant, Immanuel. 1998/1793. *Religion Within the Boundaries of Mere Reason*, translated by Allen Wood and George di Giovanni. Cambridge: Cambridge University Press.

Kavka, Gregory. 1978. "Some Paradoxes of Deterrence," in *Journal of Philosophy*, Vol. 75, No. 6, pp. 285–302.

Kavka, Gregory. 1983. "The Toxin Puzzle," in *Analysis*, Vol. 43, No. 1, pp. 33–36.

Korsgaard, Christine. 1996. *Creating the Kingdom of Ends*. Cambridge: Cambridge University Press.

Korsgaard, Christine. 1996. *The Sources of Normativity*. Cambridge: Cambridge University Press.

Korsgaard, Christine. 2008. "The Myth of Egoism," in *The Constitution of Agency*. Oxford: Oxford University Press, pp. 69–99.

Langton, Rae. 1992. "Duty and Desolation," in *Philosophy*, Vol. 67, No. 262, pp. 481–505.

Langton, Rae. 2007. "Objective and Unconditioned Value," in *The Philosophical Review*, Vol. 116, No. 2, pp. 157–185.

Lyons, David. 2001. "Ethical Relativism and the Problem of Incoherence," in Paul Moser and Thomas Carson (eds.), *Moral Relativism: A Reader*. New York: Oxford University Press, pp. 127–141.

Mackie, J.L. 1977. *Ethics: Inventing Right and Wrong*. Harmondsworth: Penguin Books.

Manne, Kate. 2014. "Internalism About Reasons: Sad But True," in *Philosophical Studies*, Vol. 167, No. 1, pp. 89–117.

Markovits, Julia. 2010. "Acting for the Right Reasons," in *The Philosophical Review*, Vol. 119, No. 2, pp. 201–242.

Markovits, Julia. 2011. "Internal Reasons and the Motivating Intuition," in *New Waves in Metaethics*, edited by Michael Brady. Basingstoke: Palgrave Macmillan, pp. 141–165.

Markovits, Julia. 2011. "Why Be An Internalist About Reasons?," in *Oxford Studies in Metaethics*, Vol. 6, edited by Russ Shafer-Landau. Oxford: Oxford University Press, pp. 255–279.

Mele, Alfred R. 2003. *Motivation and Agency*. New York: Oxford University Press.

Mill, John Stuart. 1979/1861. *Utilitarianism*, edited by George Sher. Indianapolis: Hackett Publishing Company.

Millgram, Elijah. 1995. "Was Hume a Humean?," in *Hume Studies*, Vol. XXI, No. 1, pp. 75–93.

Nagel, Thomas. 1970. *The Possibility of Altruism*. Oxford: Oxford University Press (Clarendon Press).

Nagel, Thomas. 1997. *The Last Word*. New York: Oxford University Press.

Narveson, Jan. 1972. "Moral Problems of Population," in *The Monist*, Vol. 57, No. 1, pp. 62–86.

Nozick, Robert. 1974. *Anarchy, State, and Utopia*. Oxford: Blackwell Publishers Ltd.

O'Neill, Onora. 1985. "Between Consenting Adults," in *Philosophy and Public Affairs*, Vol. 14, No. 3, pp. 252–277.

O'Neill, Onora. 1989. *Constructions of Reason: Explorations of Kant's Practical Philosophy*. Cambridge: Cambridge University Press.

O'Neill, Onora. 2003. "Constructivism in Rawls and Kant," in *The Cambridge Companion to Rawls*, edited by S. Freeman. Cambridge: Cambridge University Press, pp. 347–367.

Parfit, Derek. 1984. *Reasons and Persons*. Oxford: Oxford University Press (Clarendon Press).

Parfit, Derek. 1997. "Reasons and Motivation," in *Proceedings of the Aristotelian Society*, Supp. Vol. LXXI, pp. 99–130.

Parfit, Derek. 2011. *On What Matters* (Volumes One and Two). Oxford: Oxford University Press.

Railton, Peter. 1986. "Facts and Values," in *Philosophical Topics*, Vol. 14, No. 2, pp. 5–31.

Rawls, John. 1955. "Two Concepts of Rules," in *The Philosophical Review*, Vol. 64, No. 1, pp. 3–32.

Rawls, John. 1971. *A Theory of Justice*. Cambridge, MA: Harvard University Press (Belknap).

Raz, Joseph. 1979. *The Authority of Law: Essays on Law and Morality*. Oxford: Oxford University Press (Clarendon Press).

Raz, Joseph. 1986. *The Morality of Freedom*. Oxford: Oxford University Press.

Raz, Joseph. 1990. *Practical Reason and Norms*. Oxford: Oxford University Press.

Scanlon, T.M. 1998. *What We Owe to Each Other*. Cambridge, MA: Harvard University Press (Belknap).

Shafer-Landau, Russ. 1998. "Moral Judgement and Moral Motivation," in *The Philosophical Quarterly*, Vol. 48, No. 192, pp. 353–358.

Shafer-Landau, Russ. 2003. *Moral Realism: A Defense*. Oxford: Oxford University Press.

Showalter, Elaine. 1993. "Hysteria, Feminism, and Gender," in *Hysteria Beyond Freud* (by Sander L. Gilman, Helen King, Roy Porter, G. S. Rousseau, and Elaine Showalter). Berkeley: University of California Press, pp. 286–336.

Sidgwick, Henry. 1981/1874. *The Methods of Ethics*. Indianapolis: Hackett Publishing Company.

Singer, Peter. 1972. "Famine, Affluence, and Morality," in *Philosophy and Public Affairs*, Vol. 1, No. 1, pp. 229–243.

Smith, Michael. 1993. "Realism," in *A Companion to Ethics*, edited by Peter Singer. Oxford: Blackwell Publishers Ltd.

Smith, Michael. 1994. *The Moral Problem*. Oxford: Blackwell Publishers, Ltd.

Smith, Michael. 1995. "Internal Reasons," in *Philosophy and Phenomenological Research*, Vol. LV, No. 1, pp. 109–131.

Stratton-Lake, Philip. 2000. *Kant, Duty, and Moral Worth*. London: Routledge.

Strawson, Peter. 1974. "Freedom and Resentment," in *Freedom and Resentment and Other Essays*. London: Methuen & Co., Ltd., pp. 1–25.

Sturgeon, Nicholas. 1994. "Moral Disagreement and Moral Relativism," in *Social Philosophy and Policy*, Vol. 11, pp. 80–115.

Sullenberger, C. 2009. Interview with Katie Couric, *60 Minutes*. New York: CBS News, 8 February 2009. Television.

Taurek, John. 1977. "Should the Numbers Count?," in *Philosophy and Public Affairs*, Vol. 6, no. 4, pp. 293–316.

Walden, Kenneth. 2012. "Laws of Nature, Laws of Freedom, and the Social Construction of Normativity," in *Oxford Studies in Metaethics*, Vol. 7, edited by Russ Shafer-Landau. Oxford: Oxford University Press, pp. 37–79.

Williams, Bernard. 1981. *Moral Luck*. Cambridge: Cambridge University Press.

Williams, Bernard. 1985. *Ethics and the Limits of Philosophy*. Cambridge, MA: Harvard University Press.

Williams, Bernard. 1993. *Morality: An Introduction to Ethics*. Cambridge: Cambridge University Press (Canto).

Williams, Bernard. 1995. "Internal Reasons and the Obscurity of Blame," in *Making Sense of Humanity*. Cambridge: Cambridge University Press, pp. 35–45.

Williams, Bernard. 2002. "'Ought,' 'Must,' and the Needs of Morality." Unpublished.

Wood, Allen. 1996. "General Introduction," in Immanuel Kant's collected *Practical Philosophy*, edited and translated by Mary J. Gregor. Cambridge: Cambridge University Press, pp. xiii–xxxiii.

Wood, Allen. 1999. *Kant's Ethical Thought*. Cambridge: Cambridge University Press.

Wood, Allen. 2011. "Humanity as End in Itself," in *On What Matters*, Volume Two, edited by Samuel Scheffler, Oxford: Oxford University Press, pp. 58–82.

Index of Topics and Persons

Index of Examples

Printed and bound by CPI Group (UK) Ltd, Croydon, CR0 4YY